The Millenarian Piety of

Roger Williams

The Millenarian Piety of

Roger Williams

W. Clark Gilpin

The University of Chicago Press
Chicago and London

W. CLARK GILPIN is assistant professor
of church history at the Graduate
Seminary, Phillips University.

Library of Congress Cataloging in Publication Data

Gilpin, W Clark.
  The millenarian piety of Roger Williams.

  Bibliography: p.
  Includes index.
  1. Williams, Roger, 1604?–1683.
2. Millennialism—History of doctrines.
I. Title.
BX6495.W55G54   286'.1'0924   78–20786
ISBN 0-226-29397-1

Contents

Preface

This study of Roger Williams began at the University of Chicago in a seminar with Jerald C. Brauer and Robert Streeter on New England Puritanism. Together with Martin E. Marty, they served as the advisers for its development into a Ph.D. dissertation and have made valuable suggestions for subsequent revision.

In the beginning , when this study was a seminar paper, its original topic was Roger Williams's relations with the Indians of New England. As a result of entering Williams's work at this point rather than through the more usual avenues of his concern for religious liberty or the separation of church and state, two questions were posed for later research. First, what were the relations, if any, between Williams's social and theological opinions about the Indians and his more famous views on liberty of conscience, the church, and the state? Second, what factors in Williams's own development or in his historical context led him to view the Indians as he did, since, as will be seen, his opinions were unusual among the New England settlers? Thus the continuing concern of the study has been to examine the development and varied dimensions of Williams's thought in their interrelationships and in relation to their historical setting.

Citations from sixteenth and seventeenth century texts exactly follow the edition cited. The only exception to this is that the occasional, and inconsistent, practice of transposing the letters *u* and *v* or *j* and *i* has been altered to conform with modern usage. In references to dates, the year is considered to begin on 1 January, rather than in March as the Puritans usually reckoned.

1 Religious Experience and Religious Vocation

In late spring, 1644, Roger Williams was in London, having returned from the New World in order to secure a charter legally establishing the colony of Rhode Island and Providence Plantations settled by him in 1636. While in the city, his mind was occupied in drawing together scattered thoughts and papers to compose his most famous treatise, an attack, as its title explained, upon *The Bloudy Tenent, of Persecution, for Cause of Conscience*. Arguing there for complete religious liberty and the separation of church and state, Williams not only made himself infamous among contemporaries but also contributed to modern Western culture one of the most important early manifestos of religious freedom. Indeed, once stated by Williams, these principles developed a vitality and independent history of their own, a history which has profoundly shaped subsequent understanding of the man himself. For, as his friend John Milton wrote in that same year, "Books are not absolutely dead things, but do contain a potency of life in them to be as active as that soul whose progeny they are." But Milton went on to observe that books also "preserve as in a vial the purest efficacy and extraction of that living intellect that bred them,"[1] and the present study of Roger Williams seeks to recover that "living intellect," the fertile source of singularly potent ideas and of a tumultuous, often brilliant, public career.

Roger Williams's ideas were greeted with consternation in the seventeenth century. From his arrival in New England in 1631 until his death fifty-two years later, Williams pursued a career of dissent which provoked passionate controversy by challenging the cherished assumptions of his age regarding the nature of the church and its place in the social order. Public reaction to publication of *The Bloudy Tenent* in 1644 was typical; confronted by its proposal that religious liberty rather than uniformity was the means for achieving social tranquility and religious peace, one of his contemporaries retorted that Williams disguised as milk for the body politic ideas which were actually "Rats-bane."[2] But Williams was not merely a perennial critic of the standing order, and his former opponents looked on with amazed pleasure when his convictions led him to conclude his public career by debating the Quakers, a people who, like Roger Williams himself, had long been in the forefront of the struggle for religious freedom. He was a man willing to follow what he believed to be the truth and to defend its most unpopular, even its most unlikely, consequences. To discover the principles out of which such a man acted is both the major fascination and the major interpretive problem for any who would understand the career of Roger Williams.

Such an understanding begins with the recognition that English Puritanism molded Williams's religious orientation and intellectual habits.[3] Puritanism had emerged in Elizabethan England as a movement dissatisfied with the church settlements imposed by the Tudors and advocating further reform of the Church of England in both its institutions and its membership.[4] Placing themselves in opposition to established civil and ecclesiastical authorities, the Puritans increasingly considered themselves "a church within the Church," gradually developing their own traditions and standards of behavior. At the level of the community this sense of distinctive identity expressed itself though practices of church discipline and worship: sabbatarianism, the singing of church covenants, or opposition to clerical vestments, for example. For the individual this same commitment expressed itself as an intense experience of religious conversion through which the individual acquired a sense of spiritual and moral identity with the community and its ideals.

Members of the Puritan movement generally perceived themselves to be living in a decisive age of history—

perhaps the final age—during which God was directing the reformation of church and society out of the corruption into which they had fallen during the Middle Ages. The godly man found this providential scheme of history most clearly revealed in Scripture, and, through the aid of the Holy Spirit, he was obliged to discriminate its working within contemporary life. Thus the constant evaluation of experience in light of biblical patterns provided a continuing impetus toward reform of the individual and society as well as a standard by which such reforms could be judged. The threat of divine judgment, both in the present moment and at the Final Moment, impressed upon each man the gravity of this reflective and introspective duty. But this common assumption that experience could, and should, be correlated with Scripture nevertheless allowed wide differences of opinion about the actual meaning of particular experiences or particular passages of Scripture. Not surprisingly, therefore, a number of different Puritan groups arose, advocating different forms of worship and piety and reflecting the different social circumstances and religious orientations of the people affected by the broad Puritan movement.[5]

Prior to 1640, by far the largest number of Puritans hoped to reform the Church of England from within, gradually removing the "popish" doctrines and practices which sullied her but never denying that she was a true church. Although differing among themselves as to whether the needed reforms should proceed toward presbyterian or congregational polities, these men agreed that reformation should be an orderly process conducted within the framework of existing social and ecclesiastical structures. The leaders of the Massachusetts Bay Company who settled New England in 1630 were Puritans of this sort; they hoped to reform the English church along congregational lines but without formally separating themselves from the established Church of England. Beginning in the 1570s, however, more extreme exponents of reform had begun to demand that the faithful totally withdraw from association with the Church of England and denounce her as an utterly false church. Known as Separatists or Brownists, these persons formed individual congregations both in England and, as exiles, in the Netherlands. It was with the Separatists that Roger Williams identified himself at the time of his arrival in Massachusetts Bay in 1631, and throughout his career he remained a spokesman of the radical wing of the Puritan movement.

In aligning himself with the "left wing" of Puritanism, Williams gave up his formal vocation as a minister and developed his talents as a religious controversialist and pamphleteer, understanding that activity as itself a religious vocation. Relishing exposure to the vast body of polemical literature emerging from the presses during the seventeenth century, he addressed in debate a wide variety of issues and opponents throughout half a century. Within this context, new ideas were continuously assimilated, old ideas altered, and the whole reorganized in order to meet the specific challenges of fresh topics and new adversaries. Williams's religious views were presented, therefore, not systematically, but through occasional pieces directed to specific historical circumstances.

As this suggests, the center of his thought is less easily discerned in his ideas about religious liberty, the church, or the state than in his ideas about himself, his religious vocation, and his place and duty in the providential order of history. Far too little is known of Williams's childhood to trace the early development of this self-understanding. But throughout the Puritan movement the process of religious conversion was decisive for character formation and vocational commitment, and some understanding of its characteristics gives much insight into Roger Williams's religious and intellectual orientation. Further, it is clear that Williams gradually came to interpret this sense of religious vocation through a millenarian understanding of history. Through his millenarian convictions he placed his role as a controversialist within the framework of God's providential plan for the whole of human history. He found himself in propitious times, and through engagement in controversy and debate he believed himself to be carrying out a religous duty in obedience to a direct call from God.

This self-interpretation is admirably expressed in Williams's published works; they are predominantly works of controversy which were dashed off in response to particular religious issues which arose during the period from 1643 to 1676. Most were published during two extended visits which Williams made to England in 1643–44 and in 1651–54.[6]

Conversion

In the experience of conversion the Puritan found his very being altered by God's intervening action, separating him from the mass of humanity and calling him to the duties and privileges of the elect. By this experience he received conviction of his salvation, and in this firm hope bent will and intellect to the greater glory of God. Such salvation depended, he was convinced, upon the free activity of God's grace; nothing man could do on his own would bring it to pass. And, since the process was conceived as both crucial and beyond human control, the believer's attitude toward it was properly one of intense self-examination in order to discern the spirit's presence and action within his soul.

To meet the needs of this introspective piety, tracts and pamphlets dealing with the nature of conversion and the characteristics by which it might be identified appeared in increasing numbers after 1600. A significant amount of this literature consisted of accounts of individual conversions, which might be published, as with John Bunyan's *Grace Abounding to the Chief of Sinners* or kept in manuscript for the satisfaction of the author and a small circle of friends. Perhaps more important, and certainly more numerous, were the published sermons describing conversion and offering the reader concrete advice about preparing for, recognizing, and cultivating its presence in his own life. Through this literature, and through the retelling of spiritual experiences within the church communities, a model of Christian conversion developed. Conversion was thus at once both a deeply personal experience of salvation and an initiation into Puritan culture.

Three examples will quickly draw the broad outlines. They are the autobiographic accounts of conversion by the Baptist preacher and author John Bunyan (1628–88), by John Winthrop (1588–1649), first governor of Massachusetts Bay, and by Thomas Goodwin (1600–1680), prominent Puritan divine and leader of the "dissenting brethren" at the Westminster Assembly.[7]

All three men began with retrospective assertions about the sinfulness of their early lives. Winthrop ruefully acknowledged that he had been a "very wild, and dissolute" youth, and Bunyan asserted that, considering his age, he had had few equals "both for cursing, swearing, lying, and blaspheming the holy name of God."[8] Whether or not such assertions were completely accurate, they set the stage for the authors' first exposure to Puritan society and development of interest in religion. For Goodwin enrollment at a Puritan college at Cambridge provided this introduction to "godly" society. For Bunyan and Winthrop marriage into a Puritan family produced the same result; the dowry which Bunyan's wife brought with her, for example, included two manuals of practical piety by Lewis Bayly and Arthur Dent.

Following this shift in social circumstance, each went through a period of outward reform and concern over the correction of individual sins. Bunyan, for example, was influenced by a sermon and a voice which "did suddenly dart out of heaven into my soul" to eschew playing games on the sabbath.[9] When not long afterward he was shaken loose from his habit of swearing, his neighbors began to remark that he had indeed become "a very godly man, a new and religious man."[10] He had arrived at a conception of Christianity which both he and Winthrop described as a "covenant of works," in which legalistic adherence to a set of ethical norms was considered sufficient for salvation. The more theologically sophisticated Goodwin described this as a period in which he had taken notice of particular sins without recognizing "the root and ground of all my other sinnings," his participation in Original Sin.[11]

But when further exposure to Puritan teachings triggered a deeper examination of their lives, it led them to identify such outward moral reform as hypocrisy. The particular situations which led to this realization were analogous: Goodwin heard a Puritan funeral sermon; Winthrop read the doctrinal works of William Perkins; Bunyan, by accident, came into contact with the members of a godly congregation at Bedford.[12] Listening to their conversation, Bunyan recognized that they were speaking of Christianity in a manner, and with a fervency, with which he could find nothing to compare in his own experience. Feeling that his legalistic struggles were doomed to failure, Bunyan assented to the proposition that "the elect only attained eternal life...but that myself was one of them, there lay all the question."[13] Bunyan's attitude toward Scripture exemplified his altered understanding; formerly he had enjoyed the Old Testament, especially the decalogue, but now he found Paul's letters emphasizing the power of divine grace, to be "sweet and pleasant."[14]

The conviction that he was powerless to effect his own salvation led each man into a period of probing self-examination, during which he sought evidence of his own election. Although this was a brief experience for Thomas Goodwin, Winthrop and Bunyan questioned their spiritual conditions for several years. But the solitary task of examining the soul raised the question of the validity of the evidence which was found there. Did these experiences confirm God's transforming presence, or rather Satan's temptations and man's delusions? For Bunyan and Goodwin, especially, the solution was to test their experiences by comparing them with those of fellow Puritans, biblical figures, Luther, or, in Goodwin's case, with the pattern which "our own divines of Great Britain do set out in their discourse of the manner of conversion."[15] The ultimate criterion was Scripture. Even occasional moments of spiritual peace could not be uncritically enjoyed unless they met its tests, since, as Bunyan stated, "unless there could be found in my refreshment a concurrence and agreement in the Scriptures, let me think what I will thereof, and hold it never so fast, I should find no such thing at the end."[16]

For each of the three men this period of testing reached a point of resolution in which he was able to acknowledge internal certainty, confirmed by Scripture, that he was numbered among the elect. In part, this was a rational statement of the conclusions of his spiritual investigations, but it also included an almost mystical sense of the presence of the Divine Spirit. Bunyan recalled, "The Lord did also lead me into the mystery of union with the Son of God"; and Winthrop wrote, "Now could my soul close with Christ, and rest there with sweet content, so ravished with his Love, as I desired nothing nor feared anything, but was filled with joy unspeakable and glorious and with a spirit of Adoption."[17] But this resolution of conversion by no means ended its influence. The rigorous habits of self-examination inculcated over its course remained to provide the core of Puritan piety, and the sense of personal warfare against sin found expression in a zealous ethical life. Having been turned to God by a process of considerable duration, the convert found himself motivated to bear the fruits of God's labors. Hence, for those who would enter the public ministry, accounts of conversion typically ended not with the experience of the spirit's regenerative power but rather with the subject's vocational decision.[18]

The spiritual itinerary of the conversion process thus oriented Puritan life at a variety of levels. In a very important sense the individual self achieved what William James called "unification," in which "religious aims" came to form "the habitual centre of his energy."[19] This culminated in the acceptance of vocation, whether as a member of the clergy or by interpretation of secular work as religious duty. And finally it was a community as well as personal event: the inculcation of the values of Puritan culture.

By such a multifaceted experience of commitment Roger Williams came, at a time unknown to us, to count himself as one who had received "manifestations of the countenance of God, reconciled in the blood of his Son unto my soule."[20] The emphasis upon growth in holiness which this experience conveyed became a characteristic quality of his personality. Human life was at once for him this "vale of tears" from whence he was beckoned to "another country" and the context of calling in which the divine will was to be embodied in moral activity.

These twin emphases of the Puritan habit of mind— eternal rest in the peace of God and the earthly emergence of the reign of God—are nowhere more evident than in the ruminations in which many Puritans engaged regarding the millennium, the thousand years prophesied in Scripture during which Christ would return to earth and reign with his faithful saints over a kingdom which would exist until the Last Judgment. By the various interpretations which Roger Williams and others gave to this millenarian hope, their personal commitment embodied in religious conversion was placed within a framework of cosmic significance, God's plan for the whole of history.

Millenarianism

In Elizabethan England millennialist theories were part of a widespread interest in a variety of predictive speculations. Prophecies concerning impending political events, most often based upon the Sibylline Oracles or twelfth century prophecies attributed to Merlin, circulated freely despite occasional legislation prohibiting their publication. During the century astrological prognostications made their appearance and began to receive wide distribution through inclusion in annual popular almanacs.[21] Fascination with millenarian ideas, as well as with these other types of prophecies, continued throughout the reigns of the early Stuarts among persons of every social, political, and religious position. It was widely assumed that some scriptural prophecies were as yet unfulfilled; and the attempt to decipher the images of Daniel and Revelation, thereby discerning the date for the advent of the millennium, was not merely a pastime for sectarian fanatics but the earnest endeavor of many renowned scientists, mathematicians, philosophers, and theologians of the age.[22] The fact that many of these calculations placed that miraculous date in the period between 1640 and 1700 would lead to their substantial influence and regular republication throughout those turbulent times.

But most important for understanding millenarianism in its Puritan setting is the recognition that, where it existed, it did not exist as some theological afterthought, some enthusiastic addendum, to a piety fully intelligible apart from it.[23] Rather, for the Puritan who espoused it, millenarianism was integral to his total religious orientation: his understanding of the providential development of world history, his image of the ideal human society, and his sense of personal responsibilities to man and to God. As will be seen, various interpretations of the millennium were current among the Puritans, but, in general, each functioned as a powerful symbol which not only described a utopian goal of social transformation but also motivated the individual to seek his own responsibilities in effecting that transformation. In setting forth the end toward which history was moving, millenarianism thereby became a symbolic means of comprehending one's personal place and duty in history. Through it, the individual perceived himself as a significant agent in the religious reformation which constituted the final drama of history, the establishment of Christ's earthly kingdom for the benefit of all mankind. Thus, in the following chapter, it will be seen that in Massachusetts Bay "reform" did not connote piecemeal repairs upon the machinery of civil and ecclesiastical government, but rather was consistently conceived as part of the apocalyptic struggle against Antichrist.

Preaching and publishing by English divines both reflected and generated this millenarian dimension of Puritan piety. Increasingly convinced that they were living in the latter days of the world, scholars and preachers, undertaking a task which Calvin had assiduously avoided, published numerous sermons and commentaries dealing with Revelation and other prophetic books of Scripture. Such works appeared from the hands of writers representing every shade of religious opinion, ardent supporters of prelacy as well as rigid Separatists, but, for the generation which settled New England and waged the English civil wars, the commentaries which would prove most influential were the erudite judgments of Thomas Brightman (1562–1607) and Joseph Mede (1586–1638). A brief examination of the manner in which these two men interpreted scriptural prophecies will illustrate a number of motifs which would persistently reappear in the writings of Roger Williams and his contemporaries.

Thomas Brightman, a Puritan writing in the last years of Elizabeth's reign, expounded millenarian views which were most strongly characterized by a nationalistic optimism. In the types and symbols of John's Revelation he discerned a record of the entire course of history from the time of Christ to the Last Judgment, and he predicted that England would play a central role in the final phase of that drama. According to Brightman's reading of Revelation, the millennial reign of Christ had already begun, about the year 1300, and had become fully manifest with the accession of Elizabeth in 1558.[24] During these final thousand years of history the church would experience a glorious purity made possible by the rule of Christian magistrates, through whom Christ would exercise his lordship by "so framing and fashioning their hearts" that they would "give themselves wholly to seek the advancing of his glory."[25] Elizabeth of England, decalred Brightman, was preeminent among these godly sovereigns, and he appealed to his readers' own experience for verification that his optimism was justified:

> And is there not a most evident proof given us of this eternall Kingdome, in that so great conspiracies and attempts, of so many and mighty enemies against *England*

alone, *our most gracious Queen,* have vanished away like
smoke, and come to nothing? He whose Scepter they
strive to overthrow, laugheth at their foolish and vain
enterprises.[26]

At the conclusion of this glorious age, three hundred years
of which had already passed at Brightman's writing, Christ
would personally return and translate his kingdom into
heaven.[27]

Explicit throughout Brightman's commentary on Revelation were two didactic points. First, he sought to demonstrate that the Pope was Antichrist and that the Turk had
been sent as a "scourge of the Christians," whose threat
would continue until all popish idolatry was forsaken. He
therefore urged all Christian princes to "make your selves,
and all your Artillery, ready against *Rome,* and raze her to
the ground."[28] Second, Brightman issued a warning to his
countrymen that, although Christ had begun his millennial
reign in England, he might remove his blessings from her if
she became remiss in her piety:

Let us in good earnest use the prescribed remedy. Wee
have need of zeale, to the intent we may attaine to a full
reformation. Wee hang as yet by Geometry, as it were,
between heaven and hell; the contagious steaming of the
Romish foggie lake doth in a deadly manner annoy us:
*Our silver is yet defiled with drosse; Our Wine is mingled with
water:* Christ will no longer indure such *midling Angels* as
ours are.[29]

In thus combining his vision of England's millennial role
with a homiletic warning against a national lapse of piety,
Brightman exercised his influence upon numerous later
godly divines.[30] In so doing he reemphasized a theme
which John Foxe's *Acts and Monuments* had already made a
staple of the English literary diet: the idea that England
was now reenacting the role of ancient Israel as a people in
peculiar covenant with God.[31]

Joseph Mede, a conforming Cambridge scholar who
dedicated one of his books to William Laud, interpreted
Revelation in a fashion different from that of Brightman.
As a biblical scholar, Mede was primarily concerned with
developing a *critical method* for understanding the
chronological and symbolic relations among the various
prophecies of Revelation, and he declined to venture

specific calculations concerning the date of the millennium.[32]

Writing in 1627, during the Thirty Years War, Mede was both chary of Brightman's optimism and doubtful of his method. Specifically, Mede denied Brightman's assumption that the literary arrangement of Revelation was simply chronological in character. Instead, Mede argued that from the fourth chapter onward Revelation was "distributed into two principall prophecies [Rev. 4–11 and Rev. 12–21], either of which proceedeth from the same time, and endeth in the same period."[33] The first prophecy disclosed the destiny of the Roman Empire, and the second prophecy predicted the dissolution and eventual reformation of the church.[34] This interpretation of the literary structure of the book had the effect of grouping the predicted cataclysmic tribulations just prior to the advent of the millennium, rather than distributing them throughout history as in Brightman's scheme. For example, Rev. 11:7 predicted a slaughter of all the faithful witnesses of Christ; Brightman had stated that this calamity had already occurred, but Mede disagreed, placing it as one of the last events prior to the millennium. Mede added that his interpretation provided spiritual edification which Brightman's chronology lacked: "The expectation of a future calamity conduceth more to piety, then an over-credulous securitie therefrom, as if it were already past."[35]

With the intensification of millenarian expectancy during the 1640s, Mede's critical method was adapted by enthusiasts who were less circumspect in applying the prophecies to their own times. Since his method dictated that a time of great disturbances would be the prelude to the thousand years of Christ's rule, persons who both searched Scripture and read the signs of the times could easily apply it to the social convulsions which accompanied the English civil wars.

In the period after 1640, millenarian controversialists like Roger Williams seldom stated their views on scriptural prophecies in the methodical fashion characteristic of Brightman and Mede. Nevertheless, when they desired corroboration for some particular aspect of their opinions, the authorities most often cited were these two men. The favorite themes of Mede and Brightman continually reappeared, though revised to meet the particular situation:

the eschatological role of England, the centrality of reformation in the final ages of history, and the implications of millenarianism for practical piety.

Roger Williams's own piety, originally shaped by the conversion experience, developed into a distinctive form of millenarianism through which he expressed his sense of religious vocation. The influence of this millenarian vision of history is evident in his published works as the religious orientation from which he approached particular questions of religious controversy. His ideas about the church, the state, and religious liberty are thus best understood in the context bounded by his sense of millennial mission and the specific controversies in which he engaged.

2

Ministry and Reformation in Massachusetts

In 1630 Massachusetts Bay Colony began taking shape as the consciously experimental expression of the hopes and anxieties of its leadership, English merchants, clergy, and gentry of broadly Puritan sympathies. These godly Englishmen hoped to transform a trading company, whose charter gave it limited power to make colonial laws, into the vehicle for founding a model Christian commonwealth. Envisioning themselves, in the famous phrases of John Winthrop, to be acting "through a speciall overruleing providence" in order to establish "a due form of Goverment both civill and ecclesiasticall," they were convinced that by divine support they could organize the colony in accordance with the pattern God had revealed in Scripture.[1] The goals of the colony thus extended beyond its character as a business venture to represent a partnership with God in "buyldinge his new Jerusalem" and emboldened early planters with the hope "to laye but one stone in the foundacion of this new Syon."[2]

In addition to these broad hopes, enthusiasm for the enterprise also gained momentum from the anxieties of its Puritan leaders. Their fears paralleled those which were precipitating the flight of other Puritans to the Low Countries and which would, in little more than a decade, eventuate in revolution. Increases in population, inflation, changes in land use, and a series of poor agricultural yields led to belief that the country gentry in their number had an unstable economnic future. Politically, they were increasingly alienated from the government of Charles I. They opposed his attempts at consolidation of power, particularly the dissolution of Parliament in 1629, and were disquieted by Catholic influences within his court. Further, the king's chief minister, Bishop Laud of London, had begun to make stringent demands for religious conformity, which the Puritans regarded as dangerous steps backward toward the errors of the Roman church and thus as dark omens for the future of English Protestantism.

Looking toward the Continent, the Puritans found their alarm confirmed by the ebbing fortunes of the Protestant cause in the Thirty Years War. They belived that because the churches of the Protestant nations had declined in their zeal for reform, God was now forcing them "to drinke of the bitter cuppe of tribulation, even unto death," and they feared that a similar judgment awaited England, if she did not turn back from her present course. Therefore, in late summer, 1629, one of the reasons agreed upon for plantation in New England was that "all other churches of Europe beinge brought to desolation it cannot be but that the like judgement is comminge upon us and who knoweth but that *god hath prepared this place for a refuge* for many whome he meaneth to save in the general destruction."[3]

The shareholders of the Massachusetts Bay Company thus perceived New England not only as a place in which to realize their most hopeful visions, but also as a refuge from social instability, political prosecutions, and, not least, divine judgment. On one hand, they connected the colony with the biblical appellations of millennial optimism: Canaan, Zion, the New Jerusalem. But on the other hand, New England was the latter-day Zoar, Lot's city of refuge as he fled from Sodom and Gomorrah, which were doomed for their failure to heed God's word (Gen. 19:17–22).

When the principals of the company arrived in Massachusetts in the summer of 1630, they faced the task of actually implementing the Christian society whose outlines they had only partially conceptualized. Without sacrificing its vitality, religious zeal had to be directed by the need for establishing internal consensus on the form of civil and religious government, maintaining cordial relations with supporters in England, and avoiding the wrath of royal authority for any deviations from English law. In the first decade of the colony's existence, therefore, a delicate process of experimentation, consolidation, and definition occurred with respect to law, church polity, and social organization. By what George Haskins has characterized as the "alchemy" of social transformation, the exigencies of the situation gradually interacted with Puritan scriptural interpretation and English custom and law to form what would be termed "the New England way."[4]

But when Roger Williams disembarked at Boston in February 1631, this process of consolidation was in its earliest stages, and his arrival introduced a highly volatile element into the complex mixture of interests and aspirations already present. During the ensuing five years, he threw his prestige as a Cambridge-educated clergyman into the advocacy of numerous disruptive ideas: that their churches publicly sever all ties with the established Church of England, that the patent by which they claimed right to the land be rejected and returned to England, and that oaths of political allegiance be disallowed. Finally, in the autumn of 1635, the leaders of the colony, recognizing that such ideas were jeopardizing their status in England and deteriorating relations among the towns of Massachusetts, decided that Williams must be returned to England. In January 1636 they dispatched Captain John Underhill to Salem to apprehend him, only to discover that Williams had already escaped into the wilderness beyond the jurisdiction of Massachusetts, there to establish the tiny colony of Providence Plantations.

From this wilderness retreat, Williams would subsequently advocate the theory of full religious liberty for which he has been lauded by later generations. But adequate understanding of those views on liberty of conscience requires recognition of their relationship to his contentious public life in Massachusetts from 1631 to 1636, a time during which Williams gave scant evidence of the large-minded tolerance today popularly associated with his name. Both his controversial pronouncements in Massachusetts and the later development of his thought had as their matrix the religious beliefs and practices of the English Separatist tradition, and it was his stringent Separatist piety which so quickly and emphatically set Williams at odds with the ideals and pragmatic decisions of the

Bay Colony leadership during the crucial early years of settlement.

Development of Massachusetts Bay Colony

In England during the spring and summer of 1629, the Massachusetts Bay Company grew out of two earlier New England trading enterprises, but in planning the Bay Colony its members gradually turned toward new purposes their experience from those previous endeavors. The first of the earlier corporations, a commercial fishing venture called the Dorchester Company, had been organized in 1623 by approximately 120 subscribers from the western counties of Devon and Dorset. The large majority of these adventurers were country gentry and merchants, but the company also included some twenty clergymen, most of whom favored moderate Puritan reform of the English church.[5] The company soon faltered, however, and its treasurer John Humfrey and the Dorchester minister John White attempted to revive it by drawing in new stockholders, primarily London merchants such as Simon Whetcombe, Matthew Cradock, and Thomas Goffe. Incorporated as the New England Company in March 1628, this second organization numbered in its membership the important Puritan preachers Hugh Peter and John Davenport, as well as several members of Davenport's London congregation.[6]

On 4 March 1629, a royal charter was obtained which transformed the New England Company into the Massachusetts Bay Company.[7] During the ensuing six months, a number of Puritan gentry from the eastern counties of Lincoln, Essex, and Suffolk were introduced into the organization, which by the time contained men of considerable education, business experience, and sense of moral purpose. As preparations were made for removal to New England, therefore, the company represented a Puritan constituency of fairly broad geographic distribution, which would provide crucial support in England for those who actually emigrated. In addition, connections with prominent families would aid in the success of the venture; John Humfrey and Isasc Johnson, for example, were married to sisters of Theophilus, Earl of Lincoln, and both Thomas

Dudley and Simon Bradstreet had served in the Lincoln household.

These influential representatives and friends would prove vital to the colony during the first decade of settlement, since its charter from the king had apparently been obtained by covertly circumventing the Council for New England, a board of aristocratic proprietors which had been granted rights to New England in 1620.[8] Members of the council, especially Sir Ferdinando Gorges, were incensed that the Massachusetts Bay Company had "surreptitiously" and "unknown to us" obtained this grant of land and, ignoring the jurisdiction of the council, "made themselves a free People."[9] The very origins of the Bay Company thus created potential enemies, enemies who later posed a serious challenge to the colony's existence.

In appropriating membership and, legally or not, land grants from earlier mercantile organizatons, the Massachusetts Bay Company came to possess as well the remnants of their colonies in the Massachusetts Bay area. Known collectively as *old planters*, the inhabitants of these outposts included such men as the Reverend William Blaxton, Samuel Maverick, and the blacksmith Thomas Walford, who had remained in the area to fish, trade, or ply special skills after the failure of Robert Gorges's colony at Wessagusset in 1624. Also living in the area were men like John Oldham and Roger Conant, who had left nearby Plymouth Colony either to trade independently with the Indians or to participate in the Dorchester Company's unsuccessful colony at Cape Ann. Struggling but resourceful, the old planters were resentful when, in 1628, the New England Company dispatched John Endecott to organize a colony at Salem which incorporated them within its jurisdiction. Additional colonists arrived at Salem in 1629, and it has been estimated that, counting Plymouth Colony, some 500 English settlers were living in New England at the arrival of the Bay Company's "Winthrop fleet" in June 1630.[10]

In addition to this small assemblage of colonists, the Massachusetts Bay Company also inherited from its predecessors a religious rationale for colonization. Commercially, the Dorchester Company had conceived its New England colony as a station for replenishing the supplies and crews of English fishing vessels returning to European markets.[11] But, particularly through the influence of the Reverend John White, it also hoped that the colony would provide an opportunity for spiritual edification of the fishermen and evangelization of the Indians. White's interest in the Indians' conversion was heightened by the millenarian conviction that the Last Days were approaching in which the Jews would be converted to Christianity. In preparation for that event, the gospel had first to be carried throughout the world, and White argued that New England colonization would advance this eschatological mission.

> Let it bee granted that the *Jewes* conversion is neare, and that the *Gentiles*, and consequently the *Indians* must needs be gathered in before that day; and any man may make the conclusion, that this is the houre for the worke, and consequently of our duty to endeavour the effecting that which God hath determined; the opening of the eyes of these poore ignorant soules, and discovering unto them the glorious mystery of Jesus Christ.[12]

Writing on behalf of the New England Company, Matthew Cradock reminded Endecott in February 1629 that the "mayne end" of the plantation was this missionary endeavor "to bringe ye Indians to the knowledge of the gospell."[13]

But as the year 1629 progressed, a year in which Charles I dissolved Parliament and William Laud increased the pressure for clerical conformity, the commercial and religious interests which had prompted organization of the earlier companies were incorporated into a different design. Although reference was still made, for example, to the responsibility for converting the Indians, this and other arguments appeared in the context of advantages to be derived from *participating in* colonization, rather than simply *sending out* colonists.[14] A New England plantation was no longer the means by which the trading company could achieve its goals; it was itself the justification for the company's existence. The concrete action which expressed this shift in purpose was the agreement signed at Cambridge in August to take to New England "the whole governement together with the Patent" of the company.[15] The planters' scheme for a Puritan haven and holy commonwealth was thus to be superimposed upon the settlements which already existed in Massachusetts and upon the rationales which had given rise to them.

The proponents of this alteration in the goals of the company felt the action required clear justification. No enterprise would prosper, they believed, whose objectives were not compatible with God's providential ordering of history, and, for this reason, they expended considerable energy examining their motives for emigration and their prospects for success. As John Cotton would remind the colonists at their departure from England, God's purposes determined the outcome of human actions, and "every plantation that he hath not planted shall be plucked up, and what he hath planted shall surely be established."[16] From this perspective, in a manuscript which circulated among potential colonists during the summer of 1629, John Winthrop concluded that the present undertaking could be distinguished from earlier unsuccessful colonization attempts.

> There were great fundamental errours in others, which are like to be avoided in this: for 1st there mayne end and purpose was carnall and not religious. 2d, They aymed chiefly at profitt and not at the propagation of religion. 3d, They used too unfitt instruments, a multitude of rude and ungoverned persons, the very scums of the land. 4th, They did not stablish a right fourme of government.[17]

The key to success, therefore, was combining religiously motivated persons within the right system of government, and this consideration obliged the serious settler to examine his individual purposes in order to ascertain if he was one whom God intended to travel to New England.

Winthrop's own case, as he deliberated upon participation in the colony, provides numerous examples of this introspection. Among the justifications for his decision to emigrate, Winthrop recorded his worsened financial situation, the inclinations of his own heart, the requests of godly acquaintances, and the agreement of other members of his household; he also considered the colony a unique opportunity for religious service.

In my youth I did seariously consecrate my life to the service of the Church (intendinge the ministry) but was diverted from that course by the counsell of some, whose Judgment I did much reverence: but it hath ofte troubled me since, so as I thinke I am rather bounde to take the opportunitye for spendinge the small remainder of my tyme, to the best service of the Churche which I may.[18]

Having decided to go to New England, Winthrop continued examining his experiences for confirmation that he was pursuing the proper course. Thus, immediately after being chosen governor of the company, he wrote his wife that this election gave him "assurance that my charge is of the Lorde and that he hath called me to this worke."[19] He demanded the same self-examination from others considering participation in the colony, and he severely agitated his brother-in-law, Arthur Tyndal, by pressing him on this point. Tyndal, feeling that his immediate answers were inadequate, withdrew for reflection and then wrote Winthrop, affirming his resolve "to master my desires, and conversacion, and to live under the Hierarchie of your church and civill government, purposed and concluded among your selves."[20]

In searching out additional colonists, the leading planters maintained this concern for proper motivation and took considerable care to avoid what Winthrop had termed "unfitt instruments." William Gager, for example, was asked to become a colonist not simply because of his skill as a surgeon, but also because the company had received "sufficient assurance" of his "godlinesse."[21] Particular diligence was exercised in obtaining ministers motivated by Puritan desires for personal piety and reformed orders of worship. Early in November 1629, a meeting with "divers godly Ministers" was called in London to evaluate the qualifications of various pastors, in order to find "hitherto able and sufficient Ministers to joyne with us" in establishing the colony.[22] Winthrop, Humfrey, and Isaac Johnson, the most substantial subscriber of the colony, corresponded about selection of ministers, tendering and receiving recommendations of such Puritan divines as Thomas Hooker, Hugh Peter, William Ames, and George Phillips. The Puritan pastors John White, John Davenport, and Arthur Hildersam were consulted concerning the suitability of ministers; and at White's suggestion two London preachers, John Archer and Philip Nye, were admitted as freemen of the company to provide a regular source of advice and spiritual edification.[23]

Arguments justifying the colony and clarifying its objectives were consciously turned outward toward the English public by two documents published in 1630. One, *The Humble Request*, carried the signatures of Winthrop, Johnson, Dudley, Sir Richard Saltonstall, the minister George Phillips, and the Lincolnshire merchant William Coddington. This brief address sought to correct any "misreport" of their intentions, by asserting that in leaving the country they were by no means renouncing allegiance to the Church of England, their "deare Mother," but rather extending her influence to new regions.[24] By reaffirming their allegiance, they hoped to avoid the epithets Brownist or Separatist. Similarly, in *The Planters Plea*, John White defended the colonists against "scandalous reports" that they were Separatists, who out of a contentious spirit were leaving England to "rayse and erect a seminary of faction."[25] There was, announced White, a great difference between the disruptive Separatist and the peaceful nonconformist who, differing slightly with English church order, chose to withdraw rather than disturb the church's harmony.[26] Both tracts stressed that, whatever hopes the colonists might hold for religious reform, they did not combine them with the harsh denunciations which Separatism hurled against the established church. This clarification was crucial for maintaining the support of Puritan moderates, who considered themselves members of the English church, who were accustomed to their ministers holding livings, or at least lectureships associated with the establishment, and who feared Separatism as a threat to social order.

Meanwhile, in New England itself, social organization had been occurring with the independence from company direction which a six-week ocean crossing necessitated. Administration of affairs resided with John Endecott and a twelve-member council, which included two old planters and the three ministers (Samuel Skelton, Francis Higginson, and Francis Bright) whom the company had appointed for the colony early in 1629. Although the Bay Company periodically sent instructions to Endecott, it left the ministers free to exercise their religious responsibilities as they saw fit, hoping only that they would "make Gods word the rule."[27]

During 1629 the Salem ministers followed the dictates of "Gods word" into revisions of church discipline which would provide Governor Winthrop and his associates an unpleasant surprise when they disembarked in New England in 1630. By July 1629, the Salem congregation was organized on the premise that a true church was created by written covenant among professing Christians, who then had sole authority to select their ministers. Any churches not constituted in this manner, such as the English parishes, required further reform and could not be recognized as authentic churches.[28] Thus, although Skelton and Higginson had served English parishes and were appointed and paid as ministers by the company,[29] both men denied that these were sufficient reasons for them to assume ministry at Salem. Instead, they asserted that authority to call a minister could be exercised only by "a company of beleevers . . . joyned togither in covenante." The congregaton followed this procedure, and, having compacted "to walke togither in all ye ways of God," they elected Skelton pastor and Higginson teacher.[30]

In thus affirming its autonomy, the Salem church implemented principles espoused by a diverse collection of English congregationalists over the preceding four decades. Initially, these ideas had been advanced by the Separatist churches as justifications for their existence apart from the national church. Since the time of the Elizabethan Separatists Robert Browne and Henry Barrow, conceptions of the church parallel to that applied at Salem had been enunciated by every major Separatist spokesman; they were concisely summarized by one of them, John Smyth, when he defined the visible church as "two, three, or more Saincts joyned together by covenant with God & themselves, freely to use al the holy things of God, according to the word, for their mutual edification, & Gods glory." Such a covenanted community, Smyth added, was "the only religious societie that God hath ordeyned for man on earth" and therefore the only one capable of electing church officers.[31] Those who submitted to its covenant submitted to the moral and religious discipline which it exercised through these duly elected officers.

The "stiffer sort" of Separatists combined this congregational polity with repudiation of the Church of England as
a false church, a charge prominent in the gospel soon to be
preached by Roger Williams at Salem. Apologies for separation by such leaders as Henry Barrow, Henry Ainsworth, and Williams's contemporary, John Canne, asserted
three grounds for their conviction that the Protestant
establishment was no true church: its worship was con-
taminated with the "popish trumperies" of Catholicism,
its parishes were "cages of uncleane birds" mixing the
godly and the profane in their membership, and its polity
confused the sacred and secular realms by allowing its
officers, the bishops, also to act as officials of the state.
What genuinely godly person, asked Henry Barrow, could
hope to find "a true visible established church" in the midst
of "this generall falling away from the gospel ... this universall corruption and confusion of all estates, degrees,
persons, callings, actions, both in the church and commune wealth?"[32] Faced with this apostasy by the establishment, Barrow announced that "God calleth all his
servantes out of confusion, and will not have them live in
dissipation or disorder, but only in this order [separated
congregations] which he hath prescribed in his worde."[33]
For strict Separatists such as Henry Barrow, the divine call
out of "dissipation" required complete abstention from
public or private involvement in the parish assemblies and
repentance for all former associations there.

The severity of these demands for purity had provoked a
long series of disputes and polemical tracts. Many of these
debates occurred between the extremists and the Puritans
who remained part of the national church, but disagreement also arose among and within the separated congregations themselves. By the second decade of the seventeenth
century, a more tolerant version of the Separatist ecclesiology had found its champions, including John Robinson in
Leiden and the Plymouth colonists, who were a segment of
Robinson's congregation. Although they too affirmed the
autonomy of their separated congregations, these more
temperate spirits recognized common aspirations relating
them to reformers within the Church of England and permitted their members to attend Puritan sermons. John
Robinson, for example, wrote A Treatise of the Lawfulness of
Hearing of the Ministers in the Church of England, demon-

strating that such limited contacts were neither actual communion with, nor approval of, the church's faults but merely recognition that spiritual edification is not "inclosed by any hedge, or ditch, divine or human, made about it, but lies in common for all, for the good of all." Robinson made significant distinction between his separation from public communion with the Church of England and his allowance of private association with its godly members or with "things lawful" in its practice.'[34] Furthermore, both Robinson and, at Plymouth, William Brewster advised applicants for admission to their covenant that denunciation of the Church of England was not approved. If applicants began such statements, they would "stop them forthwith, shewing them that wee required no such things at their hands, but only to hold forth faith in Christ Jesus ... and submission to every Ordinance and appointment of God, leaving the Church of *England* to themselves."[35]

During the reign of James I, there also began to appear congregationalists who were intent upon remaining *within* the Church of England, who lamented its need for reform but nevertheless believed it a true church.[36] Henry Jacob, for example, insisted that he was not a Separatist, but endured imprisonment in 1604 for advocating the reform of English Protestantism along congregational lines; a church, he said, was created by "a free mutuall consent of Believers joyning & covenanting to live as Members of a holy Society togeather in all relgious & vertuous duties as Christ & his Apostles did institute & practice in the Gospell."[37] Jacob implemented this ideal in 1616 by forming a church in London which "Covenanted togeather to walk in all Gods Ways" and then chose and ordained him as its pastor.[38] Nor was Jacob's church alone in its views; during these same years, the tenets of nonseparating congregationalism were also advanced by such reforming preachers as William Bradshaw, Robert Parker, and Paul Baynes. But it was in the relative freedom of the Low Countries that English churchmen had opportunity, in the early 1630s, to bring this position to full expression. There, especially through the influence of William Ames (1576–1633), the theory and practice of this ecclesiastical "middle way" between episcopacy and separation were developed by a number of ministers, including three—John Davenport, Thomas

Hooker, and Hugh Peter—who would play important roles in the establishment of New England congregationalism.

At the time the Salem church was organized in 1629, the boundaries separating these three types of covenantal congregationalism were not, in practice, always clearly drawn. There did exist distinctly different attitudes toward the Church of England, as to whether it was a true or false church and whether covenanted persons should have public or even private association with it. But despite these definite—and important—differences, regular correspondence, debate, exchange of ideas, pulpit visitations, and movement of members began early in the century. Moreover, in both England and Holland were congregations which admitted Separatists to membership as well as those of the nonseparating persuasion. These factors set a context in which the religious beliefs and practices of individuals, groups, and occasionally whole congregations were subject to marked change and development. The history of Henry Jacob's church in London provides numerous illustrations of these points. Established in 1616 on the principle of nonseparation, the church nonetheless "gave notice" of its formation to London Separatists and considered them "brethren in the common faith" throughout its early years. Under the ministry of John Lathrop, who succeeded Jacob in 1624, internal debate over separation from the Church of England kept the congregation in ferment, and, by 1641, it had become the parent congregation of London's most important Baptist preachers and churches. In 1645 its own pastor, Henry Jessey, a friend and correspondent of John Winthrop, was rebaptized.[39] Thus, when the Salem colonists covenanted together in 1629, they were not relating themselves to a clearly defined communion, party, or denomination but were instead drawing upon a patchwork tradition of English congregationalism which was still very much in process of development.

Covenantal congregationalism, of course, already had its representatives in New England, the Plymouth colonists, but their direct influence upon the decisions made at Salem was apparently limited.[40] Certainly Salem's newly elected pastor, Samuel Skelton, was acquainted before he left England with congregational theory and the controversies it had engendered. In addition to works of practical piety by John Dod, Henry Scudder, and Lewis Bayly, the small library which he brought to the colony contained treatises by the Separatists Henry Ainsworth and John Robinson describing the "communion of saints" in church covenant as well as tracts attacking Separatism by Richard Bernard, Stephen Bredwell, and John Paget.[41] Samuel Sharpe, ruling elder of the Salem church until his death in 1656, may also have had prior knowledge of Separatist congregationalism, since he had been a proprietor of Plymouth and had sold his holdings to its governor, William Bradford, only shortly before becoming interested in the Massachusetts Bay Company.[42] Likewise, Salem's John Endecott was pleased to discover that the judgment of the Plymouth church concerning "ye outward forme of Gods worshipe" did not differ from his own long-standing views on the subject.[43] But whatever the precise historical sources of its polity, events of the ensuing twelve months suggest that the church discipline practiced in Salem inclined toward the Separatist end of the congregationalist spectrum.

In Salem the deviations from conformity appearing in ecclesiastical organization and in the ministers' prayers and sermons aroused the opposition of two council members, John and Samuel Browne.[44] Although several old planters also were conformist in their opinions, they apparently did not intercede in the controversy, and Endecott ordered the two brothers to return to England for disturbing the peace of the colony. Upon reaching England, the Brownes complained to the company but received little satisfaction, since its major concern was the protection of its reputation. To that end, the company's officers first confiscated letters which the Brownes had sent to "their private freinds heere in England," and then wrote warnings to Higginson, Skelton, and Endecott that any aspersions "cast upon the state heere" were ill considered and might "make us obnoxious to any adversary."[45] The company's actions thus paralleled the position stated in *The Humble Request* and *The Planters Plea;* it sought to avoid any implication that it planned separation from, or disruption of, the established church settlement.

But when Johnson, Winthrop, Dudley, Coddington, and their fellows actually arrived at Salem in early summer, 1630, they found that this earlier reproof had done little to mollify tendencies toward separation in the Salem church.

Skelton refused to baptize Coddington's child and denied participation in the Lord's Supper to all four men, because, as members of the Church of England, they were not members of "any particular reformed church."[46] To add to the injury, a member of John Lathrop's covenanted congregation in London presented himself at the same time and, on the basis of "testimony" from that church, was admitted "not onely to the Lord's Supper, but his child unto Baptisme."[47] Winthrop and the others wrote back to England for advice on church discipline, and John Humfrey compiled for their direction statements on polity from the hands of William Ames and others "best studied in these thinges."[48] In sending these statements, Humfrey pleaded that proof "to the good people here that wee goe not away for Separation, the apprehension whereof ... takes deepe impression in them" would do much to restore confidence among those displeased by early reports of the colony.[49] John Cotton, meanwhile, wrote Skelton, giving a detailed refutation of Skelton's assumption that "none of our congregations in England are particular reformed churches, but mr Lathrops & such as his."[50]

The newly arrived settlers did not, however, await the advice of Ames, Humfrey, and Cotton. They asked the Plymouth colonists to join in the observance of a fast day on 30 July, at which time Winthrop, Dudley, Johnson, and the minister John Wilson formed the Boston church by signed covenant. In succeeding weeks they added others to their congregation, and in late August a second fast day was held at which the church chose Wilson pastor, Increase Nowell elder, and William Gager and William Aspinwall deacons. In confirming Wilson in his office, they "used imposition of hands, but with this protestation by all, that it was only as a sign of election and confirmation, not of any intent that Mr. Wilson should renounce his ministry he received in England."[51] By this affirmation that the Church of England was indeed a true church, however much in need of reform, the Boston colonists initiated development of the New England way on the priniciples of nonseparating congregationalism.

But even this form of congregationalism would have been too radical for Puritans who shared John Cotton's views in 1630. In his letter of reprimand to Samuel Skelton, Cotton expressed an understanding of church covenants significantly different from those being acted upon at Salem or Boston. According to Cotton, "explicite & solemne covenant" was an aid to "neerer fellowship with god & one another" rather than an "essentiall cause of the church without which it can not bee." Covenants, therefore, did not constitute a church but instead were valuable teaching devices which promoted the moral and spiritual "wel being & continuance of a church," and Cotton noted that "some congregations in England" were using them for just this purpose. He argued further that, understood in this manner, the established church itself employed covenants, since

> it is not a vayne thing, that the whole state in Parliament in the beginning of Q[ueen] Elizabeths raigne did renounce popery under a penalty to embrace the gospell of Christ. for such a thing was Asa his covenant, even a law of the chiefe members of the state in the name of the rest.[52]

By denying that explicit congregational covenant was the essential mark of a true church, Cotton could justify remaining a parish minister within the Church of England while seeking its reform. To his mind, both John Robinson and the ostensibly unseparated Jacob-Lathrop church had overemphasized discipline as the mark of a true church by their exaltation of the covenant. This, he reminded Skelton, was to go beyond the example of the apostles, who did not withdraw from the churches at Corinth and Galatia even though these contained "sundry scandalous persons both for life and doctrine."[53] Thus, even though by the end of the decade John Cotton would be New England's most distinguished apologist for congregationalism, in 1630 his convictions had not yet developed in that direction, and he spoke for many Puritans who then perceived any variety of congregationalism as a dangerous solution to their quarrels with the religious establishment.

The winter of 1630–31 found the fledgling colony presenting only the indefinite first features of its later ecclesiastical policy. Opinion ranged from the conformity of the old planters to the Separatist practices of Samuel Skelton, with the most influential settlers pursuing a course of reform without renunciation. Still, even the nonseparated congregationalism developing at Boston would be considered radicalism in England, and the subscribers of the company clearly recognized that any decisions they made concerning church discipline would have to be defensible at home, not only to the crown, but also to the Puritan party within the Church of England, which for some time to come would be supplying them with goods, capital, and manpower necessary for maintenance of the colony. It was the arrival of the Separatist "firebrand" Roger Williams which forced colonial leaders to begin deciding the direction the congregational way would lead in New England.

Roger Williams's Separatist Piety

In England in the spring of 1629, at the same time the Bay Company was developing plans for its New England venture, Roger Williams was serving as household chaplain to a wealthy Essex Puritan, Sir William Masham. Such a post was then a relatively common refuge for the minister who, because of a "tender conscience," could not accept a position within the established church, and while so employed Williams would meet and wed Mary Barnard, a maid to Masham's stepdaughter. Having recently departed his studies at Cambridge, Williams stated that he had refused both a "New England call" and "2 severall livings proferred" to him in order to retain the "libertie affoorded" by his chaplaincy.[54] Apparently this liberty included not only freedom from conformity to the common order of worship but also freedom from daily parish responsibilities, since Williams had opportunity to spend part of his time in London acquainting himself with the current of public affairs.[55] But despite his satisfaction in 1629, Williams would shortly leave Masham's service and sail for New England, propounding there a "reformation without tarying for anie" which immediately provoked controversy with the leading colonists.

Too little is known of Williams's youth to trace the precise sources of the theological opinions he espoused in Massachusetts. The son of a London guildsman of the Merchant Tailors, the young Roger Williams possessed abilities as a shorthand scribe which for a time were employed by the famed jurist Sir Edward Coke, under whose auspices he obtained his education at Charterhouse School and, with a modest scholarship, at Pembroke Hall, Cambridge, Concerning his religious development, Williams later recalled that following his conversion his spiritual "questions and troubles" had revolved not around his personal reconciliation with God but rather around his "sanctification and fellowship with the holiness of God."[56] During the last years of his studies at Cambridge, these introspective uncertainties about religious purity seem to have led him out of conformity into Separatism. In January 1627 he had completed the A.B. by subscribing his adherence to the Three Articles, thereby accepting the king's supremacy in ecclesiastical affairs and the religious authority of the Thirty-Nine Articles and the Book of Common Prayer. During 1629, however, Williams discontinued his studies toward an advanced degree, forfeited his scholarship, and refused two beneficed appointments, actions which suggest a growing alienation from the religious establishment.[57] Further, he now *opposed* use of the prayer book and, while traveling in Lincolnshire with John Cotton and Thomas Hooker, "presented his *Arguments* from *Scripture*, why he durst not joyn with them in their use of *Common prayer.*"[58] Williams's rejection of read prayers, although at this date too radical for Cotton and Hooker, was already a common view among the Separatists; as early as 1590 Henry Barrow had judged that the ill effect of written prayers was "utterly to quench and extinguish the Spirit of God, both in ministerie and people."[59]

Williams's opposition to common prayer in this early debate with Cotton and Hooker was indicative of the general religious orientation toward which his quest for "fellowship with the holiness of God" was turning him. He was convinced that personal piety could rightly express itself only through the worship and discipline of a properly ordered church. Participation in "spirituall societie," he asserted, "is the fayrest evidence of Adoption. If this Pin breakes all falls."[60] But, although he concurred with the view being adopted in New England that the scripturally authorized shape for "spirituall societie" was the covenanted congregation, he entertained an extremely strict conception of the qualifications for admission to the covenant. The heart of the covenant ideal was the requirement that membership be restricted to professing and practicing Christians, "visible saints," and among New England churches it would later become expected that potential members should not only evince doctrinal knowledge and moral uprightness but also be able to give suitable account of their conversion experiences.[61] From Williams's perspective, however, such professions were *not* by themselves sufficient for acceptance to church membership; in addition to demonstrating the traits of personal godliness, applicants must also publicly repent their former associations with the Church of England, whose worship and polity deviated from "the first and most ancient path" established by God in the New Testament.[62] To Williams's way of thinking, eligibility for church membership required repudiation of "those inventions of men," those "ordinances ministered by Antichrist's power," which had sprung up within medieval Catholicism and which still tainted the Church of Engalnd: clerical vestments, read prayers, episcopal polity, or the mixing of godly with impious persons in the parish church. The Christian must "come out from that former false Church or Christ, and his Ministrie, Worship, &c. before he can be united to the true Israel."[63]

The corollary to this principle was, of course, that anyone who had not thus "come out" would defile the Christian rites if allowed to participate in them. In 1636 John Cotton quoted Williams on this point, stating that when the ordinances of Christian worship were "'practiced by persons polluted through spirituall deadnesse and filthinesse of Communion, they [the ordinances] become uncleane unto them, and are prophaned by them.'"[64] These rigid requirements for church membership were designed to protect the purity of the covenanted community from the contagion of false Christianity, which could be spread by contact with the diseased English church or any of its members. Thus, when Williams later ministered at Salem, he would not receive persons into "Church-fellowship untill they first disclaime[d] their Churches in *England* as no Churches" and "rejected all Communion with the Parish Assemblies, so much as in hearing of the Word amongst them."[65]

By these declarations, Roger Williams emphatically threw his support to the most radical of the Separatists. For them the church covenant represented no mere matter of ecclesiastical politics; it was instead a demonstration of personal devotion and a refuge from spiritual dangers and pollutions. The piety of such persons finds clear expression in the opinions of John Canne, one of their number who was publishing tractarian literature and controverting non-separated Puritans in Holland at the same time Williams was laboring for the Separatist cause in Massachusetts. Canne's *Necessitie of Separation from the Church of England* (1634), in the opinion of Roger Williams, "unanswerably proved" the rightness of separating from the Church of England in order "to seek out the true way of Gods worship according to Christ Jesus."[66] Although the ideals of Canne and Williams would later diverge dramatically, in the early 1630s they spoke with a single voice for the "necessitie" of separated congregations.

Canne's appeal turned on the argument that true piety consisted not simply in a state of mind or an inclination of the soul, but equally, in the expression of that spiritual inclination through purified worship and public testimony. He attacked Puritan reformers within the Church of England for denigrating the importance of true forms of worship in the hierarchy of personal godliness. Such erroneous teaching, Canne averred, not only made false division between the components of true piety, but, worse, represented a cowardly justification for their failure to separate from the established church. He fully agreed with Henry Barrow that such unseparated reformers "boast of a false gift when they speake of their inward sanctification. Christ doth not reigne in the heart of anie that wil not submit all their outward actions to be ruled by him also. Christ will have the whole man both bodie and soule to serve him."[67] By this reasoning, any who remained in communion with the false ministry of the established church were guilty of "spiritual whoredom against the Lord" and in their misguided efforts at worship offended God's "nostrils with the stench" of "trash" and "unclean persons." Only in public separation from false religion did the individual authentically express his devotion to God and protect himself from the divine wrath which would descend upon disobedience. "It showeth," Canne concluded, "that the love and zeal of God is much in us, when our care is to worship only in his own ordinances, and to leave the contrary.... For one infallible evidence of true conversion is to see the filthiness of idolatry, and to cast

away the same with reproach.... To communicate in a
false worship causeth pollution to the soul."[68] For Canne,
as for Roger Williams, convictions regarding church order,
discipline, and reformation were intimately bound up with
ideas about personal piety—about "fellowship," as Williams described it, "with the holiness of God."

By their insistence that repentance and purification
must accompany personal godliness as prerequisites for
church membership, Roger Williams and other radical
Separatists were not denying the existence of truly faithful
saints among the nonconformists. But they were warning
the individual that, if his faith did not include a longing to
worship within the order of a pure church, it gave poor
evidence of indeed being true faith. And, further, they were
warning that even true faith, if it did not seek out
"spirituall societie," would be stunted in its growth, disor-
dered in its expression. There was, wrote the Separatist
John Wilkinson in 1619, an incompleteness of the piety of
nonseparated Puritans; he compared them to a loose
"heape of stones" which had not yet been constructed into
a house.[69] In 1644, recalling his controversies in Massachusetts, Roger Williams made the similar observation
that many of the saints required a further experience of
God's spirit to draw them out of false worship.

> Although I confess that godly persons are not dead but
> living Trees, not dead, but living Stones, and need no
> new Regeneration ... yet need they *a mighty worke of
> Gods Spirit* to humble and ashame them, and to cause
> them to loath themselves for their Abominations or
> stincks in Gods nostrils (as it pleaseth Gods Spirit to
> speak of false Worships).... hence it is that I have
> known some precious and godly hearts confess, that
> the plucking of their souls out from the Abominations of
> false worship, hath been *a second kind of Regenration*.[70]

Repudiation of the Church of England, Williams believed,
issued directly from personal religious experience, as a
"worke of Gods Spirit" comparable to the experience of
conversion. Scrupulous attention to matters of church polity was an integral part of the individual's spiritual growth.

Thus, among the identifiable forms of congregationalism
in New England, Roger Williams was a representative of
the most extreme or radical type. In Massachusetts Bay the
actions of the minister John Wilson and the magistrates

John Winthrop and Thomas Dudley implied belief that the individual could live a pious life despite external connections with nominal Christians in the English parishes. And even at Plymouth it was not considered a danger to the Christian's spiritual health to attend preaching in the established church. But for Roger Williams the piety of the individual and the sanctitiy of the congregation could be protected only by completely disconnecting them from the Church of England, which was, he felt, irretrievably defiled by remnants of Catholicism.

Upon his arrival in New England Williams was asked to join the Boston congregation (perhaps even offered the position of teacher later held by John Cotton), but he refused because the members would not publicly declare their repentance for having previously communed with the English parishes. For them to have done so would, of course, have run counter both to their public declarations in England and to the express opinions of their supporters there such as John Humfrey and John Cotton. Williams declared, dissatisfied, "I durst not officiate to an unseparated people, as, upon examination and conference, I found them to be."[71] Instead, he traveled to Salem, where Samuel Skelton entertained notions more satisfactory to Williams's Separatist scruples. But when Williams accepted the Salem church's call to the office of teacher, the court of assistants in Boston wrote to them that the appointment should not be made without first "advising with the council."[72] Following this intervention by the civil authorities, Williams and his wife again moved, settling at Plymouth in late spring or early summer 1631.

In the Pilgrim colony Williams, like other immigrants reared among the merchant and artisan classes of England's cities, soon turned to agriculture for a livelihood. He "wrought hard at the hoe" to provide for himself and his wife and, with the assistance of John Winthrop, obtained some cattle in 1632.[73] Meanwhile, although he held no church office, Williams regularly "prophesied" in a fashion Governor William Bradford found "well approoved" by the members. By the fall of 1633, however, Bradford was disconcerted to find that Williams had begun

> to fall into some strang oppinions, and from opinion to practise; which caused some controversie betweene ye church & him, and in ye end some discontente on his parte,

by occasion wherof he left them some thing abruptly.
Yet after wards sued for his dismission to ye church
of Salem, which was granted, with some caution to them
concerning him, and what care they ought to have of him.[74]

After returning to Salem, Williams assisted the ailing
Samuel Skelton in his pastorate, but again was not elected
to any official post in the congregation.

During Williams's two-year absence in Plymouth, Governor John Winthrop and his associates had made considerable
progress toward their goal of establishing a Christian commonwealth. Among the most notable developments was
the decision in May 1631, that "noe man shalbe admitted
to the freedome of this body polliticke, but such as are
members of some of the churches within the lymitts of
the same." Despite the presence of the old planters among
the freemen already admitted, this new restriction was
understood as a means of insuring the integrity and sound
judgment of the body of men responsible for electing magistrates.[75] In the following year, after consultation among
the Boston, Plymouth, and Salem churches, it was decided with reference to Increase Nowell that no man should
hold the positions of magistrate and ruling elder of a church
at the same time.[76]

By concentrating political power in the hands of church
members at the same time that they separated political and
ecclesiastical offices, the colony leaders hoped that "gods
institutions (such as the government of church and of
commonwealth be) may be close and compact, and co-
ordinate one to another, and yet not confounded."[77] But
this functional separation of church and state by no means
released the latter from religious responsibility: "Over religious and moral offenses the civil government exercised
jurisdiction concurrent with but broader than that of the
individual churches; while the churches were responsible
for disciplining only their own members, the state was
responsible for the spiritual welfare of every man within its
borders, whether church member or not."[78] In this manner, not merely the churches but the total society could be
organized according to divine law, since "when a commonwealth hath liberty to mould his owne frame . . . the
scripture hath given full direction for the right ordering of
the same, and that, in such sort as may best mainteyne the

euexia [vigor] of the church."[79] For this reason, although ministers no longer held civil office as they had in 1629, they were regularly consulted by the magistrates on matters of civil policy, a practice which became especially marked after the long-awaited arrival of John Cotton and Thomas Hooker in September 1633.

Imposition of congregationalist ecclesiology and this political rule by the saints had quickly aroused opposition; in 1631 both Philip Ratliffe and Henry Linne were banished for their public clamor and letters back to England decrying the colony's church and civil order. Similarly, Thomas Knower was "sett in the bilbowes" for threatening to challenge in the English courts the colonial authority to punish his alleged offenses.[80] In England grumbling letters from such malcontents, together with reports spread by returning sailors, began to concern supporters of the colony and at the same time to raise the hopes of its enemies. Letters from Puritan friends to the Winthrops, father and son, reiterated the fear already conveyed by John Humfrey that the colony was slipping into Separatism. In March 1633, the London merchant Francis Kirby reported to John Winthrop, Jr., that

> your friends heere who ar members of your plantacion have had much to do to answer the unjust complaints made to the Kinge and counsell of your government there . . . . I know I shall not need to advise you that the prayeinge for our kinge be not neglected in any of your publique meetings, and I desire that you differ no more from us in Church government, then you shall find that we differ from the prescript rule of gods word.[81]

The "unjust complaints" to which Kirby referred had been gathered by the head of the New England Council, Sir Ferdinando Gorges, who hoped that revocation of the colony's patent would further his own attempt to establish a New England plantation. He organized a group of dissidents banished from Massachusetts to petition the Privy Council, before whom, according to Governor Winthrop, they asserted that Massachusetts Bay's "ministers and people did continually rail against state, church, and bishops" of England.[82] The colony was spared royal intervention when Richard Saltonstall, John Humfrey, and

Matthew Cradock met with the Privy Council and pointed out the colony's potential military value as a source for masts, cordage, and other naval supplies.

Thus, when Roger Williams returned to Salem in the early autumn of 1633, godly desires for "a due form of Goverment both civill and ecclesiasticall" were meeting opposition in England as well as in Massachusetts. And even among the leaders of the colony, zeal for reformation in conformity with supposed biblical precepts was bound up with disagreement over what particular practices and institutions those precepts authorized. Roger Williams's presumption that true reformation meant reformation upon Separatist principles was destined to tumultuous failure, but his strident advocacy did much to force more careful delineation of church and civil order in Massachusetts.

Religious Controversy, 1633–36

Two minor questions which arose not long after Williams's return to Salem illustrate the scrupulous efforts of the Salem church to conform its practice to that of the apostolic era—and perhaps thereby to demonstrate a superior zeal for reformation. The first concerned whether women should wear veils during worship and hinged upon interpretation of Paul's comments to the Corinthian church on that subject (1 Cor. 11:2–16). William Hubbard reported in 1630 that Samuel Skelton had begun to advocate the veiling of women soon after Francis Higginson's death in 1630 and that Skelton was later joined in this opinion by Roger Williams.[83] Other ministers of the colony doubted that Paul's words could be interpreted with such literal simplicity. In 1634, during his weekly lecture at Boston, John Cotton discouraged the use of veils by proposing "that where (by the custom of the place) they were not a sign of the women's subjection, they were not commended by the apostle." At this, Salem's John Endecott rose in such heated opposition that Governor Winthrop "interposed" and broke off debate.[84] Richard Mather shared Cotton's doubts that the use of veils could be proved from Scripture and, in response to queries from England in 1636, defended the New England churches against any suggestion that requiring women "to be veyled in the church" was a com-

mon practice among them.[85] But the restitutionist impulse
was far stronger in the youthful Williams, and the requirement that women be veiled, in its intent to recreate
the apostolic church order, was of a piece with his long-
standing refusal "to doff and don [his hat] to the Most
High in worship," because this customary bit of English
piety lacked a scriptural warrant.[86]

A second minor disagreement occurred in the fall of
1633, when the ministers began holding meetings at which
"some question of moment was debated," once every two
weeks. Both Skelton and Williams objected to this practice,
fearing that it might develop a presbyterial authority in-
jurious to the liberty of the individual congregations. The
other ministers actually agreed with this principle of autonomy, but they considered *consultation* among ministers
and congregations perfectly acceptable. From the first,
they had regularly conferred among themselves or with
the Plymouth church on matters of polity, and even the
writings of such staunch Separatist congregationalists as
Francis Johnson and Henry Ainsworth provided prece-
dents for this advisory relation among churches.[87]

In both cases, the extreme degree to which the Salem
ministers asserted congregational distinctiveness and independence paralleled the town's resistence to the increasing concentration of power in Boston. It should be
remembered, for example, that at this same time Salem
was receiving intense criticism from Thomas Hooker, John
Haynes, and Deputy Governor Dudley for its failure to
share in the expenses of fortifications at Boston. The matter
was resolved by the court only after these Newtown citizens had sent a letter "full of bitterness and resolution" to
Governor Winthrop.[88]

But in late December 1633 the opinions of Roger Williams
took a turn which, in the minds of the magistrates, far
overshadowed disputes over the niceties of church polity.
At that time he presented the court of assistants a treatise
he had written at Plymouth; this "large Book in Quarto"
declared that the royal patent granting the land on which
the colony was settled should be rejected and returned to
England. Coming as it did in the midst of Gorges's attempts to have the colony charter recalled, such a pro-
nouncement must at best be described as politically naive,
especially since the young minister embellished it with

abusive characterizations of the Stuart monarchs. In his manuscript Williams argued that the king's grant did not give legal title to the land, which could be legitimately occupied only if purchased from its true owners, the Indians. Although the treatise itself is no longer extant, John Winthrop recorded four major points at which he and the other magistrates found it particularly objectionable. First, Williams charged James I with a lie for saying that he was the first Christian prince to discover New England. Further, he asserted that Charles I had used his profession of Christianity as a false justification for taking land from its rightful owners, simply because they did not happen to be Christian. Third, he identified Charles with the ten sovereigns whom Revelation prophesied would "give their power, and autoritie unto the beast" and wage apocalyptic warfare against "the Lambe." Finally, persons who called Europe *Christendom* were, Williams decreed, blasphemers.[89]

Williams was not the first to ponder the prior claims of the Indians to land which European kings were granting to their own subjects. Since the age of the Elizabethan explorers, tracts publicizing colonization had proposed religious or legal considerations favoring the English title to land in the New World over that of its native claimants. Robert Gray, for example, had written in 1609 that "a Christian king" might lawfully subdue barbarian peoples, if his conquest would bring them to "humanitie, pietie, and honestie."[90] In 1629 John Winthrop had outlined a somewhat more sophisticated legal argument which distinguished between a "natural" and a "civil" right to the land. All men, Winthrop declared, have a natural claim to land which "lies common" and untended; the Indians clearly held such tenure in New England. But a civil right took precedent over this right of common usage and was achieved whenever men "improve the Land" by enclosure, settled habitation, and the pasturage of livestock. If the Indians were left land "sufficient for their use," so Winthrop developed his case, the English settlers might by civil claim "lawfully take the rest, there being more than enough for them and us."[91] In Winthrop's opinion, the Puritans' right to the land was further confirmed by the fact that during the winter of 1633 smallpox had virtually emptied the area of Indians. By this event, he wrote John Endecott, God's special providence had legitimated the English title, since "if we had no right to this lande, yet our God hathe right to it, and if he be pleased to give it us (takinge it from a people who had so longe usurped upon him, and abused his Creatures) who shall control him or his termes?"[92]

Of these various justifications for the English land title, Roger Williams directed his most acerbic criticism against the argument that the responsibilities and prerogatives of a "Christian" monarch or nation justified the acquisition of Indian lands. As Winthrop saw at the time and as Edmund S. Morgan has recently observed, Williams opposed the patent primarily because he denied the assumption that "a prince's Christianity gave him a more valid claim to the land than that enjoyed by the heathen natives."[93] In advancing this argument, Williams exhibited not simply religiously motivated humanitarianism but more specifically the extent to which Separatist ideology informed his perception of the practical affairs of the colony. To lament, as one recent biographer has, that "there is not a shred of logical correspondence between King Charles and the ten kings of the earth" cited by Williams from Revelation is to misunderstand the extent to which Williams's piety prompted his advocacy of Indian rights.[94]

The clearest point from which to begin reconstructing Williams's argument is Winthrop's statement that the youthful Separatist had accused of blasphemy those persons who referred to Europe as Christendom. Williams, it should be recalled, strictly adhered to the principles of congregationalism; in his mind the "one holy Nation of the *Christian Israel*" consisted solely of "the Church gathered unto *Christ Jesus* in particular and distinct *congregations* all the World over."[95] This would lead him to argue, in *The Bloudy Tenent* (1644) and *Christenings Make Not Christians* (1645), that the terms Christian or Christendom could not properly be applied to a *nation,* since only the *church* actually consisted of God's chosen people. All nations, even the most civilized, were therefore in the religious sense *heathen*—not a part of the church.[96] Civil states could not legitimately acquire special privileges by claiming that they were, as a whole, Christian. Williams went on to note that the misconception of a geographic Christendom had arisen during the medieval hegemony of Catholicism and was thus yet another antichristian pollution which the true

Christian was duty-bound to purge.[97] By this reasoning,
when an English king justified his actions by referring to
his rights as a Christian prince, he was placing himself in
league with the Catholic Antichrist. In accepting land
claimed by this irreligious pretense, the colonists, Williams
warned, were accepting a share of the king's guilt and
perhaps also a share of the divine wrath which such impiety might provoke. It was quite probably in this context
that Williams accused James of lying for calling himself a
Christian prince and identified Charles with the ten antichristian kings portrayed in Revelation. Thus the same insistence on ecclesiastical purification and reformation
which was the foundation of his strict views on church
membership showed itself in another aspect in his demand
that the colony reject its royal patent. The blasphemous
presuppositions of the patent imperiled both Indian land
and English sanctity.

After the magistrates met to discuss the treatise in December 1633, Winthrop wrote John Endecott in Salem to
obtain Williams's retraction. Both Endecott and Williams
responded; the latter was apologetic, professing "only to
have written for the private satisfaction of the governor" of
Plymouth and "offering his book or any part of it, to be
burnt." After conferring with the ministers of the Boston
church, John Wilson and John Cotton, the magistrates decided that the tract was obscurely written and not so
dangerous as it had first appeared. Even men accustomed
to biblical rhetoric found Williams's writing overburdened
with "allegoryes," and Winthrop complained that it "ex-
ceeds all that ever I have read (of so serious an Argument) in
figures and flourishes." Consequently, when Williams
"appeared penitently" at the January meeting of the court
and "gave satisfaction" of his loyalty to the king, the matter was dropped.[98]

In England both George's and Charles's government
were also working for return of the charter, but with a far
different motivation than Roger Williams. During the
spring and summer of 1634 Archbishop Laud was extending his influence in Charles's regime and was placed at the
head of a committee for the regulation of colonies. In July
the magistrates received word from Matthew Cradock that
they should return their charter to England, but they decided not to do so. In September rumors reached the col-

ony that a fleet of ships was being sent to "compel us, by force, to receive a new governor, and the discipline of the church of England."[99] The colony hurried the construction of fortifications, but the threat never materialized. Undeterred by the precarious situation of the colony, Williams soon resumed his preaching against the patent. He was summoned to appear at the November meeting of the court, but, once again, no action was taken.[100]

According to John Cotton, the magistrates did not proceed against Williams because Cotton, on behalf of his fellow ministers, presented a "Request to the Magistrates, that they would be pleased to forbeare all civill prosecution against him [Williams], till our selves (with our Churches) had dealt with him in a Church way."[101] The new governor, Thomas Dudley, doubted the power of persuasion to change Williams's opinions, and his doubts proved justified. An attempt was made to shift the ground of the debate by using Winthrop's distinction between natural and civil titles to the land, but Williams would not relent. He replied that the Indians used land for hunting which they might not actually occupy or cultivate, and that their title was thus analogous to the claims held on forest preserves by nobles in England. Nothing could be said to alter his conviction that holding the patent constituted a "Nationall sinne."[102]

Just at the time Williams renewed his preaching against the patent, the magistrates received the equally alarming news that the English flag at Salem had been mutilated by having the cross cut out of it. Investigation determined that John Endecott had ordered the act on the presumption that "the red cross was given to the king of England by the pope, as an ensign of victory, and so a superstitious thing, and a relique of antichrist."[103] In later years William Coddington, William Hubbard, and Cotton Mather laid blame for the incident with Roger Williams, whose zealous preaching for reformation kept Salem simmering over religious matters. But contemporary accounts demonstrate that the matter should not be explained so simply. During the following six months, considerable public agitation developed against the presence of the cross in the flag, opposition espoused by several prominent figures, not solely by Endecott and Williams.

Although condemning the physical defacement of the

flag as a regrettable act of "indiscreet zeale," a potent minority of magistrates and ministers shared Endecott's basic opinion that the cross was "an Idoll, unlawfull to be continued."[104] Contemporary letters numbered John Winthrop and John Cotton among these iconoclasts. Indeed, Israel Stoughton reported that Winthrop was *"so zealous against the cross"* that rumor made this the reason for his failure to be reelected governor in 1635.[105] Strident controversy over the issue delayed the court's decison in Endecott's case and prompted suggestion of a new design for the flag, omitting the cross.[106] An uneasy resolution was achieved in the spring of 1635, when Thomas Hooker challenged the zealots and halted debate with the argument that, despite its idolotrous significance for "papists," Protestants could legitimately reinterpret and use the flag "in a Civill way." Christian charity, he counseled, favors this conclusion and in such matters will generally "preferre peace before contestation and heart burninge."[107]

The incident of the flag exemplifies the manner in which the impetus toward root and branch reformation could divide colonial opinion and rapidly induce unsettling controversy. It illustrates as well the limited extent to which the colonial leadership would heed Roger Williams's interpretation of reformation. They, as did most English Protestants, identified the papacy with the Antichrist of biblical prophecy, and "reliques" of papal influence such as the cross in the ensign could thus be depended upon to rouse their holy ire. But when Williams advanced the more extreme interpretation that Antichrist also defiled the Church of England and pleaded for reformation by separation, they would not follow.

In April 1635 the court of assistants again interrogated Williams; on this occasion he had been preaching against the imposition of a loyalty oath upon male residents of the colony. His sermons had advanced this unwelcome thesis from the fact that not all residents were church members and the assumption that taking an oath was an act of Christian worship. "A magistrate," Roger Williams declared, "ought not to tender an oath to an unregenerate man, for ... we thereby have communion with a wicked man in the worship of God, and cause him to take the name of God in vain."[108] For identical reasons he stated that regenerate persons should not pray with the unregenerate, even members of their own family. In the case of the loyalty oath, this extreme demand for religious purity was construed by the magistrates as a clear breach of civil order, since it encouraged several citizens to refuse the oath, making it difficult for the magistrates to "discerne how the people stood affected to the publick Safety" during the present crisis in relations with the crown.[109] For this reason, Williams was debated by other ministers at the April meeting of the court, and Winthrop felt that his position was clearly refuted, noting that Endecott, who at first shared Williams's view, eventually gave way.[110]

Roger Williams never relented in his opposition to the use of oaths in the conduct of civil affairs. While in England in 1644, for example, he forfeited monies won in a lawsuit and was judged in contempt of court for refusing to take his oath as a witness. Likewise, in 1652 he concluded his tract *The Hireling Ministry None of Christs* with a public challenge to debate the proposition that civil oaths were a misuse of Christian faith in God.[111]

In his preaching about the patent, the flag, and the resident's oath, the course of Williams's thought began with the principle that the rites and symbols of proper Christian worship could be used only within a covenanted congregation. To require others to use them in any form not only forced those persons into sin but also profaned the symbols. He rejected the idea that true Christianity was coterminous with a Christian political state, or Christendom. Such an idea, for him, was a remnant of Catholicism, and Catholicism was the dominion of Antichrist. The idea of Christendom bred false pride among civilized Europeans, the assurance, for example, that they had right by reason of superior piety to the land of native peoples. The patent, the flag, and the resident's oath were examples of the manner in which the false idea of a Christian state, a distortion of the true idea of the confessing church, could endanger individual souls and disfigure the symbols of Christianity by using them for illegitimate purposes.

After Samuel Skelton's death in August 1634, Roger Williams had continued to preach at Salem in an unofficial capacity, until the church appointed him teacher in the summer of 1635. Since the magistrates were then dealing with Williams for his opinions about oaths, they considered "calling of him to office ... a great contempt of authority."[112] The ministers were asked to define the limits for civil regulation of church affairs and replied that preachers who "obstinately maintain such opinions, (whereby a church might run into heresy, apostasy, or tyranny, and yet the civil magistrate could not intermeddle, (were to be removed, and that the other churches ought to request the magistrates so to do."[113] Meanwhile, the ministers continued their attempts to urge Williams to a change of mind; John Cotton, in particular, "spent a great part of the Summer in seeking by word and writing" to satisfy Williams's scruples on the points at issue.[114]

In July 1635 Salem petitioned the court for land in the area of Marblehead Neck, but the magistrates refused this request because the Salem church, in contempt of authority, had chosen Williams teacher. Incited by this action, Williams and elder Samuel Sharpe wrote a heated letter to the churches of Massachusetts on behalf of the Salem congregation, demanding that the magistrates be disciplined as church members for using their civil powers to interfere in matters of church order.[115] By August relations were severely strained, and Williams notified his congregation that conscience compelled him to renounce communion with the churches of the colony, "as full of antichristian pollution." Unless the Salem church also renounced connection with them, he would be forced to withdraw from its fellowship as well.[116]

By this declaration, Roger Williams's Separatist vision of reformation demonstrated its fundamental incompatibility with the desire to establish a holy commonwealth. For Williams the purity of the separated church was the paramount consideration, and, like Separatists since the time of Henry Barrow, this impelled him to depart from any who thwarted his quest for holiness. In Engalnd, the Separatists had not denied that the prince had an obligation to establish true faith and discipline and, if necessary, to enforce its practice. But, they had observed, the prince clearly was not living up to this obligation, and God had therefore commissioned them to pursue religious purification independent of state support. Williams apparently came to Massachusetts expecting no such "foot-dragging" from godly magistrates, but when he found that they seemed to prize social order above what he believed to be religious purity, he followed in disillusionment the well-worn path of the Separatist reformers.

In October Williams was brought before the court, with Governor John Haynes presiding and all the ministers present. There he engaged Thomas Hooker in disputation but did not retract any of his stated positions. The morning following the debate with Hooker, it was decided that Williams would be expelled from the jurisdiction of the colony. Pleading illness, he was granted six weeks before the sentence became effective, and this was later extended until spring with the provision that he cease all public exposition of his views. In January, however, the court learned that Williams had continued to express himself at religious gatherings in his home. It was then decided to return him to England, "because he had drawn above twenty persons to his opinion, and they were intended to erect a plantation about the Naragansett Bay, from whence the infection would easily spread into these churches, (the people being, many of them, much taken with the apprehension of his godliness)."[117] Learning of the plans for his deportation, Williams escaped into the wilderness before he could be forced onto a ship bound for England.

After his departure, the church at Salem continued to have a small group of dissidents who espoused the Separatist views which Williams had held. But with the appointment of Hugh Peter as the congregation's pastor in the spring of 1636, difficulties gradually subsided. Williams himself maintained contact with many people in the Bay Colony, especially with John Winthrop. Since Williams had begun in 1632 applying himself to learning the Indian languages, he soon became valuable to Massachusetts Bay as an informal diplomat among the various tribes of the area. When, in October 1636, for example, the colony made a treaty with the Narragansett tribe, the magistrates decided that "because we could not well make them understand the articles perfectly, we agreed to send a copy of them to Mr. Williams, who could best interpret them to them"[118] The fact that he was of the same social group as the other leaders of the Bay and shared many of their religious concerns caused him to be tolerated by them as long as possible and, even though his views became anathema, never to be rejected personally. Sir William Martin, writing to Winthrop not long after Williams's flight, gave what was probably a typical evaluation of Williams: "He is precipitate and passionate, which maye transporte him into error, but I hope his integrity and good intentions will bring him at last into the waye of truth, and confirme him therein."[119]

But despite the broad sympathies established by similar social class and common religious experience, distinct theological differences did exist between him and his peers. John Cotton clearly delineated these in a sermon which he preached at Salem not long after the departure of Roger Williams. In that sermon, Cotton asserted that it was not adherence to precise forms of worship which was the foundation of the church, but rather the *personal covenant* of God with the believer through the mediation of Christ. Thus the church is maintained by the grace of God and not by any work of the believer; even if Christians "break Covenant, yet if they keep close unto Christ, they have the Covenant, although they break it."[120] In what was surely a direct reference to Roger Williams, Cotton asked the Salem church to consider the nature of its covenant:

> Suppose the Church Promise never to defile themselves more with any Pollutions of the Sons of men, but they do defile themselves, then the Covenant is broken; they did Covenant they would not come into false Assemblies, & that they would have no fellowship with them, that did allow of false Assemblies; but this Covenant cometh to be broken: if this be your Covenant, it is but a Covenant of Works.[121]

Personal regeneration was the foundation of the covenanted congregation; to demand, as Williams had done, that it be coupled with personal purification was, in Cotton's opinion, to base church order on human works.

Williams's view of the theological issues at stake was stated in a letter which he wrote to John Winthrop in October 1636. Both its content and its perspective pointed toward the controversial literature which would make him famous in the following decade. In the letter Williams reiterated the Separatist distinction between the personal salvation of the Christian and the Christian's responsibility for proper worship of God. In making this distinction, he declared, he was not questioning the power of divine grace, exalting human works, or disputing the godliness of individual persons. But he was insisting that healthy, alert faith seeks expression in a rightly ordered church, and he was therefore distressed that the members of the Massachusetts Bay churches remained "asleepe" in impure forms of worship. In a reference to Rev. 5:1–5, in which John weeps because no one is worthy to open a scroll held in the right hand of God, Williams lamented this sleepy condition of the saints: "I must (and O that I had not Cause) grieve, because so many of Zions daughters see not and grieve not for their Soules Defilements, and that so few beare John Companie in weeping after the unfolding of the Seales which only Weepers are acquainted with." He felt that he had acted on God's behalf as a witness to awaken Massachusetts to further reformation, and he hoped that "the Seede sowne" through his efforts would "arise to the greater puritie of the Kingdome and Ordinances of the Prince of the Kings of the Earth." [122]

Thus the two themes which ran through the letter to Winthrop were Williams's religious sorrow over the present impurity of the Churches and his millennial hope that God would restore them. For the present, he believed that "Gods people must yet mournfully reade the 74, 79, 80, and 89 Psalmes, the Lamentations, Daniells 11th, and Revel. 11, 12th, 13th," which "argue Gods forsaking his people in respect of the visible Kingdome of the Lord Jesus." And he promised to "mourne dayly, heavily uncessantly till the Lord looke down from Heaven, and bring all his precious living stones into one New Jerusalem." [123]

Despite the conflict and sorrow which his ideas had engendered, Williams reminded the governor, they both sincerely sought "the way to lost Sion." It was a sentiment which encapsulated the perspective from which Williams pursued both his ministry in Massachusetts and much of his later career. Again and again he would affirm the shared conviction which bound him to the congregationalists of old and New England. They—far more than Anglican bishops, Scottish Presbyterians, Quakers, or American Indians—were the people before whom he sought to stand as prophet. But the irony and power to be found in his writings would in no small measure stem from the contrasting conceptions of "lost Sion" held by Williams and this, his chosen audience.

3 Pilgrimage toward the Millennium, 1636–43

In the holy commonwealth of Massachusetts Roger Williams's obsession with personal and ecclesiastical purity had engendered religious controversy; in the unrestricted environment of Providence it compelled him to seek the ecclesiology which duplicated that of the apostolic era. The years from 1636 to 1643, therefore, witnessed a spiritual pilgrimage by Williams, a pilgrimage which led him out of Separatism and, finally, out of the confines of any formal church fellowship whatever. In his alterations of religious opinion during these years, contemporaries likened him to the early English Baptist, John Smyth, and, indeed, the impetus for change seems to have been identical for both men. Writing in 1608, Smyth had answered his critics that

> wee professe even so much as they object: That wee are inconstant in erroer: that wee wou'd have the truth, though in many particulars wee are ignorant of it: We will never be satisfied in indevoring to reduce the worship and ministery of the Church, to the primitive Apostolic institution from which as yet it is so farr distant.[1]

With similar "inconstancy in error," Williams briefly adopted the Baptist position in 1639, but he soon rejected it and instead averred that no *authentic* church existed anywhere in the world. With that declaration, he laid aside his ministerial functions, pursued a living as a merchant and farmer, and fulfilled his sense of religious obligation by refining his skills as a polemicist and tractarian.

In this outline form, Roger Williams's religious quest has often been recounted. Modern historians have explained his eventual denial of the existence of true churches by asserting that it resulted when Williams extended to its most radical limit the ideal of church purity present among all New England Puritans: Williams "looked so eagerly for a pure visible Church that the kind of Church he looked for became increasingly invisible to him."[2] From this perspective the difference, for example, between John Cotton and Roger Williams was less a difference of belief than of attitude—the difference between a moderate and an extremist. This interpretation finds admirable summary in the judgment of Winthrop S. Hudson that "what distinguished Roger Williams from his fellow New Englanders was not a disagreement upon fundamental presuppositions but the singleness of devotion with which he pursued the implications of assumptions common to them all."[3] The presence of broad continuities between Williams's thought and that of other Puritans should not, however, be allowed to obscure the fundamental shift in Williams's theological position which occurred between the years 1636 and 1643. This critical alteration in Williams's opinions not only accounts for his withdrawal from formal church fellowship but also delineates the general orientation of his piety throughout the rest of his career. It was a change which involved not merely pursuing the implications of commonly held assumptions but also firmly rejecting some basic tenets of covenantal congregationalism.

Central to Williams's theological reorientation was the adoption of a distinctive form of millenarianism as the axis of his religious thought. Apocalyptic expectations which had earlier been a peripheral aspect of his Separatist piety were now organized into a millenarian vision of history through which he reinterpreted the character of religious reformation and his personal role in that reformation. Frustrated hopes in Massachusetts and physical isolation in Providence had set him adrift from the dominant archetype, reformation conducted by a holy commonwealth. Now, the influence of ideas associated with the early English Baptists and his own engagement in writing polemical letters and manuscripts regarding the nature of the church and religious liberty would press him toward a new, and more radical, formulation of his hopes.

Quest for the Authentic Church

The various Baptist congregations which would affect the career of Roger Williams were offshoots, by and large, of English Separatism. Although their early development is often obscure, it is clear that by the first decade of the seventeenth century English congregations had appeared in the Low Countries which, like the Separatists, totally rejected the legitimacy of the Church of England. They also shared with the Separatists a belief in congregational polity and in the power of professing Christians to establish such autonomous churches voluntarily. They differed, however, in demanding that their members be rebaptized, since they considered false and invalid the infant baptism practiced by the official church and by the Separatists.[4]

The *earliest* Baptist congregations also differed from the Separatists in rejecting the doctrine of predestination of the elect. Emphasizing instead that Christ had died for all who truly repented, believed, and were baptized, members of these congregations came to be known as *General Baptists.* The most important of these Baptist churches developed out of a Separatist congregation in Amsterdam pastored by John Smyth and Thomas Helwys. After a dispute in 1609 the congregation split, and in 1612 that part led by Helwys returned to London to witness its beliefs among its countrymen. From this London Baptist conventicle, under the leadership first of Helwys and then of John Murton, came important early tracts on liberty of conscience which would influence Roger Williams during the period from 1636 to 1643.

In the 1630s, first in England and then in New England, there began to appear congregations of *Particular Baptists,* that is, persons who combined the demand for rebaptism with Calvinist views on predestination. In London the most influential of these churches were composed of persons who broke away during this decade from the covenanted congregation pastored by John Lathrop. Roger Williams shared the Calvinist belief in the predestination of the elect and considered returning to England in 1636, in order "to helpe the Lord against the mighty" by associating himself with these London churches. And, in the 1640s, Particular Baptists such as Mark Lukar and the printer Gregory Dexter would emigrate from London to Rhode Island.

In both England and New England the leaders of the Baptist congregations were generally persons who, like John Smyth and Roger Williams, were "inconstant in error" and who followed a path of religious quest through moderate Puritanism and Separatism to the Baptist confession. The argument which justified this shift of ecclesiastical allegiances had been clearly delineated by Thomas Helwys in *The Mistery of Iniquity* (1612). Utilizing the apocalyptic images of Revelation, Helwys expressed the urgency and importance of church reform by describing it as rejection of, or escape from, the practices and doctrines of Antichrist. He defended the Baptist position by asserting that it alone both reproduced apostolic practice and completely isolated itself from antichristian impurities. This call for reformation carried with it an imperative for the individual person; Helwys insisted that persons who remained unseparated from Antichrist would "perish to everlasting destruction, although they do it ignorantly: A hard doctrine wil this seeme to the most: But the moueth of the Lord hath spoken it."[5]

The Christian must therefore have a care for his religious associations, and Helwys set out to expose those "false Prophets" who, wittingly or unwittingly, had leagued themselves with Antichrist, that "Man of sinne." Like most of the early English dissenters, Helwys identified the beast of Rev. 13:1–10 with the spiritual power of Rome, but he went on to assert that the prelatical government of England, because of its greed, its tyrannical and persecuting spirit, and its adherence to false ceremonies, was the very image of that beast (cf. Rev. 13:11–18). He then declared that the Puritans and Separatists, in very important respects, were among the false prophets who had not yet withdrawn from the influence of these two beasts and thus were in danger of damnation.

The Puritans had strayed from the narrow path by allowing their ministers to accept ordination at the hands of the English bishops. Ordination, Helwys argued, was not to be performed by bishops but rather by the individual congregation; in not following this procedure, the Puritans had "broken the Covenant of the lord in polluting and abolishing this his holy Ordinance."[6] The Separatists had received sufficient spiritual light to reject ordination from the prelates, but their purported separation, it appeared to

Helwys, was inconsistent and incomplete. This was the case because, although the Separatists declared the falsity of the English church, they continued to accept as valid their infant baptism within that church. Such a baptism, since it did not include the recipient's personal affirmation of faith, did not seem to Helwys to conform to the apostolic pattern: "The Baptisme of the new Testament must needs be a spiritual basptisme of *water & the spirit*, Joh. 3. 5. with which baptism infants cannot be Baptized," because they are as yet incapable of personal faith.[7] Thus both the Puritans and Separatists had halted their efforts at reform in positions which still inconsistently maintained antichristian pollutions. Only the Baptists, said Helwys, had completed this journey out of the wilderness of false Christianity.

In articulating the need for reform through apocalyptic scriptural images, Helwys expressed himself in a mode common throughout Puritanism. But in three prominent respects, Helwys's argument was quite similar to that of Roger Williams while the latter was in Massachusetts Bay. First, like Williams, Helwys stressed the importance of adherence to proper outward forms of worship for the individual's progress in sanctification. Like Williams, he was convinced that even nominal connection with the Church of England was spiritually damaging. Finally, he concurred with Williams's belief that only those who had completely separated themselves from such pollutions were spiritually qualified to form authentic churches. In Helwys's assessment, both Puritans within the Church of England and Separatists supposedly outside it failed to meet these three criteria.

Not surprisingly, then, Roger Williams's eventual espousal of the Baptist position resulted from religious development which existentially reiterated the line of argument in *The Ministery of Iniquity*. In letters to Winthrop and Cotton during the year immediately after his banishment, his major theme, an echo of Helwys, was his accusation that reformation was incomplete among the New England churches. For this reason Williams warned that in matters of Christian worship, "though you have come farr yet you never came out of the Wildernes to this Day."[8] While too many Protestants remained mired in antichristian error, Williams remarked in 1644, "multitudes of Gods Witnesses (re-

proached with the names of Brownists and Anabaptists)
have kept themselves from the error of the wicked, and
grow in grace and knowledge of the Lord Jesus, en-
devouring to clense *themselves from all filthiness both of flesh
and spirit, and to finish holiness in the feare of God.*"[9] But this
process of cleansing was far from easy. Williams judged
the consequences of the medieval apostasy to be so severe
that God's people had separated themselves from God, even
been forsaken by him, in their practices of worship and
church discipline. In 1636 his advice for the times was to
"abstract your selfe with a holy violence from the Dung
heape of this Earth."[10]

In the following two years Roger Williams took his own
advice and with "holy violence" separated himself from
any persons who might hinder his efforts to "finish holiness in the feare of God." According to John Winthrop,
this quest so consumed Williams that for a time he refused
to worship with any other than his wife.[11] At the same
time, the exodus of religious dissidents into Rhode Island
continued; Williams spent considerable time conversing
with the "antinomian" prophetess Anne Hutchinson and
aided William Coddington, John Clarke, and others recently departed from Massachusetts in establishing the
colony on Aquidneck (Rhode Island). In March 1639, Winthrop recorded that Katherine Scott, a sister of Anne
Hutchinson, had "emboldened" Williams to profess the
principles of "Anabaptistry." Rejecting that final institu-
tional link with the Antichrist, their baptisms in the
Church of England, Williams and Ezekiel Holliman,
another former resident of Salem, rebaptized each other
and some dozen like-minded individuals who would com-
prise the Baptist church at Providence.[12]

The decision to be rebaptized was reached amid considerable intellectual activity. Williams's departure from Massachusetts had by no means put an end to controversy,
and since that time he had developed his thoughts in
rough manuscripts and carried on an extensive, often
polemical, correspondence examining the nature of the
church, scriptural justifications for religious liberty, and
the evangelization of the American Indian. Revised to meet
the demands of a new context, this material formed the
basis for the works he would publish during his trip to
England in 1643–44. During 1636 and 1637, for example, he

exchanged letters with John Winthrop, John Cotton, Hugh Peter, and Peter Bulkley concerning his grounds for separation and his objections to attending preaching within the Church of England.[13] One of the letters from Cotton somehow came to be published in London in 1643, and Williams made public his reply in *Mr. Cottons Letter Lately Printed, Examined and Answered* (1644). Similarly, Williams's famous treatise on religious liberty, *The Bloudy Tenent, of Persecution* (1644), was essentially a commentary upon a General Baptist tract on "soul freedom," a letter by John Cotton, and a manuscript by the Massachusetts ministers on the relation of ecclesiastical and civil power, all of which Williams had received shortly after his settlement at Providence. Inquiry from England, meanwhile, led him to comment upon the origins of the American Indians and the prospects for their conversion,[14] topics to which he would return in *A Key into the Language of America* (1643) and *Christenings Make Not Christians* (1645).

As reading and reflection stimulated his pen, they also prolonged his theological ferment, and, having once become a Baptist, Williams did not long remain one. Instead, he concluded that the Roman apostasy had so disrupted the visible state of the church that no authentic congregations could exist until Christ initiated the millennium by sending new apostles to recreate the church. Hence, only a few months after being rebaptized by Holliman, Williams departed the Baptist congregation at Providence, never again to county himself the member of any church.[15] At the basis of this decision to renounce his rebaptism lay a fundamental shift in Williams's theological position, a shift which both ordered his understanding of religious vocation and established the presuppositions for his later controversial writings.

Williams's Millenarian Vision of History

It had long been a prominent contention of the radical Separatists, men such as Henry Barrow, John Smyth, John Canne, and Williams himself, that both Roman Catholicism and the Church of England, because they had fallen away from apostolic doctrine and discipline, were no longer true churches at all. Faced with this lamentable fact, the Separatist reformers asserted the possibility, indeed the necessity, of churches being formed independent of established ecclesiastical authority. It became the central tenet of congregationalism that a true church was created by the confraternity of the godly in church covenant; the Holy Spirit empowered the saints to constitute themselves as a body with full authority to call ministers and administer sacraments. Among the Baptists, believer's baptism tended to replace the covenant as the formative act of church fellowship, but the principle involved remained the same: the Holy Spirit, "given unto them immediatlie from heaven, & not by meanes of any State, Prince, Priest, Prelate whatsoever," provided the foundation of church authority.[16] In this form, Puritan congregationalists had articulated a doctrine of authority which undercut the hierarchical authority exercised either in Catholicism or in the English church.

It was precisely this covenantal conception of the church, which Roger Williams had himself previously advocated, that he now denied. Churches, he said, were not formed by covenant, but by *apostolic ministers* commissioned by Christ, who converted persons through the preached word and then gathered them into church fellowship. Asserting that this was the way churches had been created in New Testament times, Williams went on to argue that the only properly commissioned apostles who had ever existed were those who had ministered during the earliest era of the church and could trace their authority directly back to Christ himself. When this succession of ministers was broken by the corruption of the medieval church, the Christians of the world were left without means of forming themselves into congregations or administering sacraments.[17] Only at the millennial advent of Christ's true apostles would authority be restored and the church reconstituted. Until that restoration (which Williams at this time believed was near at hand), conscience compelled him to abstain from sacraments in any of the supposed churches of the world.[18] Williams, in other words, rejected either covenant or believer's baptism as the formative act of church fellowship in favor of a doctrine of *apostolic succession*.

The seriousness with which he held this view at the time

he left the fellowship of the Providence Baptists is well illustrated by Isaac Backus's story of the events within that church immediately after Williams's departure:

> Mr. Pelatiah Mason, who was born near Providence Ferry in 1669, told his sons (three of whom are now public preachers in Swanzey) that he had heard from the fathers of that day, that in the trial they then had, they heard that the Queen of Hungary, or some in those parts, had a register of a regular succession from the apostles, and they had thoughts of sending Mr. Thomas Olney (who succeeded Mr. Williams as their pastor) into that country for it; but at length concluded that such a course was not expedient, but believing they were now got into the right way, determined to persevere therein.[19]

Williams thus continued in his views with few, if any, followers in New England. But this shift in his conception of the nature of the church and the basis of its authority defined the shape of the millennium for which he worked and hoped throughout the rest of his life.

Williams persevered in this lonely religious quest because his millenarianism was not evanescent enthusiasm, nor the product of fleeting religious excitement. It emerged from deeper wells of his personality, and it was integral to broader convictions about the providential ordering of history. His pondering of history began with that commonplace of Puritan thought, the conviction that Christianity was slowly passing out of a centuries-long eclipse during which it had been robbed of inner spiritual power, had declined into error-laden formality.[20] These centuries were the dominion of Antichrist foretold in Revelation and, according to popular exegesis, their destined span of 1260 years was nearing its expiration. According to Williams, the effect of this apostasy had been the destruction of the visible church, "a total routing of the *Church* and *Ministry* of *Christ Jesus*, put to flight, and retired into the *Wildernesse of Desolation*."[21] But during their wilderness retreat, God had not wholly deserted his people; he continued, throughout the reign of Antichrist, to raise up a scattered band of spiritual Christians in every age. These true Christians, although unable to recover or reestablish the authentic church, nevertheless had carried on a witness against Antichrist and his corruption of Christianity. Especially since the Reformation, they had been waging a spiritual battle against false state religions, often suffering for their faith. Their proper task was not to found churches but rather to denounce error in the Christianity of their time, thereby purging it in preparation for Christ's millennial restoration of the true church.[22] For such faithful witnesses—and Williams aspired to be numbered among them—glory waited in Christ's coming rule:

> If him [Christ] thou seekest in these searching times, mak'st him alone thy white and soules beloved, willing to follow and be like him in doing, in suffring: although thou find'st him not in the restauration of his Ordinances, according to his first Patterne. Yet shalt thou see him, raigne with him, eternally admire him, and enjoy him, when he shortly comes in flaming fire to burne up millions of ignorant and disobedient.[23]

In this manner, Williams strongly contrasted the church of his own day, a church scattered in the wilderness, with Christianity in its authentic form. He believed that the glorious church of the latter days would bring the godly out of the wilderness by repristinating the doctrine, discipline, and spiritual authority of ancient, apostolic Christianity. This primitivism constituted a characteristic emphasis of his piety; the goal of God's providential plan for his church was the precise restoration of its original pattern, and Williams now awaited the apostles whose preaching would bring that plan to realization.[24]

In discussing the substantive qualities of the pristine church, either during the apostolic era or at the millennium, Roger Williams emphasized that the inward spirituality of its members would be manifested through external forms of worship. For this reason, Williams consistently stressed the importance for the *authentic* church of outward practices: laying on of hands at ordination, baptism by immersion, or apostolic succession of ministers.[25] But for the church in the wilderness, the church of his own day, Williams found that this bond between spirit and form had been sundered. God now acted upon men's souls not by the ordinary means of his ordinances but by the direct intervention of his Holy Spirit: "I believe that where the ordinary power of *Gods* hand in his holy *Ordinances* is withdrawen, it is his *extraordinarie* and immediate *power* that preserveth and supporteth his people against *Men* and *Devills;* as in particular, during the *reigne* of *Antichrist* in stirring up and supporting the . . . *Witnesses.*"[26] Forms of worship were, for the present, mere husks; the grace-filled Christian lacked proper ways of worship for expressing his piety: "Gods people in their persons, Heart-waking, (Cant. 5. 2.) in the life of personall grace, will yet be found fast asleep in respect of publike Christian Worship."[27] But at the millennium, the conjunction of spirit and form would again be possible in Christian worship, and laying on of hands or baptism by immersion, for example, would again communicate spiritual power and authority.

Both Williams's primitivism and his conviction that spirituality should express itself through outward religious practice stood in partial continuity with his earlier opinions in Massachusetts Bay. One example from that period was his concern about the use of veils by women or hats by men during worship services. Robert Barclay has noted that these qualities of piety were also common among early Baptists, who

> held strongly to outward baptism, and the outward Lord's supper, supplementing it often by a "love-feast." They often washed each other's feet, used "the kiss of charity,"' as well as the imposition of hands in receiving a member; and along with their views of the purely spiritual nature of the christian religion, there was a certain leaning to the visible and outward.[28]

What distinguished Williams's new opinions from his own earlier views and from those of the Baptists was, of course, that he now projected into the millennium the possibility of expressing spirituality through external symbols and ordinances and abstained from them during the present dispensation.

Thus, with his change of opinion about the nature of the church's spiritual authority, and his consequent belief that new, legitimate apostles were required to create churches, Williams's piety was decisively reorientated toward the millennium. Only with its arrival could he enjoy the fellowship of the church in its true form. He was prohibited fellowship in anything less than that heavenly Jerusalem by his conviction, characteristic of radical Puritan piety, that all who received the "mark of the beast" by participating in impure churches would suffer eternal punishment (Rev. 14:10–11).

As will be seen in later chapters, two characteristics of this millenarian vision of the church differentiate it from the two major trends of Puritan millenarianism from the civil wars to the Restoration. First, Williams's extreme primitivism cannot be overemphasized; when he spoke of the millennial rule of Christ, he referred quite specifically to a restoration of the church to what he conceived to be its apostolic form. In this, he differed from most English millenarians who, in the tradition of Thomas Brightman, believed that Christ's 1,000 year reign would extend over both state and church, creating a holy commonwealth in which the true saints would exercise both political and ecclesiastical power. Second, Williams considered the most prominent quality of the pristine church to be that its members, regenerate Christians, would express their spirituality through or by means of the outward and visible ordinances of Christian worship. This opinion differed from the tendency among many radical Puritans to envision the millennium as the establishment of an entirely new form of Christianity. They argued that God was inaugurating a new spiritual age in which Christians would not be edified through ordinances of Christian worship but through the immediate ministrations of Christ or the Holy Spirit within them. From this perspective, the army chaplain John Saltmarsh advised his readers that the millennium would witness the establishment of a spiritual kingdom within the saints: "The Lord Jesus *his coming* is *in Spirit* and *glory,* in *revelation* in his *Saints;* he shal *come to be glorified in his Saints.*"[29] These two broad trends in Puritan millenarianism appeared sometimes in combination, sometimes in opposition, but their differences from Roger Williams's conception of the millennium have decided importance for understanding the religious controversies in which Williams engaged after 1643.

The sources for Williams's millenarian views are uncertain, although the years immediately following 1639 do seem to have witnessed a general heightening of interest in millenarian speculation on the part of New Englanders. Between 1639 and 1641, for example, John Cotton preached three series of sermons on Revelation which were later published in England.[30] Likewise, at Windsor, Connecticut, Ephraim Huit composed a homiletic commentary on the book of Daniel.[31] In 1639 the lawyer Thomas Lechford, who lent some of his writings to Roger Williams, wrote a work on scriptural prophecy which was immensely unpopular with Thomas Dudley and others of the Massachusetts magistrates. Like Williams, Lechford concluded that the only true church was one in which "Apostles and Evangelists" could trace their authority by the "imposition of hands from one another, downe from the days of the Apostles." In Lechford's case, however, this conclusion led him not out of all churches but rather back into conformity with the Church of Engalnd. Denied fellowship in the churches and limited in his law practice by the magistrates, Lechford soon returned to England.[32] Among the Rhode Island saints there also was speculation on the millennium, and John Winthrop interviewed a son-in-law of Anne Hutchinson who shared Roger Williams's belief that "there were no gentile churches (as he termed them) since the apostles' times, and that none now could ordain ministers."[33] But, with this last exception, these interpretations of scriptural prophecy bore little similarity to Williams's opinions. Indeed, as will be seen Williams's understanding of the millennium was directly opposed at almost every point to that held by such men as Cotton and Huit. However, since Williams did become acquainted with the ideas of the General Baptists during this time, it should be noted that the opinion that new apostles must come to restore the church had circulated among people associated with Thomas Helwys and John Murton.[34]

The years following Roger Williams's banishment from Massachusetts were, therefore, crucial ones for his religious development. During this time he engaged in controversial writing which would form the foundation for his later publications in England. He experimented with a variety of church forms in his quest for the purity of the apostolic congregations. And, most importantly, he arrived at a new conception of the church's spiritual authority which brought to the fore the millenarian dimensions of his theology. At his arrival in England in 1643, each of these factors would influence the manner in which he addresed the religious issues being debated during the English civil wars.

4 Christian Vocation for a Revolutionary Age

Roger Williams's eschatological reading of history placed the Christians of his own time in a transitional period, a "wilderness" era during which a revitalized Christian community was fervently anticipated but not yet to be enjoyed. Christ would soon send new apostles to rebuild spiritual Jerusalem, but until then the saints lacked authority to establish or administer true churches. By this opinion Williams did not, however, counsel passive waiting for Christ's coming. Instead, his millennial expectations expressed both a definite program of religious reformation and a demanding regimen of personal piety. In these latter days, he was convinced, God was appointing individual Christians to play responsible roles in the church's restoration. Williams found these eschatological religious responsibilities symbolically delineated in Revelation, and he identified the witnesses or martyrs of those pages with persons he regarded as the specially chosen Christians of his own time. Further, he hoped that he himself was numbered among these witnesses, and Williams's interpretation of the social role of the apocalyptic witness thus became the paradigm for his own sense of religious vocation. During his first trip to England, he publicly expounded this conception of the eschatological witness and his task in *Mr. Cottons Letter Lately Printed, Examined and Answered* and *Queries of Highest Consideration*.

Roger Williams arrived in London in June 1643, with the intention of obtaining a charter for Rhode Island, which

would provide it some legal protection from the encroach-
ments of its colonial neighbors. The Parliament from which
he sought this formal recognition had been engaged in
active warfare against Charles I since the preceding October. By the time of Williams's arrival, the opposing sides
in the Civil War had reached a military stalemate, and Parliament was looking north to Scotland for troops which
would sway advantage in its favor. Among the Scots, however, the potential alliance was not perceived as merely
military, and that most Protestant of peoples expected—as
part of the agreement—that the English Parliament would
begin to refashion English Protestantism in the pattern of
"the best Reformed churches." Thus the need for Scottish
military assistance precipitated the work of ecclesiastical
reform which had long been a general concern among Parliament's predominantly Puritan constituency.

During the summer and autumn of 1643, Parliament expressed its commitment to reformation by gathering the
Westminster Assembly of Divines and by signing the Solemn League and Covenant with the Scots. Throughout the
following year religious radicals attacked both the Assembly and the Covenant as improper vehicles for religious
reformation, and Roger Williams's *Mr. Cottons Letter Lately
Printed, Examined and Answered* and *Queries of Highest Consideration*, published in February 1644, were prominent
documents of this sectarian polemic. In their witness
against Parliament and the Westminster divines, the two
tracts witnessed as well to the intellectual and religious
energies generated by Williams's decade of controversy,
isolation, and rumination. In 1644 convictions wrought in
the wilderness would propel him into his calling as one of
the most acute controversialists of the era.

Millenarianism and Public Policy

The Westminster Assembly, from its inception, was an instrument of Parliament. Parliament not only nominated
the individual members of the Assembly but also in-
structed it upon its general topics of debate. Thus, in establishing the Assembly, Parliament restricted it to an
advisory role, believing that "the Divines should consult
and advise on matters and things *proposed to them* by both
or either of the Houses, and give their advice and counsel

as often as required; and in all cases of difficulty refer to the authority which had called them together."[1] With this limited mandate, the Assembly began meeting on 1 July 1643; its active membership ranged from sixty to ninety and was composed almost entirely of Puritan clerics.

Having manifested the sincerity of its desires for reformation by calling the Westminster Assembly, Parliament next sent three commissioners to Scotland to negotiate the actual alliance. Leader of the mission was the younger Sir Henry Vane (1613–62), already an acquaintance of Roger Williams and subsequently one of his closest friends. Vane had settled briefly in New England, arriving there in October 1635, shortly before Williams's banishment. Still in his early twenties at that time, Vane had promptly been elevated to the governorship of the colony, perhaps largely in deference to the prominence of his father in Charles's court. He served as governor during the Pequot War and had regular dealings with Williams, who was the primary English negotiator with the Indians during that conflict. Vane's brief governorship was rendered tumultuous when the "antinomian controversy," ignited by the outspoken doctrinal pronouncements of Anne Hutchinson and John Wheelwright, split the colony into two hostile factions. Vane's own religious orientation, which emphasized the indwelling of the Holy Spirit in the believer, aligned him with Hutchinson and Wheelwright; he was defeated in the election of magistrates in 1637; and in August of that year he departed Massachusetts and returned to England. Since the calling of the Long Parliament in 1640, Vane had served as an able and increasingly influential lieutenant to that body's uncrowned king, John Pym.

Accompanied by the Puritan clerics Stephen Marshall and Philip Nye, Vane and the English commissioners arrived in Scotland to find their potential allies ill-disposed to any civil compact which was not at the same time a religious covenant among the two nations and God to guarantee the victory of God's cause.[2] After considerable negotiation, the Solemn League and Covenant was composed in a manner which affirmed a mutual desire to reform religion but left ambiguous the precise substance of such a reform. Since Parliament expected advice on the substantive matters of polity to come from the Westminster Assembly, it requested that the Scots appoint representatives to that

body. Of the eight Scottish appointees, six actually
traveled to Westminster and took leading roles in the debates of the ensuing months, the ministers Robert Baillie,
George Gillespie, Alexander Henderson, and Samuel
Rutherford and the two laymen Archibald Johnston and
Lord Maitland.[3] Both the Westminister Assembly and the
House of Commons swore to the Covenant in late September and made provision that it should be imposed
upon each citizen over the age of eighteen; by these acts
the Covenant became a symbol of adherence to the parliamentary party.

In mid-October of 1643, Parliament directed the Assembly to leave the work with which it had begun, revision of
the Thirty-Nine Articles, and turn its attention instead to
the reform of church government. The parliamentary di-
rective quickly disclosed the amorphous character of Puritan ecclesiology. The divines generally agreed that the
church should be reestablished without "popish" ceremonies, the Book of Common Prayer, and what they regarded as the tyranny of prelatical episcopacy, but beyond
this negative agreement existed considerable indecision
and difference of opinion. In the main, they favored an
inclusive national church such as that in which they had
been reared, and they looked with suspicion upon congregationalist doctrinaires who would forsake the
neighborhood parish for a gathered congregation of visible
saints. They were committed to an educated ministry as
the surest leadership for the church, but this "presbyterian" sentiment was tempered by a distaste for the hierarchical authority so rigidly exercised in the Scottish system
of church courts. Their traditionalism was such that many
showed significant enthusiasm for Archbishop Ussher's
proposal for a limited episcopacy in which deliberative
synods at each ecclesiastical level would limit the bishop's
power by the need to have the clergy concur with his acts.
This desire, then, for a comprehensive and orderly polity,
one overbalanced neither toward rigid hierarchical authority nor toward the seeming anarchy of gathered congregations, marked the broad channel through which would
flow the diverse thinking of those Puritans commonly
grouped as the English Presbyterians.[4]

The Westminster divines were not, however, afforded
the luxury of resolving their uncertainties about church

polity by the celebrated English capacity for "muddling through." Instead, three self-conscious groups of lobbyists immediately began to exercise their concern, from the pulpit and in the press, over the direction which the reform of church government should take. The first of these groups was the Scottish delegation to the Westminster Assembly. Each of the four clergymen in its number preached before Parliament during this period and published the text of his remarks.[5] Quite naturally, they advocated the adoption of presbyterianism on the Scottish model as the surest route to the attainment of the reformed religion, civic liberties, and public welfare which were the objectives of the Solemn League and Covenant.

A second lobby advocated congregationalism quite similar to that which predominated in the New England churches. These congregationalist spokesmen—known in England as Independents—were primarily dissenting clergymen recently returned from self-imposed exile during which they had served as pastors to English churches in the Netherlands. Like Cotton, Davenport, and Hooker in New England, they were not Separatists but did argue that the individual congregation had scriptural authority to manage its own affairs. Within the Assembly this position was espoused by the five "dissenting brethren," Thomas Goodwin, Philip Nye, Sidrach Simpson, William Bridge, and Jeremiah Burroughes. In the city they were supported by a small number of ministers such as John Archer, who had also spent time as a pastor in Holland and who, like Philip Nye, had earlier served as a spiritual adviser to the Massachusetts Bay Company. Another ardent and articulate Independent was John Goodwin, pastor of the congregation in Coleman Street, London, formerly ministered to by John Davenport. Goodwin's theological views, and especially his advocacy of broad religious toleration, gradually set him apart from the other Independent ministers, but at this early date in the civil wars he was among the most active and effective pamphleteers for "the congregational way." Finally, two other energetic proponents of the gathered congregation were on the scene, the New England clerics Thomas Weld and Hugh Peter. The two had been commissioned by the Massachusetts magistrates to travel to England in 1641 and represent the colony's interests there. Part of their charge upon departure had been to promote religious reform in England, and they had published several expositions of the New England way as guides for old England in her quest for full reformation.[6]

The third lobby was composed of London's religious radicals, who, since the opening of hostilities between Parliament and Charles I, had taken advantage of the consequent freedom from restraint to expound their views more publicly. Primarily Separatists and Baptists, they had, of course, comprised the religious underground for many years but now saw the opportunity to press for a right to gather and preach unencumbered by civil or ecclesiastical regulation. As one of their number, a London coachman and lay preacher named John Spencer, had expressed the matter in 1641, "true understanding of scripture" was granted not by human institutions but by the spirit of God, and any man thus had the right of "exercising his gift" in the interest of religious reformation.[7]

Upon his arrival in London, Roger Williams lost little time in establishing a wide network of contacts among the members of these contending lobbies. He made or renewed numerous friendships among the lay and clerical supporters of the parliamentary cause, an important asset in his successful petition for a parliamentary charter for Rhode Island. By the summer of 1644, even the Scottish commissioner Robert Baillie, although horrified by Williams's singular ecclesiology, would count him "my good acquaintance."[8] Nor did Williams fail to associate with London's Separatist and Baptist congregations, to whose fellowship he had considered returning at the time of his banishment. Many of these congregations were offshoots of the church gathered by Henry Jacob in 1616 and pastored since 1637 by Henry Jessey. And after a letter from John Cotton to Williams was published by unknown means in London in 1643, Cotton suggested that the person responsible was a member of Jessey's church who was "well affected" to Roger Williams, one Sabine Staresmore.[9] Likewise, when Williams arrived in England in 1643, his printer for *A Key into the Language of America* was the Baptist Gregory Dexter. The two men became close friends, and Dexter's shop, where the printing ranged from military "intelligences" to John Milton's *Of Prelatical Episcopacy*, may well have been an important setting for Williams's reintroduction to the English religious and political scene. Both Dexter and Mark

Lukar, another London Baptist, emigrated to Rhode Island soon after Williams's visit to England.[10]

The diversity of Williams's associations during his sojourn in England betokens the manner in which his millenarian religious orientation had led him to the margins which separated Presbyterian and Independent spokesmen on the one side from the sectarian pamphleteers on the other. His tracts spoke in defense of the separated congregations and their rights to gather, ordain their own ministers, and pursue reformaton without external regulation; and his apocalyptic imagery of religious purification drew much of its fervor from their peculiar piety. At the same time, the audience which he addressed most directly was that group of indeterminate size, numbered formally among the Independents, whom Williams liked to designate as those who "seekest in these searching times." Not infrequently laymen of position and influence, such as Henry Vane or Oliver Cromwell, they were firmly committed to the pragmatic necessity for social order while simultaneously attracted by the sectarian vision of the communion of saints, commitments which the common wisdom of the day declared fundamentally incompatible. The obligation of the state for the oversight of religion was thus an increasingly problematic issue for them, rendering their piety and perhaps their policy susceptible to the arguments of the witness from Providence. To souls bedeviled by such questions of policy, Williams made the case for the possibility of an enduring social order which respected liberty of conscience, fostered religious reformation, and protected the public peace. Although recognizing that his solution was too distant from the assumptions which had thus far guided the parliamentary party to be widely accepted, Roger Williams nevertheless hoped that his "humble and faithfull suggestions" would serve Parliament and the Westminster Assembly like medicine from the Good Physician, becoming the common "spittle and clay, with which sometimes *Christ Jesus* opens the eyes of them that are borne blinde."[11]

Debate among Presbyterians, Independents, and sectarians concerning questions of church government was quickly perceived as a threat to the unity of the parliamentary party. This concern prompted conciliatory efforts during November and December 1643, efforts which were heightened in early December, following the death of the principal parliamentary leader, John Pym.[12] During this time Independent and Presbyterian ministers in London met and agreed to suspend religious controversy during the war, with Stephen Marshall acting as mediator between the Scottish commissioners and the five Independents. Writing in the name of the Presbyterian and Independent leaders within the Assembly, Marshall then prepared a paper designed to publicize their common mind. It announced that the Assembly was settling questions concerning reform of the English church with all possible speed and asked the people, as Robert Baillie summarized its argument, "to wait patientlie for the Assemblies minde, and to give over that most unseasonable purpose of their own reformations, and gathering of congregations." After limited debate the Assembly approved Marshall's proposal and published it on 23 December as *Certain Considerations to Dissuade Men from Further Gathering of Churches.*[13] It underscored the agreement of Presbyterians and Independents that reform should be left to the Assembly and to Parliament and opposed the activities of the London sectaries who, like the Elizabethan Separatist Robert Browne, were advocating their own "reformation without tarying for anie."

The sectarians had no inclination to heed the Assembly's appeal for moderation. They passionately defended the right of congregations to direct their own affairs independent of advice from Westminster, and they quickly attacked Parliament's plan to require each citizen over eighteen years of age to swear to the Solemn League and Covenant. The Separatists and Baptists considered the Covenant an attempt to impose Presbyterianism thinly disguised as support for Parliament. In London, they prepared a petition to Parliament which stated that they would "not take up arms for the Scots prisbitry, which is as antychristian or more then the English prelacy." They warned that, if the Covenant were imposed, three regiments of them would lay down their arms.[14] Philip Nye went to them as an emissary from the city's representatives to the Assembly and persuaded the sectaries not to publish the tract,[15] but objections to the Covenant continued to come to the Assembly's attention.[16]

Dissuaded from petitioning Parliament, the sectaries attempted to present their views before the Westminster Assembly. At the end of December, a group of them brought to the Assembly copies of a book by "an old English Anabaptist at Amsterdame" which asserted that the nation was "bound in conscience" to tolerate all religious views.[17] When some members of the Assembly proposed that this document be read, the suggestion was vehemently opposed by the Independents Thomas Goodwin and Philip Nye. At the time, members of the Assembly "marvelled at" the violence with which the Independents rejected recognition of the sectarian pamphlet, but the essential reasons for their reaction have, in another context, already been traced in detail. Like the clerics and magistrates of Massachusetts Bay, the English Independents were struggling to avoid being classed as Separatists intent on social and religious disruption. Like the leaders of the Bay colony, they shared with the Separatists the concept of congregational autonomy, but, also like the Bay colonists, they rejected the Separatist assertion that any church not so formed was an utterly false church. In order to exonerate themselves from the connection with Separatism, the Independent ministers published in early January 1644 *An Apologeticall Narration.*

The *Apologeticall Narration* was aptly named. It narrated those experiences in England and in the Netherlands which had led its authors to their present views on church polity, and it defended those views by emphasizing their broad agreement with the Reformed churches and their assiduous avoidance of the schismatic errors of Separatism.[18] The authors had fled England during the decade of Laud's hegemony because of their objections to the *"dark part"* of Christian worship: "those superstitions adjoyned to the worship of God, which have been the common stumbling block and offence of many thousand tender consciences, both in our own and our neighbour Churches, ever since the first Reformation of Religion."[19] But once in the Netherlands, they had felt "a farther necessity of enquiring into and viewing the *light part,* the positive part of *Church-worship* and Government," and in order to discover these principles of polity they had adopted as their guide the "Primitive Churches recorded in the New Testament."[20] Armed with this touchstone, they stood in the Netherlands as "unengaged specators" evaluating the examples of the various Reformed churches. The most beneficial example was the practical piety of the "good old Non-conformists" of England who had meditated and expounded upon Christian religious experience—"*the power of godlinesse* and the profession thereof, with a difference from carnall and formall Christians"—with an excellence found in no other nation.[21] They also considered the organization of the New England congregations, and, finally, they observed the warning provided by the "fatall miscarriages and shipwracks of the Separation" in which zeal for religious purity fractured congregations and antagonized the state.[22]

From their evaluation of these and other attempts at reformation, the Independent ministers concluded that three principles delineated the proper steps in organizing churches. First, their ultimate authority was Scripture; there they "found principles enough, not onely *fundamentall* and essentiall to the being of a Church, but *superstructory* also for the wel-being of it, and those to us cleare and certaine." Second, they sought to avoid making present judgments about church polity a binding law which would exclude "further light" from God's word revealed in Scripture and experience. Finally, they did not condemn the practices of other churches but steered a safe course on moot questions by following the customs of most Reformed churches.[23] These rubrics, they declared, had led to their belief that each congregation was a complete expression of the church which should, nevertheless, voluntarily associate with other congregations for advice and support. Thus each church had full authority to administer discipline through its appointed officers, but did so in general conformance with the practice of associated congregations. They considered this the authentic pattern of the apostolic churches: "We believe the truth to lye and consist in a *middle way* betwixt that which is falsely charged on us, *Brownisme*; and that which is the contention of these times, the *authoritative Presbyteriall Government* in all the subordinations and proceedings of it."[24]

The five authors further declared that they lived in an auspicious age in which all the churches, including the English church, stood in need of further reformation. To be sure, for many years England had experienced considerably less ecclesiastical reform than had neighboring nations.

But during those same years, asserted the Independents, the godly people within England had greatly increased their knowledge and practice of true Christian piety. While God had withheld outward reform from the English churches, he had instead "blessed them with the spiritual light (and that encreasing) of the power of Religion in the Practique part of it, as having in his infinite mercy on purpose reserved and *provided some better thing* for this Nation when it should come to be reformed, that the other Churches might not be made *perfect without it,* as the Apostle speaks."[25] Like Thomas Brightman, the Independent divines envisioned England playing a central role in the latter-day glory of the church.

During the same month, the Scottish commissioners responded by expressing their own views on polity under the title *Reformation of Church-Government in Scotland, Cleered from Some Prejudices.* In an argument similar to that of the dissenting brethren, they asserted that reformation of the Church of Scotland had used the practice of the New Testament churches as its pattern and guide.[26] But unlike the Independents, they did not claim a personal role in effecting this reform; rather it had been the accomplishment of John Knox and the early Scottish Protestants. Thus the tract described church government in Scotland as the product of labors by the Scottish reformers, those "instruments which the Lord used in the blessed work of Reformation."[27] Through their exceptional piety and industry, they had made the Church of Scotland a paragon among Reformed churches:

> Some of them had a propheticall Spirit manifested in divers particular and wonderfull predictions, and some of them were honoured to be Martyrs, & sealed the truth with their blood. So that in them, in the people of God converted by them, and in the Reformation brought about by the blessing of God upon their labors, against al the Learning, pride, Policy, and abused power of the time, there was to be seen *a representation of the Primitive and Apostolike times* and a new resurrection from the dead.[28]

As a sign of his approval, God had extended a "wonderfull blessing upon their order and Government" by preserving the Scottish church from heresies and schisms and by making it the instrument for the advance of Christ's king-

dom and the conversion of many souls.[29] The commissioners argued that Scotland and England alike should recognize these attainments and hold fast to the reformed polity
which they had received "upon the warrant of the word,
and by the teaching of the spirit with the certainty of
faith." Although they did not deny the truth of the Independents' claim that men should be ready to receive "more
light from the word and Spirit of God," even concerning
"what needeth further to bee reformed in the Church of
Scotland," they warned that "we ought to be resolute and
unmoveable in so far as we have attained."[30] Not Independency but Scottish Presbyterianism thus represented
the wise middle course in reformation between tyrannical
prelacy and schismatic and turbulent Separatism.[31]

In this fashion, both Independents and Presbyterians
justified their respective plans for reform by maintaining
that through them the structure and piety of the apostolic
churches would be restored from the decline suffered during
the Middle Ages. The twin assumptions that Scripture revealed both a scheme of church government and a predictive interpretation of history were used to justify their
opinions by locating them within a cosmic plan. Such a
view of the course of history was highly compatible with
millenarian enthusiasm, and many of the Independents
and some of the Scots used the apocalyptic image of an
approaching millennial age to interpret the goals of their
respective reform efforts. At the broadest level, then, Independents, Scottish commissioners, and Roger Williams
all agreed that in these latter days Christians had particular
responsiblity to carry out reforms which would prepare the
way for a glorious restoration of the church. However, in
describing the persons who should effect reform and the
method by which they should proceed, the Scots and Independents used the rhetoric of the millennium in a fashion quite different from that of Roger Williams.

Since returning from the Netherlands in 1641 and 1642,
the Independent ministers had published several tracts,
including texts of sermons delivered before Parliament,
which expounded an eschatological reading of contemporary history. According to their view, the reformation of the
sixteenth century had begun a definite, but gradual,
movement out of popery toward a golden age in which the
purity and peace of the church would be restored and the

saints would establish a godly commonwealth. Thus Thomas Goodwin explained in a fast-day sermon before the House of Commons that, since Antichrist had desolated the true church "and defiled Gods worship in all the parts of it ... the restauration of them become a work of time: The holy Ghost Age after Age gradually revealing pieces of the platform of it; the *Spirit* by degrees *consuming* and dispelling the darknesse that Antichristianisme had brought in, by light shining clearer and clearer to the perfect day, which is the *brightnesse of Christs comming.*"[32] This conviction that progressive revelations would culminate in the church's latter-day glory was the implicit intellectual framework for the argument, used in the *Apologeticall Narration*, that the older Protestant churches were incompletely purified. Congregational polity benefited from more recent revelations, from "further light" which God was bestowing upon his people as the millennial age approached.

According to the congregational divines, the first glimmerings of the millennium were already shining in the Independent churches. But in order for reformation to be advanced throughout England, this congregational way required the active support of Parliament. Their constantly reiterated theme before Parliament and in the press was, therefore, the cooperation between the congregationalists and the House of Commons in promoting Christ's kingdom.

One of the early expositions of the theme was a fast-day sermon preached in the Netherlands, probably by Thomas Goodwin,[33] and later published under the title *A Glimpse of Sions Glory* (1641). Acknowledging the influence of Thomas Brightman, the author reckoned that the millennium would actually begin about 1650 and reach perfection about forty-five years later. By founding congregations formed on the apostolic pattern, the saints were "furthering this great Worke" of establishing the New Jerusalem. In this manner, God had begun "the raising of the Church ... among the meaner sort of People, among the Multitude." But reformation by congregations of common people was ordinarily "mixed with much confusion, and a great deale of disorder." Therefore, God was now stirring up "the Great ones of the Land," especially the Houses of Parliament, to organize and advance the reformation.[34]

This increase of piety among saints and magistrates, predicted the author, would lead to earthly felicity for the
church, security from her enemies, numerous conversions,
union among all churches, and outward prosperity for the
saints.[35] Similar hopes were expressed by John Archer in
The Personall Reigne of Christ upon Earth, which appeared in
five editions between 1641 and 1643. Archer, too, predicted
that the millennial timetable would begin about 1650 and
culminate about 1700, with Christ ruling through his saints
over the churches and the civil states of the world.[36] Godly
ministers and the pious magistrates of Parliament had been
chosen to prepare the way for Christ's millennial rule, said
Archer, and he identified them with the two witnesses
depicted in Rev. 11:3–12.[37]

Thus, in both tracts, the symbol of the millennium referred to a purified church protected and nurtured by the
laws of a godly commonwealth, and both saw this state of
affairs prefigured in cooperation between the Independent
congregations and Parliament: "The nearer the Time
comes, the more clearly these things shall bee revealed.
And because they begin to be revealed so much as they doe
now, we have cause to hope the Time is at hand."[38]

In their sermons before Parliament, the Independents
particularly stressed the responsiblities of the magistrate in
protecting and purifying the church during this eschatological age. Jeremiah Burroughes expressed the
opinion of the group when he said, speaking to Parliament
in 1641, "You Right Honorable, are the *annoynted of the
Lord,* I mean set a part from your Brethren, to the great
worke of the Lord that He is doing in this latter age of the
world."[39] God effected his purposes through mortal "instruments," and in the foundation of Christ's monarchy
the men of Parliament were the most critical of those
agents.

With the outbreak of hostilities between Parliament and
the king, this argument was quickly extended to interpret
the military conflict as a righteous war waged against those
who impeded the divine march toward a reformed church
and society. Burroughes, William Bridge, and John Goodwin claimed that evil courtiers and papists had misguided
Charles. Parliament was now fighting not to usurp the
king's rights but to protect him from betraying his trust:
the preservation of his subjects' rights and the promotion of

reformed religion.[40] Apocalyptic language provided an easy interpretation of the war as a struggle between evil and righteousness:

> There are two Captaines in the world, under whose command all the world serve, this Lord of Hosts, and the Devil, for he also hath his Armies fighting for him, the Dragon and his Angels; all wicked men are under him, and fight for him: his great Live-tenant is *Antichrist.* It is no dishonour to run from these Commanders, to get under the Banners of the Lord of Hosts.[41]

Among the Scottish commissioners similar convictions about the latter-day glory of the church were espoused by Samuel Rutherford, George Gillespie, and Archibald Johnston.[42] According to the Scots, however, it was not the Independent congregations which were the forerunners of the church's restoration but rather the Presbyterianism of their own land. Even Robert Baillie, who was inalterably opposed to literalistic millenarian speculations, considered the times auspicious and believed that the intervention in England marked the first step by which godly military power would impose Reformed church polity throughout Europe.[43] But in 1643 and 1644, millennial enthusiasm among the commissioners found its clearest spokesman in the youngest of their number, George Gillespie (1613–48). Applauded by Baillie for his learned contributions to debate in the Westminster Assembly, Gillespie subsequently participated in the debate over religious liberty by publishing *Wholesome Severity Reconciled with Christian Liberty* (1645), which controverted Roger Williams's *Bloudy Tenent, of Persecution.*

Gillespie expressed his millennialist theories quite distinctly in a sermon preached before Parliament on 27 March 1644. At that time, Gillespie proposed that Ezek. 43:11 predicted the existence of "a more glorious Church in the latter dayes."[44] This golden age, declared the young cleric, is near at hand, and if one considers "the great revolution and turning of things upside downe in these our dayes, certainly the work is upon the wheele: the Lord hath pluckt his hand out of his bosome, he hath *whet his sword, he hath bent his bow, he hath also prepared the instruments of death,* against Antichrist."[45] In fact, according to Gillespie's calculations, the 1260 years of the beast's reign

had come to an end in 1643, "at this very time of ours."
This might not mean the immediate destruction of Antichrist, "but assuredly, the acceptable yeare of Israels
Jubilee, and the day of vengeance upon Antichrist, is
comming, and is not farre off."[46] Christ is even now
storming the battlements of false worship: "Christ hath put
Antichrist from his utterworks in *Scotland*, and he is now
come to put him from his inner works in *England*."[47] In
Gillespie's opinion, these divine initiatives determined the
duty of Parliament. Scotland's example provided England
with a presbyterian pattern of government "found in the
Word of God" and indicated the goal toward which reformation was moving. Therefore, without delay, Parliament
should begin to support the establishment of presbyteries
in selected spots throughout England to serve as forerunners or prefigurements of Christ's millennial kingdom.[48]

In summary, although the Independents and the Scots
interpreted contemporary upheavals in church and society
by means of enthusiastic millennial expectations, they consistently stressed that God's agencies in these overturnings
were men of means and established authority. It was the
ordained, godly clergy and the members of Parliament
who were divine instruments acting to bring down Babylon and raise the New Jerusalem. Thus their apocalyptic
language expressed not only their general sense that they
lived in climactic times but also their firm conviction that
their God remained a God of order. Their millenariansim
was quite compatible with their circumspect statement of
policy in *Certain Considerations to Dissuade Men from Further
Gathering of Churches* which, it will be recalled, urged that
reformation be left in the hands of the Assembly and Parliament. They differed on the nature of church government
and articulated this difference in terms already discussed,
but they emphatically agreed that God was revealing his
millennial schemes through preaching and legislation by
the leaders of the parliamentary party.

The Witness and His Task

In *Queries of Highest Consideration*, Roger Williams proposed testing the assertions of the Scots and the Independents that their respective programs of reformation were
based upon the authority of Scripture. Such a test, Wil-

liams asserted, would demonstrate that neither of the dis-
agreeing parties would succeed as reformers precisely because of their "joint Agreement" in opposing the "Truth
and Purity" of Christ's "last will and Testament."[49] To
prove that this was the case, he posed twelve sets of questions for the authors of the *Apologeticall Narration* and *Reformation of Church-Government in Scotland.* By the answers
he presupposed, Williams denied that either of the contending groups had scriptural authority for the manner or
the substance of their proposed reforms.

As this suggests, his brief pamphlet raised some fundamental issues concerning the character of religious reformation. To be sure, in the course of his argument Williams
addressed many of the causes popular with his sectarian
colleagues; he opposed the Solemn League and Covenant,
advanced the Separatist position on congregational autonomy, and appealed for religious liberty. But his central thrust drove much deeper, addressing four principal topics. He questioned, first, whether the Westminster
Assembly and Parliament were actually the proper *agents*
of reform. He then suggested that the entire nation of
England should not be the *object* of religious restoration.
Third, he raised questions about the *methods* which his opponents were employing to effect reformation, and, finally,
he repudiated the *evidences* which they adduced from contemporary events as certifications that God looked with
favor upon their reforms. Each of these points of opposition
issued from Williams's convictions about the nature of the
church and his particular millenarian reading of the course
of history. They eventuated in a program of religious reformation markedly different from that espoused by either
the Scots or the dissenting brethren.

Williams had lost little time before appearing on the field
of controversy. The Independents' *Apologeticall Narration*
and the Scots' *Reformation of Church-Government* had issued
from the presses during January 1644; he responded with
his *Queries* in early February.[50] Although the tract was
anonymous, contemporaries in both England and New
England were aware that Williams was the author.[51]

He began his argument, as he had in his unsuccessful
struggle to reform the Massachusetts churches, with the
thesis that church discipline was the responsibility *solely* of
the individual congregation and its officers. For this reason

Williams repudiated the assumption of the Independents and the Scots that Parliament had responsibility for advancing religious reformation. Williams reminded his adversaries that Parliament represented the nation, not the gathered churches, and to use it to reform the church was to impose the will of the unregenerate masses upon the church and, by implication, upon Christ himself. "Is not this," asked Williams, "to subject this *holy Nation* [the church], this heavenly Jerusalem, the Wife and spouse of Jesus, *the pillar and ground of Truth*, to the vain uncertain and changeable Mutations of this present evill world?"[52] He therefore notified Parliament in his preface that his arguments were intended to dissuade them from engaging in religious reform:

> Concerning Soules, we will not (as most doe) charge you with the loads of all the Soules in England, Scotland, Ireland: wee shall humbly affirme, and (by the help of Christ) maintaine, that the Bodies and Goods of the Subject is your charge: Their Soules and yours are set on account to those that professe to be the Lights and Guides, the Messengers and Embassadors sent from Heaven to them.[53]

But if Parliament had no proper role in directing reformation, who was responsible? Who were the authentic "Messengers and Embassadors sent from Heaven" for this purpose? Williams emphatically denied that they were the members of the Westminster Assembly. Citing Acts 15:1–35 as his scriptural authority, Williams declared that the Assembly lacked power "to reforme or forme a Religion" because it did not represent individual congregations. Instead, the Assembly was composed of national representatives appointed by Parliament.[54] Even by calling themselves an "Assembly of Divines," they appropriated a title which rightfully belonged to each congregation, or assembly of saints.[55]

When he turned his attention to the persons who were the objects of reformation, Williams observed equally serious wanderings from the scriptural path. In attempting to reform the religious practice of the entire nation, his opponents were forgetting that only regenerate persons could have fellowship with God. Is it not impossible, queried Williams, actually to reform any but spiritually living per-

sons, those who have experienced the second birth of conversion? For this reason Williams asked the Scots and the
Independents "whether since you professe to be Builders,
you have not cause to feare and tremble, least you be
found to reject the *Corner stone,* in not fitting to him only
living stones?"[56]

In *Cottons Letter...Examined,* his companion piece to
Queries of Highest Consideration, Williams examined the entire issue of personal qualifications for church membership, but in the present context he directed his point
against plans to impose the Solemn League and Covenant
throughout the nation. The duty of the clergy in these
times, he said, was to acquaint persons "with their conditions and how impossible it is for a dead Stone to have
Fellowship with the *living God,* and for any man to enter
into the Kingdome of God, without a second Brith."[57] Instead, by imposing the Covenant, they would be encouraging hypocrisy and a false sense of security among
persons who were yet unregenerate.[58]

Williams was most disturbed, however, by the assertions of the Scots and Independents that one justification
for war against Charles was the desire of the godly for
religious reformation. Williams denied that Christ had
given authority to conduct war for his sake, and he asserted to the contrary that physical violence over religious
differences was likely to provoke divine judgment. He
questioned their identification of contemporary military
struggles with the apocalyptic battles portrayed in Daniel
and Revelation. According to Roger Williams, those were
not physical, but strictly spiritual, battles waged by faithful
preaching and prayer; John's Revelation spoke of no
"other Ammunition and Artillerie, used by the Saints, but
what we find in *Pauls* Christian Magazine, *Ephes.* 6."[59]

Williams concluded his tract by raising questions which
indicated the directions in which he felt reformation
should proceed; he began by placing responsibility in the
hands of a religious elite, the witnesses or martyrs of
Christ.[60] In calling certain of his contemporaries *witnesses,*
his precise meaning resulted from a complex combination
of apocalyptic scriptural symbols, English martyrology,
and his own theological orientation. His specific scriptural
reference was to a Greek word, *martys,* employed in Revelation. That book envisioned two witnesses (Rev. 11:3–12)

who would testify on behalf of Christ throughout the 1,260 days following destruction of the holy city by the gentiles. At the end of that period, these prophets would be killed by "the beast" and their bodies would lie in the streets for three and one-half days. God would then resurrect the witnesses and, in full view of their enemies, raise them up into heaven. Williams's exegesis of this apocalyptic vision transformed it into a concept for interpreting both contemporary events and his own religious experience.

According to Williams's exegesis, the witnesses were true witnesses not because they had been put to death but rather because of their prophetic activity. Christ acknowledged them as "his *Martyrs* or *Witnesses*" because they had been "testifying his holy *Truth* during all the *Reign* of the Beast."[61] Without rejecting the martyrological understanding of the witness as one who had died for the faith, Williams emphasized the distinctive work of the witness, the act of bearing testimony to the gospel. It was because they were witnesses for religious truth that they suffered and died at the hands of their enemies; suffering was a consequence of their identity as Christ's chosen prophets.[62]

Since Williams considered Revelation a symbolic presentation of historical development from the time of Christ to his own age, he interpreted the witnesses' prophetic task as actual activity by historical persons. For Williams, one fact dominated that historical development: the dissolution of the Christian church caused by the apostasy of medieval Catholicism. Within this context, the witnesses preached and wrote as informal groups of individual Christians in a world which lacked authentic visible churches. Those were faithful witnesses who had "prophecyed in *Sack-cloath* 1260 dayes or years (prophetically) I say mourned for the routing, desolating of the Christian Church or Army: and panted and laboured after the most glorious *Rally* thereof, and *Restauration*."[63] Williams specifically identified these laborers for a restored Christianity with the leaders of religious dissent: Wycliff, the Waldensians, the Hussites, Luther, and Calvin. He drew upon the martyrological writing of John Foxe—himself an "excellent *witness* (or Martyr) of God"—for biographic references to sixteenth-century English dissenters. Faithful witnesses with theological views closer to his own included the Separatists Henry Barrow and John Canne and the Baptist layman Samuel How.[64] Thus the two witnesses of Revelation symbolically represented all those Christians who had persevered in dissenting against religious errors throughout the centuries.

As this suggests, Williams specified the proper content of the witnesses' testimony as an attack upon the errors of behavior and belief which had crept into the church during the Middle Ages. When various witnesses, such as Luther or Calvin, proceeded beyond preaching against false Christianity and began establishing churches, they failed to duplicate the polity of the apostolic era.[65] Until Christ renewed the church at the millennium, Williams believed, attempts at forming churches would inevitably result in "great *mistakes* and *wandrings* from the first *Patternes* and Institutions of *Christ Jesus*."[66]

In this manner, Roger Williams's exegesis of Revelation called contemporary Christians to pursue specific responsibilities. This ministry of the witnesses was primarily negative; they were to purge the church of all impurities in order that Christ at the millennium might restore its pristine qualities. In his *Queries* he described this process of reformation by drawing upon the distinction made by the dissenting brethren between the *dark* and *light* parts of reformation. Williams suggested that "the Sufferings of Gods Witnesses since the Apsotacie, have . . . been only right against the *darke* part, the Inventions, Abominations and Usurpations of Anti-christ, according to Rev. 11." Not until "the finishing of the Testimonie, with the slaughter of the Witnesses, and their 3 dayes and halfe last great oppression be over and past" will the *"light* part," or positive restoration of the church, begin to "arise in its brightnesse."[67] But suffering which the witnesses endured upon behalf of Christian truth would find reward in the millennium, when those who had persevered would rule with Christ: "These *Witnesses,* these *Prophets,* are probably those one hundred forty four thousand *Virgins,* mysticall *Israelites,* twelve times twelve, which stand with the *Lamb* on *Mount Zion,* against the *Romish Beast,* and are the same Number sealed *twelve times twelve, Revelations* 7."[68]

Such an interpretation clearly contrasts with the millenarian opinions of the Scots and Independents. They emphasized a progressive unfolding of divine truth, a process already begun and destined to be gloriously consummated in the very near future. From this perspective, existing institutions—their churches and Parliament—were anticipations or harbingers of Christ's godly commonwealth and purified church. Persons already in authority, the ordained clergy and the members of Parliament, were acting as divine agents to initiate still greater reformation. Certainly, they expected dramatic occurrences in approaching days, but at the same time they stressed the continuities between those times and the present. Roger Williams, on the other hand, focused his millenarian beliefs on the discontinuity which he perceived between existing institutions and the church's millennial glory. In his view, no true churches or church officers existed at present, nor would they until Christ restored them. Only informal activity by individual witnesses, preaching, praying, and publishing, indicated God's preparative work in the world. But even this underscored discontinuities between the present and the millennium; the task of the witness was to cry down old errors, not to announce the first glimmerings of new truth.

Williams's interpretation of the reformation process primarily implied that the witnesses required complete freedom to speak and write as their consciences directed them. Only if they were left unfettered by the state could the witnesses carry out their eschatological task of razing the popish additions to Christ's holy temple. He pointed out that both the Scots and the dissenting brethren professed to desire and expect "a greater Light" of divine direction in reformation. Yet at the same time they had begun "to Persecute all other as Schismatiques, Hereticks, &c., that beleeve they see a further Light."[69] In consequence, Williams had been forced to circumvent the book licensers and publish his *Queries* anonymously, an illegality which he attempted to justify in his preface addressed to Parliament. The clergy responsible for licensing books, Williams warned, were screening out any that did not closely agree with their own opinions. He cautioned Parliament that "by such Circumscribing and immuring of your selves by such a Guard (their Persons we honour and esteem) it is rarely possible that any other Light, but what their Hemispheare affoords, shall ever shine on your Honours Souls, though ne're so sweet, so necessary, and though it come from God, from Heaven."[70]

At the same time that Roger Williams published his *Queries* concerning the proper reformation of church government, he was presented an opportunity to compose a second polemic on the same subject, *Mr. Cottons Letter Lately Printed, Examined and Answered.* This opportunity was occasioned by the appearance, near the end of 1643, of a brief tract entitled *A Letter of Mr. John Cottons.* Originally written to Roger Williams in 1636, shortly after his banishment from Massachusetts, Cotton's letter confuted two reasons which the rigid Separatist had offered for breaking communion with the Massachusetts churches.[71] As has been indicated in previous discussion of those events, the first reason Williams had given was that the members of the Bay congregations were not properly fitted for church membership. They might indeed exhibit the evidences of personal regeneration, but they had not yet fully and publicly separated themselves from the "Antichristian pollutions" of the Church of England. They had not, for example, explicitly repented hearing sermons in the English parishes. Second, Williams had claimed that the Massachusetts churches lacked sufficient respect and compassion for the London Separatists, who were suffering persecution for practicing in England the congregational discipline which New England churches practiced in peace. Cotton's letter responded that both Williams and the London Separatists bred factions and dissension by their insistence on denouncing the Church of England. Such fanaticism, said Cotton, obscured the more important matters of personal edification and individual godliness, and Williams should not expect the churches of Massachusetts to look with favor upon it.[72]

The English publication of Cotton's letter came at an appropriate time; since mid-October 1643, the Westminster Assembly had been debating matters of church government, specifically the duties of church officers.[73] The letter from Cotton to Williams concerned these very matters: the proper exercise of church discipline and the nature of Williams's responsibilities as teacher of the church at Salem. In addition, both the Presbyterians and Independents of the Assembly were then engaged in publicly repudiating the Separatist position and attempting to discourage the

further formation of individual congregations. This issue of
relations with the Separatist churches was, of course, also
a prominent topic of Cotton's letter.

Williams, while claiming he had had no hand in its publication, admitted that the appearance of Cotton's letter at
this time was providential indeed.[74] Not only was Williams
in England and able to reply, but these very issues of
church reform were now evoking "resolutions of so many
fearing God, to seek what Worship and Worshippers are
acceptable to him in Jesus Christ."[75] As an aid to these
godly Englishmen in their quest for the authentic Christian
society, he published in early February 1644, *Mr. Cottons
Letter Lately Printed, Examined and Answered.* Although the
tract's subject was the religious dispute which preceded
Williams's banishment from Massachusetts, it was composed in a manner which both accentuated the contemporary relevance of those earlier debates and displayed
Williams's credentials as an authentic witness for Christ.[76]

As in *Queries of Highest Consideration,* Roger Williams was
concerned to deal with the issue of church reform. But in
this case he approached that topic from the perspective of
personal piety rather than public policy, addressing not
Parliament and the Assembly of Divines, but the "impar-
tiall" Christian reader, the godly "seeker" after Christ.[77] In
so doing, Williams developed the classic Separatist argument that the quest for individual sanctification must
necessarily embark the saint upon the search for a church
fellowship restored to the true apostolic order. John
Cotton—and in this he seemed to Williams representative of
many Puritan clergy—was a man of eminent personal godliness who had accommodated rather than face the full
rigors of this spiritual journey. And Williams therefore
held up an alternative paradigm for the saints, the witness
of Christ, "willing to follow and be like him in doing, in
suffring," even though such discipleship might withdraw
him from the comfort and prestige of a place among the
settled clergy or the regular parish assemblies.

In portraying the witness and his task it is noteworthy
that, unlike the other two controversial tracts which Williams published during this visit to England, his answer to
Cotton was *not* anonymous. Since it was unlicensed, this
meant that Williams was subject to the same legal penalties

which he claimed had forced him to withhold his name from the title page of *Queries of Highest Consideration*. Further, in organizing his arguments, Williams took advantage of the first opportunity to insert an account of his banishment from Massachusetts, despite the fact that, as John Cotton later emphasized,[78] this information had no direct relevance to the issues at hand. This insertion becomes all the more interesting when it is recalled that Williams never discussed his exile in *The Bloudy Tenent*, to whose arguments for religious liberty it would have been considerably more pertinent. Thus an initial question posed by the structure of *Cottons Letter . . . Examined* is the significance of its autobiographic dimenson.

Williams's format was to reprint a section of Cotton's letter and then respond selectively to it. Cotton's opening paragraph stated that Williams had banished himself from church fellowship by refusing to associate with non-separating congregations. Williams used this comment to introduce into the first several pages of his answer an extended account and interpretation of the events surrounding his exile from the colony. These pages portrayed his disputes in the Bay through the apocalyptic images of the struggle between Antichrist and Christ's suffering witnesses.

Williams asserted that, in his preaching at Salem, his opposition to the patent, his rejection of civil oaths, and his repudiation of the English parishes, he had been acting "as a faithfull Watchman on the walls to sound the Trumpet and give the Alarum" concerning "publike sins, for which I beleeved (and doe) it pleased God to inflict, and further to threaten publike calamities."[79] By referring to himself as a faithful watchman, Williams identified his activities with the watchman of Ezek. 33:1–6, who had been commissioned by the voice of God to warn his city of approaching enemies. If the watchman failed to blow his trumpet, God would hold him responsible for any persons killed. But having trumpeted his concern for their spiritual welfare, Williams found that the churches were "resolved to continue in those evils, and persecuting the witnesses of the Lord presenting light unto them." He had at that point separated from all the churches of the Bay, an act which he hoped was "the act of the Lord Jesus sounding forth in me (a poore despised Rams horn) the blast which shall in his owne holy season cast down the strength and confidence of those inventions of men in the worshipping of the true and living God."[80] Thus, Williams concluded, Cotton was quite correct in saying that Williams had voluntarily departed the New England congregations; this had been his proper duty as Christ's "poore despised Rams horn."

But, Williams informed his readers, the matter had not ended with his separation; he had then been banished from the colony. And if Cotton called this banishment self-imposed, he was using the "language of the Dragon." Such "expressions of the Dragon" were well-known among "the witnesses of the Lord Jesus rent and torne by his persecutions" (cf. Rev. 12:1–17) because they implied that these faithful saints were responsible for their own sufferings: they were being justly punished, not persecuted, for their schismatic, heretical, and inflammatory opinions.[81] In order to dramatize his suffering at the hands of the authorities, Williams made much of the fact that he had departed the colony in January. In phrases reminiscent of the Apostle Paul's summation of his missionary journeys, Williams recounted how in that midwinter flight he had been "exposed to the miseries, poverties, necessities, wants debts, hardships of Sea and Land, in a banished condition" and reduced to "distressed wandrings amongst the Barbarians . . . destitue of food, of cloths, of time."[82] Having suffered such deprivations, he had written to Cotton that "if I had perished in that sorrowfull Winters flight; only the blood of Jesus Christ could have washed him from the guilt of mine," since, Williams claimed, Cotton had advised the magistrates on his sentence.[83]

A dramatic picture is drawn. Roger Williams, the "despised and afflicted" witness for Christ, is hounded out of Massachusetts by John Cotton, "swimming with the stream of outward credit and profit, and smiting with the fist and sword of persecution such as dare not joyn in worship with him." Drawing a reference from Rev. 2:14, Williams asked his readers to decide whether he or Cotton had acted like "the Witnesses of Christ Jesus," who spoke with "the sword of the Spirit, the holy word of God," and who had acted "most like to *Balaam*," who drew Israel off into idolatry.[84] Through this interpretation of his exile, Williams presented himself to his audience as one of the divinely chosen witnesses for Christ who were preparing the way for their Lord's millennial return. The credentials of these inspired prophets were filled by two requirements: forthright testimony on behalf of the gospel, and willing suffering for having so testified. Williams described himself as having met both requirements and reminded his readers in a marginal note that *"Christ Jesus speaketh and suffereth in his witnesses."*[85]

In Williams's opinion, eschatological witnesses were appointed to this religious vocation neither by presbyteries nor by congregations, but by direct, divine inspiration: "Christ Jesus by the secret motion of his own holy *Spirit* extraordinarily excited, incouraged and sent them abroad."[86] The events surrounding his exile from Massachusetts soon convinced him that he had been so called. In October 1636, John Winthrop had written asking what Williams felt he had gained by maintaining his Separatist practices in the face of so much opposition, and Williams answered,

> I confess my Gaines cast up in mans Exchange are Losse of Friends, Esteeme, Maintenance, etc. but what was Gaine in that respect, I desire to count losse for the Excellencie of the Knowledge of Christ Jesus my Lord etc. To his all glorious Name I know I have gained the honour of one of his poore Witnesses, though in Sackcloth.[87]

He therefore felt that "my tribulacion hath brought some Consolation and more Evidence of his Love, singing Moses his Song and the Lambes in that weake victorie which (through His helpe) I have gotten over *the Beast, his picture, his Marke,* and *Number of his Name* Revel. 15.2.3."[88] By claiming such a victory over the Beast, Williams was claiming, according to his own exegesis of Revelation, to be numbered among those 144,000 saints who would reign in the millennial church.[89] God had called him to the vocation of the witness, and he was now "ready not only to be Banished, but to Die in New England for the name of the Lord Jesus."[90]

The conviction that God spiritually appointed individuals to perform eschatological tasks was a characteristic aspect of sectarian enthusiasm. This is not to deny connections between this opinion and the notions of more moderate Puritans concerning eschatological calling, but, according to Presbyterians and Independents, appointment to a millennial role fell upon legally designated social officials. The Lord's annointed, as revealed to moderate spirits, were members of Parliament and ordained ministers. But for the enthusiasts with whom Williams associated, the divine spark might fall upon men from any social station. As William Tindall has observed, these sectarian prophets "depended upon inspiration and revelation, upon openings, trances, illuminations, visions, and celestial voices for what they did or said. The mysterious direction of God exempted them from dependence on man and lent to their actions and speech an unquestionable authority. . . . The voice of God gave them fine words in the night and directed their controversial pen."[91] Having no access to traditional religious authority or, like Williams, having rejected traditional offices because of their antichristian taint, the radicals depended upon evidences of divine inspiration to lend credence to their prophecies.

In its most extreme form such millenarian enthusiasm had messianic implications. Thus, in 1591, Thomas Cartwright and other prominent Puritans were discredited by their acquaintance with three chiliastic conspirators, Copinger, Arthington, and Hacket. The three had plotted to overthrow the government; and in Cheapside, London, Hacket was proclaimed the Messiah by his two companions and, as a result, was hanged for treason.[92] In Williams's own day, John Reeve (1608–58) and Lodowicke Muggleton (1609–98) attained great notoriety by announcing that they were the two witnesses foretold in the Revelation and by traveling about sentencing "all who displeased them to irrevocable damnation."[93] Similarly, in the first decade of the century Walter, Thomas, and Bartholomew Legat "held it stifly, that their must be new Apostles, before their could be a true constituted Church," and further declared that they were those long-awaited messengers.[94] This same opinion was attributed in 1623 to that "ancient stout Separatist" John Wilkinson, whose views on church membership have already been compared with those of Roger Williams.[95] Since Williams shared this opinion that new apostles must come to restore the church, it is worthy of note that John Winthrop stated in 1639 that Williams was "expecting (as was supposed) to become an apostle; and having, a little before, refused communion with all, save his own wife, now he would preach to and pray with all comers."[96] Williams never mentioned this, and it cannot, therefore, be determined whether he ever shared the flamboyant self-appraisals attributed to the Legats and John Wilkinson. If he did, however, he soon reassessed his identity, and spent the rest of his life awaiting such apostles.

What Williams referred to as the "secret motion" of the spirit could often take the form of revelations or visions. Among the London sectarians, for example, a notable witness for the approaching millennium was the visionary Anna Trapnel. A member of the church led by John Simpson, the London Baptist and Fifth Monarchist, she was "seized upon by the Lord" in 1654 and "carried forth in a spirit of Prayer and Singing, from noon till night." In this state, she lay in bed for twelve days, expounding millenarian visions in the form of spiritual discourses and songs. She was well known to Henry Jessey, Hanserd Knollys, and their congregations, and her inspired speeches attracted throngs of pious auditors to her bedside.[97] Trapnel believed that God had commissioned her to announce the millennium and to denounce "the great Rabbies of the world," the ordained clergy; her prophecies generated such attention and, apparently, credence among the faithful that Cromwell eventually had her imprisoned.[98] Throughout the account of her experiences ran her insistence that she functioned as an instrument of God: "Thy servent is made a voice, a sound, it is a voice within a voice, anothers voice, even thy voice through her . . . and when thy Servants has done thy work, she shall be willing to lock her self in her closet again, and not to be seen of men; Oh Lord thy servant knows there is no self in this thing."[99]

In New England the most famous recipient of such illuminations was Anne Hutchinson, one of the principals in the antinomian controversy which erupted in Boston the year following Williams's banishment. Called before the magistrates to defend her leadership of regular prophesying sessions, Hutchinson recounted several "immediate revelations" which justified her actions, promised her miraculous rescue, and foretold "ruine" for her judges and "this whole State."[100] Cast out of Massachusetts, she and other members of her party were assisted by Roger Wil-

liams in establishing a colony on Rhode Island. Williams
had long coversations with Anne Hutchinson in 1638, and
it was her sister who had brief success in converting him to
Anabaptism.[101]

Another instance of spiritual calling to an eschatological
vocation was the vision reportedly experienced by the
army chaplain John Saltmarsh. Like Roger Williams,
Saltmarsh was a Cambridge-educated clergyman who had
renounced his ordination in order to identify himself with
the enthusiasts and lay preachers.[102] According to a
contemporary pamphlet, Saltmarsh told his wife on 4 December 1647 that "hee had beene in a Trance, seene a Vision, and received a command from God, to go presently
to the Army, to make knowne to them, what the Lord had
revealed to him, which would be the least work that he had
to do for them."[103] Leaving home, he arrived at army
headquarters on the sixth, appearing "as one risen from
the grave, his eyes almost fixt in his head, or rather as if he
had come out of a Trance."[104] In that condition he warned
Sir Thomas Fairfax and the Council of Officers that God
had forsaken them because they had fallen away from their
former godly principles. When the troops then asked the
chaplain if they should lay down their arms, he replied,
"No . . . God hath yet a great work to be done: In which he
will make use of Members of this Army, to do great things
for the glory of his Name." Announcing that he had completed his divine *"errand,"* Saltmarsh returned home and
died on 11 December.[105]

The enthusiasts typically interpreted such revelations as
the revival of apostolic gifts of tongues and prophecy
which would accompany the millennium. For example,
John Canne, the Separatist to whom Williams referred in
Cottons Letter . . . Examined, believed that Christ was revealing the meaning of the scriptural prophecies to certain
chosen saints. In 1653 he numbered himself among these
prophets and announced that he and others had been divinely called to act for the "fulfilling of the will and com-
mandment of God, though the same (as the world judgeth)
seem irrational, illegal, absurd, destructive to Religion,
Law, Liberty, &c."[106] Williams, of course, did not believe
that such prophets and new apostles had yet arrived, but
he theorized that, when they did, "it may please the *Lord*
againe to cloath his people with a spirit of *zeale* and *courage*

for the name of *Christ*, yea and powre forth those fiery streames againe of *Tongues* and *Prophecie* in the *restauration* of *Zion*."[107] His friend, Sir Henry Vane, was more positive and predicted that immediately preceding the millennium a spiritual ministry would arise and "be found speaking with the tongues, not of men only, but of angels, and to have also the love requisite to distinguish them from all counterfeits."[108]

Suffering for testimony to religious convictions, like the spiritual gifts of visions and prophecy, provided evidence of the witness' divine calling—as Williams's interpretation of his banishment emphasized. Suffering, in fact, was regularly construed by the enthusiasts as itself a religious experience, a manifestation of God's favor. It was in this manner, for example, that the Leveller leader John Lilburne interpreted his punishments in *A Worke of the Beast* (1638), a pamphlet with several similarities to the autobiographic sections of *Cottons Letter . . . Examined*. Lilburne had been accused of distributing unlicensed books, and his tract described how God enabled him to endure with serenity the whipping to which he was sentenced by the prelates.[109] Like Williams, he depicted himself as one impelled by the spirit to speak despite any physical danger: "I dare not hold my peace, but speake unto you with boldnes in the might and strength of my God, the things which the Lord in mercy hath made knowne to my Soule, come life come death."[110] Lilburne placed his testimony and prosecution by the bishops in the context of the apocalyptic spiritual battle against Antichrist, "in which Battell," he told his readers, "the Lord befor your eyes hath raised up some valiant Champions that fought up to the eares in bloud, therefore be couragious Souldiers and fight it out bravely, that your God may be glorified by you."[111] He described his whipping in detail and declared that he counted his suffering "my weding day in which I was married to the Lord Jesus Christ; for now I knowe he loves me in that he hath bestowed soe rich apparrell this day upon me; and counted me worthie to suffer for his sake."[112]

A particularly emphatic description of the religious experience of suffering came from the pen of Roger Williams's friend Obadiah Holmes, a Rhode Island Baptist leader. Holmes had been apprehended in Massachusetts in 1651, while attending an illegal prophesying session. Soon

afterward, he wrote a letter to the London Baptist congregations in which he reflected upon his punishment in
the hope that his remarks would prove edifying for his
English friends. He recalled that "as the stroaks fell upon
me, I had such a spirituall manifestation of Gods presence,
as the like thereunto I never had, nor felt, nor can with
fleshly tongue expresse, and the outward pain was so removed from me, that indeed I am not able to declare it to
you."[113] Williams discerned similar evidence of divine
mercy in his own difficulties in Massachusetts, and he remarked in *Cottons Letter . . . Examined,* "I have said and must
say, and all Gods witnesses that have borne any paine or
losse for Jesus, must say, that fellowship with the Lord
Jesus in his sufferings is sweeter then all the fellowship
with sinners, in all the profits, honours, and pleasures of
this present evill world."[114]

In sum, Roger Williams's portrayal of himself in the intro-
ductory section of *Cottons Letter . . . Examined* was written
in the language of sectarian enthusiasm. His claim to be an
eschatological witness, stirred up by the Holy Spirit to
testify for Christ, spoke directly to the millenarian expectations of the English religious radicals. Not Parliament, not
the clergy, but the individual preacher, illuminated by the
spirit and willing to suffer for his convictions, was the
agent of reformation in these latter days of the world;
Roger Williams shared these convictions and counted himself among those called to this spiritual vocation.

Having established his credentials with his audience,
Williams then presented the substance of his controversy
with John Cotton as a model of the direction in which
reformation in England should proceed. The focus of his
debate with Cotton had been the qualifications necessary
for church membership; Williams had argued that the
church member must not only give evidence of regeneration but also have expressly repented adherence to false
forms of worship. To be acceptable to Christ's church, the
applicant must first "come out from that former false
Church or Christ, and his Ministrie, Worship, &c. before
he can be united to the true Israel."[115] In 1644, according to
Williams, only the Baptist and Separatist churches were
preaching and suffering for this thorough reformation
based on total separation from false Christianity; the
"middle way" of reform espoused by the Independent and

Presbyterian clergy was, from his perspective, mere vacillation halfway between Christ and Antichrist.[116]

The position of the Baptists and Separatists was not, of course, the same as his own conviction that the church did not exist and would not until Christ sent new apostles to recreate it. In *Cottons Letter . . . Examined,* he only alluded to these particular beliefs of his own and did not press for their adoption by others.[117] Nevertheless, the entire tract stressed the compatibility of sectarian churchmanship with his own sense of religious mission. Both he and they were striving for the restoration of Zion, and they did not find their social and religious goals revealed in Independent and Presbyterian proposals for a godly commonwealth.

Taken together, *Queries of Highest Consideration* and *Cottons Letter . . . Examined* illustrate the connection which existed between Roger Williams's personal piety and his convictions about reformation. The clerical spokesmen for Presbyterianism and Independency tied reformation to the authority vested in Parliament and the Westminster Assembly; they applauded their respective church governments as in the first manifestations of the latter-day glory. Engaging them in controversy, Williams first declared that religious experience, not tenure in political or ecclesiastical office, provided the authority to engage in "resotration work." He therefore ignored his background as an ordained clergyman and presented himself as a suffering witness, specially called to the reformer's vocation. Second, by pointing out differences between their churches and those of the apostles (the only acceptable models for true reformation), he emphasized that the way to lost Zion passes first through iconoclasm and repentance before affording a view of its destination. Christ's witnesses must purge the church before Christ's apostles rebuild it.

5 The Liberty of the Witnesses and the Restoration of the Church

By publishing *Queries of Highest Consideration* and *Cottons Letter . . . Examined,* Roger Williams both fulfilled and described his religious vocation in the act of controverting Puritan assumptions about the manner and direction of reformation. This controversial calling and the millenarian ecclesiology which undergirded it were in part his inheritance from the rigid Separatist and Baptist traditions, in which church membership was restricted not merely to visible saints but to those who had wholly departed from all religious practices deemed unscriptural and returned to the ancient and apostolic discipline. Williams, however, had become convinced that at present such authentic worshiping communities did not exist; the form and spiritual authority of the apostolic church had been destroyed by the medieval apostasy, he believed, and could only be restored by the millennial appearance of new apostles. For this reason, he abstained from formal participation in contemporary churches and instead projected the possibility of such communion into an approaching millennial age. In preparation for that age of restoration, so Williams saw the matter, he and other Christians had been called to write and preach against religious error.

Even given this strong religious commitment, Williams's ventures into controversial publishing must have been taxing. Much of his time was already consumed by the effort to gain a colonial charter, employment for his personal maintenance, and private litigation. In addition, after

royalist forces had stopped the supply of coal from New-
castle to London, Williams engaged himself in "the service
of the *Parliament* and *City*" by helping to supply wood to
London's poor.[1] Nevertheless, public controversy remained a high priority, and the millenarian piety which
had ordered his responses to John Cotton, the dissenting
brethren, and the Scottish commissioners also provided
the framework for further publication on two seemingly
unrelated issues: religious liberty and the conversion of the
Indians.

Williams discussed the first of these two topics, religious
liberty, in his famous tract *The Bloudy Tenent, of Persecution*,
which appeared anonymously during the summer of 1644.
Liberty, he declared, would hasten completion of the witnesses' eschatological task; their testimony was the
spiritual weapon wielded by Christ in defeating religious
error, and it should neither be restrained nor replaced by
the physical weapons of the state. But until the witnesses
had fulfilled their purgative mission, no true church would
appear in the world, and Williams published *Christenings
Make Not Christians* (1645) to dissuade his Puritan colleagues from converting Indians into members of churches
whose imperfect order still linked them by a "mystical
chaine" to Antichrist. He nonetheless made hopeful preparations for action at the proper moment for the Indians'
conversion by improving his skill as a linguist. He shared
this skill in *A Key into the Language of America* (1643), which
opened for interested Englishmen the way into civil and
spiritual discourse with the New England Indian tribes.

Religious Liberty

Roger Williams later recalled that he had prepared *The
Bloudy Tenent* "for publike view" in a "variety of strange
houses, sometimes in the *fields,* in the midst of *travel;* where
he hath been forced to gather and scatter his loose *thoughts*
and *papers.*"[2] Actually, those scattered papers and
thoughts had been several years in the gathering, since the
various documents which formed the basis for his treatise
on religious liberty had been generated by the events surrounding his banishment from Massachusetts in 1636. In
fact, *The Bloudy Tenent* was essentially a commentary on
the views concerning religious toleration held by others,

and the first step in understanding its intentions is to examine the earlier documents on which it was based.

During the years immediately following his settlement at Providence, Williams had engaged in several controversies involving ministers in Massachusetts and had circulated manuscripts expounding his own views on civil and ecclesiastical policy. One circumstance which prompted Williams's writing was agitation in the church at Roxbury, Massachusetts, over the relation between freedom of conscience and his own recent exile. At that time, the teacher of the Roxbury church, John Eliot (later famous as a missionary to the Indians), wrote a treatise which explained and justified the grounds for Williams's banishment.[3] Meanwhile, one of Eliot's parishoners, John Hall, had come into possession of a Baptist tract which set forth arguments favoring religious liberty and had asked John Cotton to comment upon it. Hall was dissatisfied with Cotton's answers and sent the material to Williams for his opinion.[4] The arguments favoring religious liberty were actually a segment from *A Most Humble Supplication* (1620), a tract composed by a member of Thomas Helwys's General Baptist congregation in London.[5] Williams reprinted the Baptist arguments and Cotton's answer to them as the two opening sections of *The Bloudy Tenent*.

The third document examined by *The Bloudy Tenent* was a manuscript entitled "A Model of Church and Civil Power," which had been composed by a group of Bay ministers and sent to the church at Salem in 1635.[6] The occasion for this document was the dispute over the right of the magistrates to block Williams's appointment as teacher at Salem. It of course upheld the responsibility of the magistrates, the churches' "nursing fathers," to intercede when they and their clerical advisers deemed it necessary for the protection or advancement of godly religion.[7] Samuel Sharpe, lay elder at Salem, sent Williams a copy of the manuscript after the latter had settled at Providence,[8] and Williams responded to extensive quotations from it in the final 200 pages of *The Bloudy Tenent*.

Reflection on these documents in connection with the controversies in which he was engaged led Williams to begin formulating his own thoughts on religious liberty and the relation of church and state. By the summer of 1637, he had composed a manuscript dealing with aspects of these issues and had sent copies to John Winthrop and the minister Peter Bulkley for their evaluations; Bulkley, at least, returned written objections.[9] From what little can be known of Williams's manuscript, his opinions already showed the influence of the General Baptist literature on religious liberty, an influence which would be quite clear throughout *The Bloudy Tenent*.

The General Baptists had published a series of pleas for liberty of conscience in the decade following their return to London from the Netherlands in 1611. In addition to *A Most Humble Supplication*, which Williams cited in his *Bloudy Tenent*, the others were *A Short Declaration of the Mistery of Iniquity* (1612) by Thomas Helwys, *Religions Peace* (1614) by Leonard Busher, and *Objections: Answered by Way of Dialogue* (1615). In each pamphlet the advocacy of a complete separation of church and state provided the foundation for arguments favoring religious liberty. The power and methods of the magistrate, said the Baptist writers, are completely inappropriate for the promotion or discipline of the true Christian church. Roger Williams would make remarkably few alterations in the Baptist arguments, when, at mid-century, he too would advocate complete religious liberty. But although the position was not original with him, Williams's convictions remained as unusual and unpopular in his time as they had been when advanced by the General Baptists.

The unpopularity of Williams's plea for religious liberty is in large measure attributable to the powerful influence which the vision of a holy commonwealth exercised over conventional Puritan thought in England and America. Among Massachusetts Bay congregationalists and English Independents the conviction prevailed that God was effecting a reformation which would conform both church and society to divine law by subjecting both to godly rule. Rule by the saints was thus felt to extend beyond the community of saints to the society at large, and this impetus toward reform tended to restrict the scope of liberty. In his exceptionally clear analysis of this relation between reform and liberty, A. S. P. Woodhouse has therefore noted that "Puritanism was not only committed in all sections to the ideal of the 'holy community,' but, in most of them, strongly drawn to the establishment of its reign outside the body of the elect, where, since persuasion could be of no avail, reform must be by coercion."[10] "A Model of Church and Civil Power" and Cotton's answer to the Baptist arguments both approached the issue of toleration in relation to this desire for a reformed, godly commonwealth, and their position is thus representative not only of New England congregationalism but also of most English Puritans.

Like the general issue of reformation, the Puritans tended to interpret questions of religious uniformity and toleration through millenarian language. This millenarian perspective was presented quite specifically in Cotton's response to *The Bloudy Tenent*, a work entitled *The Bloudy Tenent, Washed, and Made White in the Bloud of the Lambe* (1647). In this tract, Cotton argued that "when the Kingdomes of the earth become the Kingdomes of the Lord (Rev. 11. 15.) It is not, by making Christ a temporall king, but by making temporall Kingdomes nursing Fathers to his Church."[11] The magistrate had the responsibility of promoting and protecting the authentic, scriptural form of church government, which Cotton identified with the "New England way." This responsibility meant both that deviations from this authentic form were categorized as error and that permission of such errors would be adverse to the cause of reformation. But through godly magistrates conforming church and society to divine law, said Cotton, God would bring into being a "visible state of a new *Hierusalem*, which shall flourish many yeares upon Earth, before the end of the world."[12]

It was in relation to this concept of the holy commonwealth that Cotton responded to the General Baptist arguments for religious liberty. Certainly, he admitted, it would be wrong for any magistrate to punish persons presenting religious truth, but no responsible governor could tolerate advocates of religious error, since such laxity would impede reformation, threaten civil peace, and invite divine judgment.[13] The magistrate was expected to employ his authority in the best interests of religion within his jurisdiction, and Cotton's discussion defined the principles which should guide civil policy on religious matters.

Cotton's analysis began with the assertion that God had laid down certain "*fundamentall* and principall points of Doctrine or Worship," departure from which would endanger salvation. The Scripture is so clear concerning these matters, said Cotton, that, after an erring individual's attention has been directed to them, "hee cannot but bee convinced in *Conscience* of the dangerous Errour of his way."[14] If, following admonition by his minister, the individual continued in error, the magistrate should step in to punish him, since his errant actions would then be against the clear dictates of his own conscience. Human governments, Cotton concluded, have "no power to make *Lawes,* to bind *Conscience.* But this hindreth not, but that Men may see the Lawes of *God* observed, which doe bind Conscience."[15] Such action by the state against the heretic who has been warned of his errors was particularly warranted in those cases in which he publicly expounded his false opinions. Such a "scandalous and heynous offender" was subject not only to excommunication but also to civil punishments in order to preserve members of church and commonwealth from "dangerous and damnable infection."[16]

It should especially be noted in this argument that the religious responsibilities of the magistrate were distinct from, but complementary to, the responsibilities of church officers. The laws of a commonwealth can never convince conscience or lead men into the body of the elect; it is the word of God in Scripture and preaching which effects such spiritual reformations. Nevertheless, the magistrate was expected to maintain the good order of the churches and the standards of orthodoxy. By protecting the church from error and disturbance, he gave the ministers and lay officers of the congregations freedom to direct full attention to their proper concern, the spiritual welfare of saints and citizens. These protective duties of the civil governors were clearly summarized in the "Model of Church and Civil Power" sent to the dissidents at Salem:

> Magistrates upon due and diligent search what is the counsell and will of God in his Word concerning the right ordering of the Church, may and ought to publish and declare, establish and ratifie such Lawes and Ordinances as Christ hath appointed in his Word for the well ordering of Church affaires, both for the gathering of the Church, and the right administration of all the Ordinances of God amongst them in such manner as the Lord hath appointed to edification.[17]

In England, in the 1640s, Presbyterians and Independents were advancing these same basic arguments for religious uniformity and the regulation of religious order by the state. Permission of religious errors within a nation invited civil disorder and impeded the course of reformation, and they called upon members of Parliament to exercise their authority for the moral and spiritual welfare of the nation by suppressing such errors. Two factors, however, inclined the English Independents to argue for greater religious tolerance than was the case with their counterparts in New England. First, they were themselves a minority party and sought to protect their rights against a too restrictive imposition of Presbyterianism. Second, their influence over political and religious decisions depended in increasing measure on their ability to maintain relations with the sectarians, especially those in the army. Thus, in the period from 1643 to 1645, they published a number of documents which expanded the basic argument employed by John Cotton in order to admit limited toleration of differing religious opinions.

In these early days of the Civil Wars, therefore, the English Independents usually discussed religious toleration in the context of defense and exposition of their "congregational way." The first and best known example of this was, of course, the *Apologeticall Narration* issued in January 1644 by the dissenting brethren of the Westminster Assembly. It pointed out the compatibility of Independency not only with Presbyterianism but also with divine truth and emphasized the wide difference between this form of congregationalism and the turbulent and schismatic opinions of the Separatists. Its conclusion was that such a polity should not only be tolerated but commended for its advances beyond Presbyterianism toward the apostolic pattern. In the ensuing months, other congregationalist documents both defended the *Apologeticall Narration* and dealt more explicitly with its appeal for toleration of the Independent congregations.[18]

In these appeals, the concept of the progressive revelation of divine truth, the gradual outpouring of "further light," which was so important to the Independents' theory of the course of reformation, was also central to their arguments concerning religious toleration. Since God was progressively revealing his purposes for the elect, it was crucial not to restrict or retard the light of truth by persecuting those instruments whom God had selected to reveal these mysteries to church and nation. Permission of differing opinions among the godly protected against the misapplication of human force in opposition to divine will. From this perspective, the author of *The Ancient Bounds* observed that both Presbyterians and Independents had changed their opinions concerning church polity in the past; he asked his Presbyterian opponents,

> Why may you not in a while see cause to exchange your present judgement for a better? Why may there not be more truth yet behind? Is that which is perfect come, or are we come yet to that measure of the stature of the fulnesse of Christ?... May not Errours for a time, have the credit of Truths? as many Episcopall Doctrines now rejected, might be instanced in; hath not every truth its set time, the *fulnesse of time* to be borne into the world?[19]

If this is so, it would indeed invite divine judgment to oppose those truths whose time has come. And one such truth, said the Independents, was the ecclesiology of congregationalism. According to the author of *A Paraenetick . . . for (Not Loose, but) Christian Libertie,* many English Presbyterians were beginning to recognize this fact. They were, he said, giving serious consideraton to the congregational way, "which they grant was the Primitive Way, and is the purest, and the *Presbyterian Way* is but a step thereto, and will rest here as its center, and end in this as its perfection."[20]

As this clearly indicates, the Independents addressed the issue of religious toleration strictly in relation to the broader concern of religious reformation. Differences *among the godly* were to be tolerated, because these might well be advancing the cause of reformation by presenting new truths. Beliefs and practices which they considered obvious and dangerous errors were another matter. Therefore, they hearkened to Cotton's assertion that fundamental religious error could not be permitted within the commonwealth. They assured the Scot Adam Steuart that, in advocating toleration of Independency, they did not intend toleration of all religious opinions and practices; "venting of any *opinion* against fundamentalls"—Judaism, Socinianism, Catholicism, Anabaptist universalism—"ought to be suppressed."[21] Such beliefs were "errors of

manifest scandall and danger to mens soules and consciences," and Parliament should prohibit their "publique
preaching or printing."[22]

The line between godly difference of opinion and the
publication of manifest error was, of course, subject to interpretation; the limits of toleration might be quite nar-
rowly or widely drawn. The *Paraenetick*, for example,
sought to gain toleration only for the conservative Independents; in its appeal to the Presbyterians no consideration
was asked for Baptists or Separatists. Its author concerned himself solely with reminding the Presbyterians of
the brief conciliatory period surrounding the publication of
*Certain Considerations to Dissuade Men from Further Gathering
of Churches* in late 1643.[23] John Goodwin, on the other
hand, advocated a wider tolerance and warned that "for
any man to endeavour or attempt the suppression of any
Doctrine, practice, or way, which is from God, is to fight
against God himselfe."[24] He advised extreme caution in
deciding which beliefs were errors and which were not; "let
it be the first-born of religious advisements and cautions to
us, not to be fierce, no, nor so much as to lift up a hard
thought against Doctrine or *Way* claiming origination and
descent from God, till wee have security upon security,
conditions as cleer as the noon-day, that they are but counterfeits and pretenders only, and stand in no relation at all,
but that of enmity and opposition unto God."[25] By this
circumspect appraisal of religious differences, Goodwin
and such army chaplains as William Dell and John
Saltmarsh soon extended the boundaries of acceptable
opinion to include within the limits of toleration the Puritan sects, Baptists, Separatists, or Seekers.[26]

By 1645, the Independents recognized that some toleration of these sectaries was necessary in order to retain their
support for the parliamentary cause against the crown and
to maintain weight of numbers against attempts at strict
imposition of Presbyterianism. At the same time, they
found that the narrow limits of toleration observed by their
fellow congregationalists in New England were a source of
considerable embarrassment to them. Therefore, in June
1645, Thomas Goodwin, John Owen, Philip Nye, and other
Independent ministers wrote to the General Court of Massachusetts advising the colony to restore Baptists to their

liberty. They recommended this course for two main reasons. First, the allegation of persecution in New England was being used to advantage by the English enemies of congregationalism; second, such severity in New England was offensive to friends of the colony who were now in places of political power in England.[27] It should be noted, however, that this friction between the Independents and New England occurred only over the *limits* of toleration and not over the *principles* by which toleration should be granted.

The English sectarians had for some time been pleading their right to assemble and preach. In 1641, for example, a London coachman named John Spencer justified the right of himself and other laymen to preach by declaring that "the scriptures doth plainely affirme, that the true understanding of scripture comes not by humane learning, by arts and tongues, but by the spirit of God."[28] Likewise, in 1643, a group of London sectarians presented the Westminster Assembly a petition calling for liberty of conscience.[29] But not until 1644, at the same time that the Independents were addressing the issue of toleration, did the religious liberties of the sectarians begin to find their champions appearing in the controversial press in considerable numbers.

Several of these tracts favoring liberty for the sects used as their basic argument the generally accepted premise that conscience will be altered by persuasion but not by physical force. Thus, the author of *The Compassionate Samaritane* observed that "conscience being subject only to reason (either that which is indeed, or seems to him which hears it to be so) can only be convinced or perswaded thereby, force makes it runne backe, and strugle."[30] Most Puritans in old and New England would have agreed that man's conscience and spirit could be turned only by the persuasive power of divine truth working upon human reason, but they would have added that the obligation to cooperate with God in establishing the holy commonwealth took precedent over consideration extended to reluctant individual consciences. To this assertion, these tracts had no direct answers. *The Power of Love* presented the usual response with the observation that, in the experience of its author, the "Anabaptists, Brownists, and Separatists" were not the threats to "order and decency" which they were popularly portrayed to be.[31] Thus, as the titles of these tracts suggest, an appeal to Christian charity appeared to be liberty's last line of defense against the stern demands of reformation.

It was at this point that Roger Williams made a significant contribution to the controversy over religious liberty. Although he employed many of the arguments used in such tracts as *The Compassionate Samaritane* or *The Power of Love,* he went a step further. By skillfully adapting the General Baptist arguments for religious liberty to a new context, Williams developed a carefully reasoned and systematic critique of the general Puritan conception of the character and purpose of reformation. By questioning the Puritan vision of the holy commonwealth, he attempted to counter the argument that the progress of religious reform could not tolerate the presence of religious error within the state. The result was clear advocacy of complete liberty for all religious opinions, even those which Williams and his fellow Puritans were convinced were absolutely false.

In outline, the construction of *The Bloudy Tenent* appears quite rigid and formal. Documents addressing the issues of toleration and the relation of church and state are subjected to close—even line by line—scrutiny and analysis by Williams. The basic thrust and balance of the book would therefore appear to be dictated by the arguments and concerns of the writers being examined, rather than by Williams himself. This, however, is not the case because of the literary device, a dialogue between *Truth* and *Peace,* by which Williams framed and ordered his analysis of the documents and their arguments. Through this technique, Williams indicated the context in which he wished his readers to place the total controversy. Therefore, an examination of the role played by these personifications provides an appropriate entrance into Williams's understanding of religious liberty and its relations to other aspects of his thought.

Following the reprinted arguments of the Baptist writer and John Cotton, Williams introduced his reader to a chance meeting between Truth and Peace, who, despite long searching, have failed to encounter each other in any corner of the world. Truth laments that they are destined to remain separated until

> The most high *Eternall Creatour*, shall gloriously create
> *New Heavens* and *New Earth*, wherein dwells *Righteous-
> ness*, 2 Pet. 3. Our *kisses* then shall have their *endlesse* date
> of pure and sweetest joyes? till then both *Thou* and *I*
> must hope, and wait, and beare the furie of the *Dragons*
> wrath, whose *montrous Lies* and *Furies* shall with himselfe
> be cast into the *lake* of *Fire*, the *second death*. Revel. 21.[32]

During the present brief encounter, they propose to discuss how this separation between them has occurred and
how, with divine assistance, it may be remedied.

Peace observes that she has been placed in opposition to
the truth; Truth's witnesses are popularly accused of being
"*contentious, turbulent, seditious*" enemies of civil and religious peace. In addition, those who style themselves the
supporters of religious truth act on its behalf by waging
"*holy War*" against those whom they deem heretics or schis-
matics.[33] The result of these misapprehensions of the nature of religious truth and the means by which it is advanced
has thus been the disruption of both civil and religious
peace. Peace among the saints is destroyed by physical punishments inflicted upon "the holy *witnesses* of *Christ Jesus*,
who testifie against . . . invented worships," but are mis-
takenly identified as heretics. Civil peace is rendered impossible by "the *Nations* and Peoples slaughtering each
other for their severall respective Religions and Consciences."[34] The arguments of the Baptist writer, says
Truth, suggest how such antagonism between the values of
truth and peace may be ended, they are written "in *milke*,
spiritually *white*, pure and innocent, like those *white horses*
of the *Word* of *truth* and *meeknesse*, and the *white Linnen* or
Armour of *righteousness*, in the *Army* of *Jesus*." Cotton's arguments, on the other hand, are written with blood because their implication is enmity among saints and states of
differing religious practice.[35]

It was Williams's contention, then, that adoption of the
principles advanced by the Baptist writer would effect two
goals. Most important, it would free the witnesses to fulfill
their eschatological task of eradicating religious error in
preparation for the millennium. Thus liberty, not uniformity, was the fundamental tool of reformation, the means
for attaining the eschatological reunion of Truth and Peace.
In addition, the Baptist principles would eliminate religious disagreement as a cuase for, or justification of, war

and physical punishments. Liberty of conscience was the means for attaining civil peace in the present and religious peace in the millennium. Williams's detailed examination of the arguments for and against religious liberty tested the validity of this contention, to which he directed the reader's attention through the literary device of conversations between Truth and Peace.

In a generation tormented by "wars of religion," first on the Continent and now at home, it was surely a tiny minority who would have disagreed with Williams's goals, but it was an equally small group who believed that the *novus ordo seclorum* could ever be achieved through liberty of conscience. This difference, in turn, implied opposing convictions about the relation between church and state. In opposition to the more usual Puritan conception of a holy commonwealth, Williams advocated the *separation* of church and state and made this principle his fundamental argument for complete religious liberty.

Williams, like the General Baptist writers, made his clearest justification for separation of church and state through an appeal to a particular typological interpretation of Scripture. In using this method he was not unique; typology had been employed as an exegetical tool throughout the history of the Christian tradition. It related the Old Testament to the New Testament by considering the events of the former as historical foreshadowings of the history of salvation which began with Christ's incarnation. The typological method had the advantage of allowing the exegete to retain the historicity of events from the Old Testament, while at the same time freeing him to attribute to them another, specifically Christian, level of meaning. Thus the Hebraic practice of circumcision might be placed in typological relation to the Christian practice of baptism or to the experience of conversion, and statements regarding it could then be applied to one or the other of these *antitypes*. As this example suggests, the method allowed considerable possibility for variation in the selection of the antitype which a particular type presaged. Therefore, although typology had the traditional function of integrating the two Testaments by lifting up the Christian significance of the first, the specific content with which it was filled depended to large extent upon the theological intent of the individual interpreter.

The typological argument advanced by Roger Williams and the General Baptists emphasized the radical difference between the religious society or community described in the Old Testament and that described in the New Testament. Only the latter form, they argued, was a model applicable to the situation of contemporary Christians, and it emphatically denied the use of civil force in the maintenance or reformation of religion.[36]

According to Williams's exegesis, the nation of Israel, as its history was expressed in the Old Testament, was a unique occurrence. It represented the only case in which an entire nation had stood in covenant relation with God. Its magistrates, the kings of Israel, had exercised both civil and ecclesiastical jurisdiction within the nation, and every individual, under threat of physical punishment, was bound to conform to the moral and religious laws delivered by God and administered by the king.[37] At the coming of Christ, however, the Jewish nation failed to heed his preaching and did not place its allegiance with him. For this failure, God "*cast* them out of his sight, destroyed that *nationall church,* and *established* the *Christian church,*" composed not of a nation but of individuals, called by God to participate in worshiping congregations.[38]

Thus God had related himself to his people through two quite different communities. The first had been a national state in which religious obedience was directed by law; the second was a community of the faithful in which obedience sprang freely from godly desires. Williams and the General Baptists interpreted the first of these religious communities, ancient Israel, as the prefigurement or type of the second, the Christian church. Entrance into the former of these chosen peoples by the physical events of birth and circumcision figuratively represented entrance into the latter by the spiritual events of conversion and the baptism of faith. Since God's dispersion of ancient Israel, no literal chosen nation existed in the world, and, on this basis, Williams asked rhetorically, "What *Land,* what *Country* now is *Israels Parallel* and *Antitype,* but that holy *mysticall* Nation the *Church* of *God,* peculiar and called out to him out of every Nation and Country."[39] The leader of the early English Baptists, Thomas Helwys, distinguished the typological relations between these temporal and "mysticall" Kingdoms in his controversial tract, *The Mistery of Iniquity*.

> The kingdome of Israell was an earthly or worldly kingdome: an earthly or worldly Temple, Tabernacle, or house: an earthly or worldly people: and the King an earthly King, who in and over all that kingdome, Temple, and people could require onely earthly obedience. But the kingdome of Christ now, is an heavenly kingdome *not of this world*: his Temple, Tabernacle, or house *an heavenly Temple, Tabernacle, or House*, his people, a heavenly, or spirituall people, *not of this world*: and the King Christ Jesus *a heavenly spirituall King* requiring spirituall obedience.[40]

The kings of Israel, in exercising religious authority, therefore prefigured or "typed out the *Spirituall King* of *Israel, Christ Jesus*"; they did *not* provide a model for the relation of church and civil power in contemporary commonwealths.[41] In abrogating his covenant with Israel, God had foreclosed the possibility of nations advancing or protecting true religion by civil means.

The General Baptists had used this typological interpretation of Scripture to deny James I and his bishops power to impose religious uniformity. The author of *A Most Humble Supplication* declared that "there is only deceit in these learned men's comparisons of the kings of Israel in the law, with the kings of nations in time of the gospel, in matters of religion. . . . And if these judicials of Moses be not now directions for the kings of nations, we read not in all the book of God, any directions given to kings to rule in matters of conscience and spiritual worship to God."[42] This of course was the same tract quoted in *The Bloudy Tenent*, and Williams made the identical point that the nation of Israel did not provide a precedent for contemporary use of civil power to regulate religious belief and practice. Modern laws denying religious liberty were arrows "drawne from the Quiver of the Ceremoniall and typicall state of the Nationall Church of the Jewes, whose shadowish and figurative state vanished at the appearing of the Body and substance of the Sun of Righteousness, who set up another Kingdome or Church (Heb. 12) Ministrie and worship: in which we finde no such Ordinance, precept or president of killing men by Materiall Swords for Religions sakes."[43]

Under the Christian dispensation, the typological argument stated, church and state had utterly separate realms of authority and methods for exercising authority. In ancient Israel one government had been responsible for both civil and spiritual order in society, but in Christian times two different governments, one political and one religious, administered these responsibilities separately. In the same manner that "the *Civill Magistrate* hath his charge of the *bodies* and *goods* of the *subject:* So," declared Roger Williams, "have the *spirituall officers, Governours* and *overseers* of *Christs City* or *Kingdome,* the charge of their *souls* and *soule safety.*"[44] To allow civil officers to tamper with the spiritual city would pervert divine will by confusing temporal and religious realms of authority.[45]

Similarly, both Williams and the General Baptists agreed that, although the state should use physical weapons to protect the physical welfare of its citizens, Christians were permitted to defend the church only with the "sword of the Spirit" wielded in preaching and religious controversy. This spiritual sword was wholly sufficient to deal with religious error in the world and required no assistance from temporal arms to defeat the Catholic Antichrist or other heresies.[46] In the apocalyptic battles yet to be fought, Williams predicted, Christ and his witnesses would use only "mystical" weapons:

> This glorious *Armie* of *white Troopers,* horses and harnesse (*Christ Jesus* and his true *Israel*) Rev.19. gloriously conquer and overcome the *Beast,* the false *Prophet* and the *Kings* of the Earth up in Armes against them, *Rev.* 19. and lastly, raigning with *Christ* a thousand yeares they conquer the *Divell* himselfe and the numberlesse *Armies . . . of Gog* and *Magog,* and yet not a tittle of mention of any *sword, helmet, breastplate, shield* or *horse,* but what is *Sprituall* and of a *heavenly nature:* All which Warres of *Israel* have been, may be, and shall be fulfilled mystically and Spiritually.[47]

The separate functions of church and state meant, said Williams, that the peace or well-being of the nation in no way depended upon the presence of true religion within its borders. He compared the church to a guild of artisans or physicians within a city; unless the guild's internal disagreements or corruptions posed a physical threat to persons and properties, the civil peace of the city was not violated.[48] Such an assertion contradicted conventional wisdom, which predicted civil disarray and divine judgment for the nation which neglected the church's welfare. Religion, said the Independent spokesman Thomas Goodwin, is the "great interest of states and kingdoms," and he found in Scripture the clear historical lesson that "God from the beginning hath in his Providence so ordered it, that the greatest and most flourishing Kingdomes and States should still have to doe with his Saints and People in all Ages, and either they have beene broken by their ill using of them, or they have prospered by their well dealing with them."[49] Williams, on the other hand, examined the historical record and found little connection between the fortunes of nations and the presence of true faith: "Many stately *Kingdomes* and *Governments* have long . . . enjoyed *civill* peace and quiet, notwithstanding their *Religion* is so corrupt, as that there is not the very Name of *Jesus Christ* among them."[50]

Whenever religious disagreement or error has appeared to disrupt civil peace, observed Roger Williams, it has been for two primary reasons. First, when a people is disturbed by hearing the truth preached, they often violently suppress it. He did not find this surprising, since, "when a Kingdome or State, Towne or Family, lyes and lives in the guilt of false God, false Christ, false worship: no wonder if sore eyes be troubled at the appearance of the light, be it never so sweet: No wonder if a body full of corrupt humours be troubled at strong (though wholsome) Physick? If persons sleepy and loving to sleepe be troubled at the noise of shrill (though silver) alarums"[51] Second, when confronted with religious errors, governments have attempted to combat them by means of physical force which, as all the Puritan parties agreed, has no power to alter conscience. Guns and swords can no more effectively dispel heresy, declared Williams, than they can scatter a fog; "tis Light alone, even Light from the bright shining Sunne of Righteousnesse, which is able, in the soules and consciences of men to dispell and scatter such fogges and darknesse."[52] He therefore concluded that breaches in the civil peace need not occur when religious doctrine—even erroneous doctrine—was professed in contradiction to that sanctioned by the state. Civil violence resulted only when the state opposed such doctrines with physical force. The authority and power of the state was neither legitimate nor effective when applied against the consciences of men. History and experience thus verified for Williams his interpretation of Christ's parable of the tares (Matt. 13:24–30) as a command to permit religious truth and error to coexist in the nations until the end of the world.[53] By such liberty of conscience the civil peace would be protected.

In all its aspects, then, Williams's argument for complete religious liberty based upon the separation of church and state rejected Puritan hopes for the establishment of a godly commonwealth. He denied that civil regulation of religious opinion and ecclesiastical order had any validity during the Christian era, when the duties of states were essentially secular. From this perspective, the assertion that the state should punish persons for what John Cotton had described as sinning against their own consciences was a confusion of modern nations with the religious community of ancient Israel. Williams therefore commented that Cotton's *"conclusion* (though painted over with the *vermillion* of *mistaken Scripture,* and that *old dreame* of *Jew* and *Gentile,* that the *Crowne* of *Jesus* will consist of outward *materiall gold,* and his *sword* be made of *iron* or *steele,* executing judgement in his *Church* and *Kingdome* by *corporall punishment*) I hope . . . to manifest to be the overturning and rooting up the very *foundation* and *roots* of all true *Christianity,* and absolutely denying the *Lord Jesus* the Great *Anointed* to be yet come in the Flesh."[54] In Williams's view, the millennial goal of reformation was not Christ's monarchy over the church and nations but only his rule over the reformed congregations of his saints.[55]

Williams believed that the mistaken concept of a Christian commonwealth had its origin in the medieval apostasy of the church. From Constantine onward, princes had "conceived themselves bound to make their Cities, Kingdomes, Empires new holy lands of Canaan, and themselves Governours and Judges in spirituall causes, compelling all consciences to Christ, and persecuting the contrary with fire and sword."[56] By this means, the authentic Christian community composed of particular congregations was replaced by Christendom, and "the *Gardens* of the *Churches* of *Saints* were turned into the *Wildernesse* of whole *Nations.*"[57] Thus, for centuries, coercion of conscience had not only disrupted *civil peace* but also destroyed *religious peace*, the well-being and good order of the church, by mixing saints and unregenerate citizens inside either national churches or "the Popes Christendome." Nor had the New England congregationalists escaped this error by limiting official church membership to visible saints, since "by compelling all within their *Jurisdiction* to an outward *conformity* of the *Church Worship*, of the *Word* and *Prayer*, and *maintenance* of the *Ministry* thereof, they evidently declare that they still lodge and dwell in the confused mixtures of the *uncleane* and *cleane*, of the *flock* of *Christ*, and *Herds* of the *World* together, I meane in *spirituall* and *religious* worship."[58]

Relgious peace, unlike civil peace, required strict separation of the church from religious errors and unregenerate, natural men; although "weeds abound in the *Field* of the *Civill State*," such impiety must be "kept out of the *Garden* of the *Church*."[59] As in *Queries of Highest Consideration* and *Cottons Letter . . . Examined*, Williams defined reformation as precisely this process of separating the church from the religious error and impiety which had arisen during the apostasy.[60] And in his opinion, chief among these errors was the belief that the magistrate had authority to punish what he considered to be religious heresy or schism. Such persecution had shielded religious error from the spiritual sword of Christ's true reformers, the spiritual officers and witnesses of his church.

In this regard, Williams examined "that admirable *Prophecie*" of Ezek. 21:26–27, which predicted an overturning of the world in which present rulers would give way to those who had been under them. "The matter" of this prophecy, said Williams, was "a *Crown* and *Diadem* to be taken from an *Usurpers* head, and set upon the head of the right *Owner*."[61] He concluded that this "mystically" referred to the kingly crown of Christ, which throughout the apostasy had been falsely worn by princes and magistrates professing to govern and protect the church.[62] But in the coming age, Christ would again be recognized as the only king of the church. Williams therefore predicted that upon Christ's "glorious head in his *Messengers* and *Churches*, the *Crown* shall be established; The *annointing*, the *title*, and the *crown* and power must return to the *Lord Jesus* in his

Saints, unto whom alone belongs his *power* and *authoritie* in *Ecclesiasticall* or *Spirituall* cases."[63]

Among the General Baptist tracts, Leonard Busher's *Religions Peace* most explicitly shared Williams's belief that the idea of a Christian commonwealth or Christendom had originally corrupted Christianity and was now thwarting its restoration. Busher argued that persecution by antichristian priests and princes "was the occasion that the apostolic church was at first scattered and driven into the wilderness," and he feared that "so long as persecution continue, so long will the apostolic church continue scattered and persecuted in the secret places of this world."[64] It was the power of preaching, not of the sword, which would subdue the errors which had arisen during the apostasy, and Busher urged freedom of speech and of the press in order that spiritual combat between truth and error could bring about the church's restoration.[65] By allowing liberty of conscience, he believed that "the apostolic church, which is scattered and driven into the wilderness and desert of this world, may be again gathered together, both Jews and Gentiles, into visible and established congregations. And that the catholic and universal church of antichrist may be consumed and abolished by his word and spirit."[66] Busher was still alive and living in Holland during the early 1640s, when Roger Williams was writing on behalf of religious liberty. At that time, Busher, like Williams, wrote in opposition to the millenarian views of the Independents, in particular against John Archer's *Personall Reigne of Christ upon Earth.*[67]

Roger Williams shared Leonard Busher's confidence that the spirit of God in his witnesses would eventually overcome Antichrist by means of three spiritual weapons: "The *blood* of the *Lambe,* The *word* of their *Testimony,* and The not loving of their *lives* unto the *death.*"[68] But while he acknowledged that only the testimony of the witnesses could restore the church, and while he argued that religious liberty would speed that task of reformation, Roger Williams feared that the vocation of the witness would not be without its perils. He therefore prefaced his *Bloudy Tenent* with this warning:

> While I plead the Cause of *Truth* and *Innocencie* against the bloody *Doctrine* of *Persecution* for cause of *conscience,* I

judge it not unfit to give *alarme* to my selfe, and all men
to prepare to be *persecuted* or hunted for cause of *conscience* . . . . O how like is the *jealous Jehovah*, the consuming fire to end these present *slaughters* in a greater slaughter of the holy Witnesses? *Rev.* 11.[69]

Evangelism and the Millennial Church

While on the voyage to England, Williams put down "in a
rude lumpe" the notes which formed the basis for his first
publication during that busy trip abroad, *A Key into the
Language of America* (1643).[70] It consisted of a compilation
of Indian words and phrases translated from the Narragansett and organized in conversational passages concerning such aspects of the native society as religion,
money, hunting practices, and family life. The author's
comments and elaborations interspersed this dictionary,
offering examples from his personal experience or
suggesting moral and religious lessons to be drawn by
Europeans. Williams hoped that through his publication of
this guide to the native language "it may please the *Father*
of *Mercies* to spread *civilitie*, (and in his owne most holy
season) *Christianitie*" in America.[71] In addition, he hoped
that his supplementary "Spirituall *Observations*" would be
"pleasant and profitable to the view" of the general
reader.[72] Thus, although it appeared in the format of a
primer, even a cursory examination of Williams's *Key into
the Language of America* soon reveals its didactic tone. His
printer, Gregory Dexter, was a Baptist who also did work
for John Milton and who soon afterward emigrated to
Rhode Island.[73]

Christenings Make Not Christians, Williams's second work
concerning the Indians, was not published until late 1645
or early 1646, after his departure from England.[74] The
brief tract was divided into two sections, the first of which
argued that the term *heathen* should not refer only to the
uncivilized American tribes but rather to all men—civilized
as well as uncivilized—who were outside the boundaries of the church.[75] The second examined that "great
point" of interest, the conversion of the Indians, and concluded that the divinely appointed moment for this event
had not yet come.[76] The tract came from the press of Jane
Coe, a minor London printer who primarily prepared
broadsides and brief "intelligences" on military engage-

ments or political news. These included four such reports
from the hand of Williams's successor at Salem, now army
chaplain, Hugh Peter. Among the much smaller number of
theological tracts printed by Coe, the only author whose
name appeared more than once was Hanserd Knollys, who
made use of her press on three occasions in 1645 and
1646.[77] Knollys, a prominent Baptist minister in London,
had lived in New England from 1638 to 1641, and it seems
quite likely that either he or Peter was responsible for the
appearance of Christenings.

Although the actual publication dates of the two pamphlets were widely separated, cross references appear in
each indicating that Williams considered them companion
pieces and had perhaps intended their simultaneous publication.[78] In any case, both interpreted the moral and religious significance of colonial relations with the Indians in
light of Williams's distinctive theology of history. It will be
recalled that he emphasized two decisive disjunctions in
history which had major implications, the first for the relation of church and state, and the second for church polity
and worship. The first of these discontinuities was the incarnation of Christ, which altered the relation between
God and his people and which meant for Williams that a
state could neither extend its jurisdiction beyond civil affairs nor claim divine sanction for its actions. The second
historical break occurred with the apostasy of the medieval
church which obliterated the original form and spiritual
authority of the Christian community. The combination of
these views with his extensive experience with the Indians
made A Key into the Language of America and Christenings
Make Not Christians the most unusual and original of all
Williams's publications.

Evangelization of the Indians had been a prominent
rationale for settlement in New England, and Roger Williams clearly shared the general interest in this project
during his first years of residence there. His active involvement with the Indians apparently began in 1632,
while he was farming and "prophesying" at Plymouth. At
that time, Williams commenced his lifelong study of native
languages and customs and developed a friendship with
the sachem Ousamaquin (Massasoit), who had been so
helpful an adviser to the Pilgrims.[79] The young En-
glishman began to consider conversion of the Indians an

important aspect of his mission in New England, and in 1632 he wrote John Winthrop of his hope that God would bless his endeavors to reach "what I long after, the natives souls."[80]

Immediately following his banishment from Massachusetts in 1636, Williams's knowledge of Indian speech and habit was directed toward much more pragmatic objectives than turning souls to God. In his flight from the Bay he had stopped first in the lands of Ousamaquin but was quickly informed by Edward Winslow, governor of Plymouth, that the area lay within the patent of that colony. Therefore, in late spring of 1636, the fugitive traveled further south and west into the territory of the Narragansetts, an important tribe with whom he had apparently made preliminary negotiations for land in 1634 and 1635.[81] There, he completed verbal agreement with their sachems, Canonicus and Miantonomu, for the land on which Providence would be located. Settlement had scarcely begun when Williams embarked upon an informal career as a diplomat, playing the role of moderator, and often mediator, between Indians and English during the Pequot War.

The Pequots were a fierce tribe whose original home was further west and who, like the English, were of rather recent entry into New England. Throughout the early 1630s, they had feuded and skirmished with the Dutch and with Williams's friends, the Narragansetts. They were therefore anxious to secure their relations with the English and agreed in 1634 to relinquish their rights to land in Connecticut, where John Winthrop, Jr., and others were developing a colony.[82] Under this treaty relative calm prevailed until 20 July 1636, when fourteen Indians killed the respected trader John Oldham aboard his ship.[83]

The Bay colonists quickly concluded that not only the Pequots but also several Narragansett sachems were responsible for the murder. John Winthrop, at the time deputy governor to Sir Henry Vane, wrote to Williams requesting help in the matter, and Williams immediately left Providence to treat with the leaders of both tribes. Several years later he dramatically recounted to Major John Mason, another prominent participant in the Pequot War, the character of these negotiations.

> Three days and nights my business forced me to lodge
> and mix with the bloody Pequod ambassadors, whose
> hands and arms, methought, wreaked with the blood of
> my countrymen, murdered and massacred by them on
> Connecticut river, and from whom I could not but
> nightly look for their bloody knives at my own throat
> also.[84]

The Pequots, meanwhile, attempted to enlist the Narragansetts as allies by playing upon their fears of English
intentions. But Williams labored "to prevent the league
between the Pequots and the Narragansetts, which work
as an agent from this colony and all the English in the land,
I (through help from God) effected."[85] As a result, Miantonomu went to Boston in October 1636, and signed an
alliance with the English.

The Pequots had by this time turned their wrath upon
the small English settlement in Connecticut, especially out-
raging the colonists with the murder of several settlers at
Saybrook. To make the situation even more critical, Edward Winslow reported to Winthrop in April 1637 that
some Englishmen were unscrupulously trading supplies to
the Pequots.[86] The Bay's alliance with the Narragansetts
remained somewhat uneasy throughout this time, and
Roger Williams constantly acted in the role of mediator. He
was first placating Winthrop, who feared "some breach of
league in Miantonomu," and then the Narragansetts, who
were "at present doubtful of reality in all our promises."[87]
Indeed, Canonicus had even accused the English of purposely spreading the plague among them, but Williams
reasoned with him that "the plague and other sicknesses
were alone in the hand of the one God, who made him and
us, and who also visited such problems on the English."[88]

With the clear weather of spring, the Connecticut colonists, under the leadership of Major John Mason, set out
on a campaign against the Pequots and quickly ended the
war in May 1637 by setting fire to the Indian fort at Mystic in
Connecticut.[89] But Williams's role as mediator between natives and English did not end with the defeat of the
Pequots. The Narragansetts, for example, would not conclude any purchases of their land by Englishmen unless
Williams was present on their behalf. It was thus through
the mediation of Roger Williams that not only later exiles

from Massachusetts Bay, but also Governor Winthrop himself, obtained land in the area. Whether or not the natives actually thought of him as "their Right hand, their Candle & Lanthorne the Quencher of their Fires," as Williams later asserted,[90] he without doubt played an important role in reducing friction and violence between the tribes and the expanding colonies.

Indian confidence in Williams stemmed in part from his respect for their right to the land, suggested in his opposition to the patent and maintained in his later activities. But, in addition, Williams's ability to separate fact from fiction was crucial for dealing with the Indians and maintaining their respect. He had few illusions about their level of morality; even of the Narragansetts he wrote that "though I would not fear a jar with them yet I would send off from being foul, and deal with them wisely as with wolves endowed with men's brains," and he was convinced that the Pequots' "treacheries exceed Machiavelli's."[91] He therefore spent a great deal of time tracing the facts of various incidents ranging from the murder of Indians by Englishmen to the escape of Indian slaves from the Bay. Coupled with his linguistic abilities, this circumspection made him the most prominent arbiter between natives and English from the period of the Pequot difficulties until King Phillip's War forty years later. Yet, with many of the Indians, especially Canonicus and Miantonomu, Williams went beyond the role of even-handed negotiator to become a friend. As he often stated, "It was not price nor money that could have purchased Rhode Island. Rhode Island was purchased by love" which existed among the sachems, Williams, and Henry Vane during the English-Narragansett alliance.[92] In this spirit the wary Canonicus would send for Williams to be present with him when he died, to "close up" his eyes.[93]

Williams's involvement in the negotiations surrounding the Pequot War did not divert his evangelistic zeal. In fact, he suggested to John Winthrop in the summer of 1637 that English inattention to the religious needs of the natives had, by provoking divine wrath, been a principal cause of the war itself:

I fear that the Lord's quarrel is not ended for which the war began, viz.: the little sense, (I speak for the general that I can hear of) of their [the Indians'] soul's condition, and our large protestations that way, &c. The general speech is, all must be rooted out, &c.[94]

For his own part, he continued to develop the linguistic skills which he felt were required to make the gospel comprehensible to his Indian auditors. Early in 1638, his expectations of success led him to notify Winthrop of plans "shortly to send you good news of great hopes the Lord hath sprung up in mine eyes, of many a poor Indian soul enquiring after God." In the same letter, he told of his discovery that the Indians believed in "plenty of Gods or divine powers" and of his own good fortune in persuading them that their belief was in error. Although on this particular occasion he had withdrawn in fear that their acceptance of Christianity would be merely formal, he nevertheless hoped that "the time is not long that some shall truely bless the God of Heaven that ever they saw the face of English men."[95]

This, however, seems to mark the conclusion of Williams's active evangelistic efforts; soon afterward, the theological reorientation which he experienced in 1639 revised his opinions concerning the mission to the Indians. Having become convinced that no true churches existed in the world, Williams thereafter entertained serious doubts that conversion of the Indians could occur until after the millennial restoration. The broad theological justifications for delaying his apostleship to the Indians appeared in Williams's *Key into the Language of America* and *Christenings Make Not Christians*. In addition, these works capitalized upon the illustrative power which, by virtue of English curiosity regarding the subject, was potential in information about the Indians. By examining the pagan Americans, Williams directed his readers' attention to what was pagan in civilized hearts and societies. Thus, doubting his authority for becoming an apostle to the Indians, Roger Williams lost no opportunity to be a witness to the English.

This complex interweaving of concern not only for "the natives souls" but also for the souls of Englishmen is particularly well illustrated by Williams's *Key into the Language of America*. As has been noted, Williams described it as an aid to communicating civilization and, in God's time, Christianity to the Indians. Externally, therefore, the format of the work was that of a dictionary of Indian phrases organized into thirty-two sections, each dealing with a different aspect of their society. These topical selections of Indian phrases were often organized to suggest conversations or dialogues and, in most cases, were elaborated with explanations of native custom or anecdotes from Williams's own experience. Following each vocabulary Williams made a general observation which indicated its significance at a second, religious or moral level of meaning. Finally, each section concluded with a poem which directed its various linguistic, cultural, and theological lessons to the spiritual edification of the reader. The structure thus paralleled that of the standard Puritan sermon: explication of the text, derivation of general doctrines, and "uses" or edifying applications of doctrine.[96]

For example, following the vocabulary of Indian phrases dealing with the weather, Williams made the general observation that the "Judgement which the Lord Jesus pronounced against the Weather-wise (but ignorant of the God of the weather) will fall most justly upon those *Natives*, and all men who are wise in Natural things, but willingly blind in spiritual." He then applied this theological point with a poem:

> English and Indians spie a Storme,
>   and seeke a hiding place:
> O hearts of stone that thinke and dreame,
>   Th'everlasting stormes t'out-face.
>
> Proud filthy Sodome saw the Sunne,
>   Shine or'e her head most bright.
> The very day that turn'd she was
>   To stinking heaps, 'fore night.
>
> How many millions now alive,
>   Within few yeeres shall rot?
> O blest that Soule, whose portion is,
>   That Rocke that changeth not.[97]

In this manner, Williams incorporated into his linguistic guide a didactic or sermonic purpose, attempting to prompt spiritual turnings and awakenings in the hearts of readers initially attracted by the curiosity of his subject.

The principal theme running through Williams's religious observations was the distinction between *civilization* and *Christianity*. A favorite technique for making this distinction was to compare the level of civility or morality among the Indians with that among Europeans; in almost every case the morality of the "savages" was demonstrated to be superior. For example, Williams observed, "It is a strange *truth* that a man shall generally finde more free entertainment and refreshing amongst these *Barbarians*, then amongst thousands that call themselves Christians."[98] Similarly, he portrayed the Indians as less inclined to commit breaches of morality, ranging from excessive use of tobacco to robbery or murder, than were Englishmen.[99] Nominally Christian Englishmen had so hardened themselves against the truths of Christianity that they were guilty of crimes and excesses which Indians—who knew neither Christ nor civilization—would not commit. The Indian became in this instance primarily a rhetorical device, against whom the English, resistant to religious and moral truth, might be contrasted:

When Indians heare the horrid filths,
    Of Irish, English Men,
The horrid Oaths and Murthers late,
    Thus say these Indians then.

We weare no Cloaths, have many Gods,
    And yet our sinnes are lesse:
You are Barbarians, Pagans wild,
    Your Land's the Wildernesse.[100]

But when making another point, Williams had no qualms about lifting up other aspects of Indian life which he considered *more immoral* than English practices. Thus he observed that "the *Mauquauogs*, or *Man-Eaters*, that live two or three [hundred] miles West from us, make a delicious monstrous dish of the head and brains of their enemies; which is yet no barre (when the time shall approach) against Gods call, and their repentance, and (who knows but) a great love to the Lord Jesus? great sinners forgiven love much."[101] Here, attempting to make the different point that man is saved by grace working through faith, Williams stressed that civility, whether among Englishmen or Indians, has no effect on the crucial question of salvation. Once again, the point was most effectively made by one of his edifying verses:

> Boast not proud *English*, of thy birth & blood,
>   Thy brother *Indian* is by birth as Good.
> Of one blood God made Him, and Thee & All,
>   As wise, as faire, as strong, as personall.

> By nature wrath's his portio[n], thine no more
>   Till Grace *his* soule and *thine* in Christ restore
> Make sure thy second birth, else thou shalt see,
>   Heaven ope to *Indians* wild, but shut to thee.[102]

Jack L. Davis's interpretation thus seems to be in error when he states regarding these lines that "Williams became increasingly persuaded that respect for spiritual things was more characteristic of Indian than English culture . . . . He suggests that God may well judge the Indians more favorably than the English."[103] Instead, Williams's actual point was that, as natural men, both Indians and English were under the judgment "of him that shortly shall appeare, / In dreadfull flaming fire."[104] The real distinction emerged between those inside and outside the covenant of grace, not between those of different cultural backgrounds.

In sum, the basic theological assertion of *A Key into the Language of America* complemented the argument for separation of church and state advanced in *The Bloudy Tenent*; since a covenant no longer existed between God and a chosen political state, there could be no intrinsic difference between governments formed by pagan Indians and those established in the so-called Christian nations of Europe.[105] In these gospel times, God's people were a spiritual nation called out of every country, and their presence within a state did not make its purpose or policies Christian. The English conviction that they were an "elect nation" thus confused the state with the church, the realm of nature with the realm of grace, civilization with true religion. Theories which implied the godliness of whole nations were, to Williams's mind, analogous to the Indian practice of painting the body:

> Truth is a Native, naked Beauty; but
>   Lying Inventions are but Indian Paints,
> 2 Dissembling hearts their Beautie's but a Lye
>   Truth is the proper Beauty of Gods Saints.

> Fowle are the Indians Haire and painted Faces,
>   2 More foule such Haire, such Face in Israel,

England so calls her selfe, yet there's
Absoloms foule Haire and Face of Jesabell.[106]

This very conception, in fact, forms a major link between Williams's career as a diplomat and his theological position of the early 1640s. Since he did so sharply distinguish between the character of the civil and religious realms, between natural and regenerate men, he could view civil power with an unusual degree of pragmatism. His career as a diplomat among, and friend to, the Indians bore out this theological interpretation of the role of government with remarkable consistency. The principle that the only crucial distinction between men lay in the matter of spiritual regeneration seems to have directed his fair and circumspect dealings with the Indians; it was certainly the principle which his *Key into the Language of America* announced to Englishmen on both sides of the Atlantic.

The first section of *Christenings Make Not Christians,* which discussed the meaning of the term *heathen,* made a quite similar point concerning the error of confusing civilization with Christianity. To call only the pagan Indians heathen, said Williams, was a misuse, since in Scripture the heathens were all those outside the church. Therefore, as the title of the tract suggested, to the extent that individuals in European Christendom were personally unregenerate, they, like the American natives, were heathens living in opposition to Christ. Williams asked,

Who are then the *nations, heathen,* or *gentiles,* in opposition to the *People of God?* I answer, All People, *civilized* as well as *uncivilized,* even the most famous States, Cities, and the Kingdomes of the World: For all must come within that distinction. I. Cor. 5. *within* or *without.*

Within the *People of God,* his Church at CORINTH: *Without* the City of CORINTH worshipping *Idols,* and so consequently all other People, HEATHENS, or NATIONS, opposed to the People of God, the true *Jewes.* [107]

The very concept of a Christian nation or Christendom was a misapprehension of the nature of the holy community; the term Christendom, indeed, was an invention of the apostasy, when all of Europe "wonderd after and worshipped the *Beast,*" the papal Antichrist.[108] And to the extent that Protestant countries styled themselves Christian nations and attempted to establish national churches, they remained *"Peninsula* or necks of land, contiguous and joyned still" to Antichrist's so-called Christendom.[109] Williams therefore issued an apocalyptic warning to English reformers who hoped to establish a godly commonwealth, by asking them, "if the Lord Jesus himselfe were here, (as he will be shortly) and were to make answer, what would they, what would he say to a CHRISTIAN WORLD? To CHRISTENDOME? And otherwise then what He would speak, that is indeed what he hath spoken, and will shortly speake, must no man speak that names himselfe a Christian."[110]

The second section of *Christenings Make Not Christians* answered English hopes for the conversion of the Indians. Williams responded to this issue by confidently stating that he could have "brought many thousands of these Natives, yea the whole countrey," to some form of Christianity. But he did not do so, because such a conversion would have been merely external or in some degree false—in his own term an "Antichristian conversion."[111]

Williams's description of "authentic conversion" indicates continuities with his earlier, Separatist views on the qualifications for church membership. In agreement with all the Puritan parties, he insisted that conversion was founded in an inward alteration of man's spirit. It must be, he said, "a turning of the whole man from the power of *Sathan* unto God, *act.* 26. Such a change, as if an old man became a new Babe . . . yea, as amounts to Gods new creation in the soule."[112] This, of course, satisfactorily demonstrated to the godly of both old and New England the utter falsity of Indian conversions effected by the Catholics, who were "by wiles and subtle devices, sometimes by force compelling them to submit to that which they understood not, neither before nor after such their monstrous Christning of them."[113] But, Williams added, *personal regeneration was only one aspect of conversion;* this "new creation in the soule" must be accompanied by "a true externall conversion" into the pattern of worship appointed in the New Testament.[114] As he had once argued in Massachusetts, Williams continued to believe that members of the true church must not only be regenerate, "living stones," but must also have "come out," or separated themselves, from the apostate and imperfectly organized churches of the world.

At the same time, Williams doubted the possibility of effecting such complete conversions, and the reasons he gave indicated the scope of the theological reshaping he had undergone since his departure from Massachusetts. True conversions, he now believed, could only be initiated by the preaching of "such Messengers as can prove their lawfull sending and Commission from the Lord Jesus, to make Disciples out of all nations," and he did not find any church in the world able to legitimately exercise this "power and authority" of sending out Christ's evangelists.[115] In addition to this lack of apostolic authority, Williams also doubted that any church had yet restored the truly apostolic form of worship into which persons were to be gathered following their regeneration.[116] The interruption of the apostolic ministry of conversion during the medieval apostasy had left the tribes of America among those "lost Nations" of the world whose entrance into the Christian faith must await the millennial advent. In 1635, in response to a query from the English divine Thomas Thorowgood, Williams had speculated that the Americans were perhaps the lost tribes of Israel; by 1643 he had come to doubt that this was the case.[117] But, whatever their identity, Williams supposed that the restitution of the church must occur before this great work of evengelism could begin. For this reason, while he granted that divine mercy might plant the regenerative spark in scattered individual souls, his reflections upon the native Americans constrained him to ask rhetorically

> whether Gods great businesse between Christ Jesus the holy Son of God and Antichrist the man of sin and Sonne of perdition, must not be first over, *Zion* and *Jerusalem* be rebuilt and re-established, before the Law and word of life be sent forth to the rest of the Nations of the World, who have not heard of Christ: The Prophets are deep concerning this.[118]

As this eschatological reference suggests, *Christenings Make Not Christians* decidedly does not represent what Jack L. Davis has referred to as Williams's "cultural relativism . . . in religion."[119] It issued, instead, from his millenarian piety; he refrained from converting the Indians not out of respect for their religious views but rather out of his deep sense of the present impurity of Christianity and his hope for its approaching reunion with the true Christ.

For this reason, Williams concentrated his attention upon gaining greater expertise in the native tongue in order to be able to discuss spiritual matters with the Indians, a task he found much more difficult than conversation on mundane affairs.[120] Although he had observed "no small *preparation* in the hearts of Multitudes of them" he saw little evidence that God's mighty work had yet begun in America and therefore would neither "*despaire,* nor *report* much," concerning the effects of Puritan evangelism.[121]

Williams's doubts about converting the Indians were thus interrelated with his personal abstention from the ordinances of Christian worship. Not until the renewal of the church would these *forms* of Christian experience be reconnected with the *spirit* or inward vitality of faith. Only those glorious latter days would witness the conversion of the Indians and the completion of Williams's own spiritual pilgrimage. This concern for pattern and authority in ecclesiastical order is well illustrated by his reaction in 1649 to the activities of his Baptist friend, the Rhode Island physician John Clarke.

> At Seekonk a great many have lately concurred with Mr. John Clarke and our Providence men about the point of a new Baptism, and the manner by dipping: and Mr. John Clarke hath been there lately (and Mr. Lucar) and hath dipped them. I believe their practice comes nearer the first practice of our great Founder Christ Jesus, then other practices of religion do, and yet I have not satisfaction neither in the authority by which it is done, nor in the manner.[122]

Because of these dissatisfactions, the conversion of the Indians was work which could only partially be fulfilled in the time in which Williams found himself. While he could be with them as a fellow wanderer in the world, he could not of his own power bring them into a church which in a very important sense did not yet, for him, exist.

In both England and New England millenarian speculations were commonly employed to place the American Indians within the providential scheme which Englishmen discerned in Scripture. But, unlike Roger Williams's opinions, these theories typically promoted rather than discouraged efforts at evangelization of the Indians. In particular, prevailing millenarian theory among the Independents characterized their churches as the harbingers or "first fruits" of the latter-day glory. From this perspective, the institution of godly religion and congregational polity among the Indians of the Americas marked the final advance of the gospel through all the nations of the world, the consummation of Christ's commission to make disciples of all nations (Matt. 28:16–20). *New Engalnds First Fruits*, a promotional tract published in 1643, gave this optimistic, millennialist interpretation to the founding of Harvard and the early evangelistic efforts of the Puritans among the Indians.

> Many godly and wise have conceived . . . that (as its very probable) God meanes to carry his Gospel westward, in these latter times of the world; and have thought, as the Sunne in the afternoon of the day, still declines more and more to the West, and then sets: so the Gospel (that great light of the world) though it rose in the East, and in former ages, hath lightened it with his beames; yet in the latter ages of the world will bend Westward, and before its setting, brighten these parts, with his glorious lustre also.[123]

Thus, just as millenarian speculations expressed a sense of urgency and purpose regarding the task of religious reformation, they also placed the conversion of the Indians within a cosmic frame, interpreting Puritan evangelistic activities as part of God's providential design for "these latter times of the world."

Enthusiasm for the project was heightened by belief that the Indians were actually Jews, the ten lost tribes of Israel, whose conversion, so it was believed, would immediately precede the second advent. By 1649, such speculation was being used to promote English support of Indian missions in New England, and it was suggested that it was not unreasonable to "*Conjecture,* that these *Indians in America,* may be *Jewes* (especially of the ten Tribes.) And therefore to hope that the work of Christ among them, may be as a preparatory to his own appearing."[124] Reports in 1651 that "many Indians to the Southward" of New England were circumcised thus did little to dampen evangelistic spirits on either side of the Atlantic.[125]

These millennialist convictions concerning the mission to the Indians were most enthusiastically applied to the task by John Eliot of Roxbury. Just as the Congregationalists had called upon godly magistrates to reform church and society in England and Massachusetts, Eliot sought their assistance in establishing Christ's kingdom among the Indians. To enlist financial and political support for his missionary work, Eliot wrote *The Christian Commonwealth*, describing how he was forming Indian communities on what he believed to be the biblical model of society.[126] His view that these communities would be the first full manifestation of the millennium was an interesting adaptation of Puritan millenarianism to the cause of Indian evangelism; a letter published in England in 1651 sets forth his opinion so clearly that it merits quotation at some length.

> I intend to direct them [the Indians] according as the Lord shall please to help and assist to set up the Kingdome of Jesus Christ fully, so that Christ shall reigne both in Church and Commonwealth, both in Civil and Spiritual matters.... And when every thing both Civil & Spiritual are done by the direction of the word of Christ, then doth Christ reigne, and the great Kingdome of Jesus Christ which we weight for, is even this that I do now mention...humane wisdome in learned Nations will be loth to yeeld to Christ so farre, much lesse will Princes and Monarches readily yeeld so farre to stoop to Christ, and therefore the Lord will shake all Nations, and put them into distresse and perplexity, and in the conclusion they will be glad to stoop to Christ. But as for these poore Indians they have no principles of their own, nor yet wisdome of their own (I meane as other Nations have) wherein to stick; and therefore they do most readily yeeld to any direction from the Lord, so that there will be no such opposition against the rising Kingdome of Jesus Christ among them.[127]

Not all New Englanders shared Eliot's optimism. Both John Cotton and Hugh Peter, although harboring hopes of Christ's approaching kingdom, doubted present success of the missionary activities. Cotton, using an argument from scriptural prophecy which was similar to that by Roger Williams, suggested regarding Indian conversions that "till the seven plagues of the seven Angels be fulfilled, wee cannot easily hope for the entrance of any New multitudes of men into the Church" (cf. Rev. 15:18).[128] Hugh Peter, meanwhile, became disillusioned for the more pragmatic reason that English funds intended for John Eliot were being misappropriated. [129]

But Roger Williams differed in his position from both these men, because his doubts about Indian missions grew out of questions about the very existence of the church. This made his behavior, especially his abstinence from formal worship, exasperating to the evangelistically inclined. Thus, in 1648, Thomas Shepard recounted a discussion between John Eliot and a Narragansett sachem. Eliot had asked why the Indians had not obtained religious instruction from Williams and received the reply that "they did not care to learn of him, because hee was no good man but goes out and workes upon the Sabbath day." Shepard included the story in his promotional pamphlet to illustrate "what the ill example of English may doe" to impede evangelization, despite any justifications which "mans shifting wits" may devise for avoiding public worship. [130]

Since Williams's beliefs regarding missionary activity were an integral part of his millenarian ecclesiology, they can be clarified by comparing them with opinions on the nature of the church held by other Puritan radicals. In particular, his conviction that the church was in a "wilderness" state in which all outward forms of worship had ceased bore definite similarities to the ideas of his close friend, the parliamentary leader Sir Henry Vane, and to the ideas of the military chaplain William Erbery. At the same time, important theological differences between Williams and these two men further delineate the precise character of his thought.

William Erbery, like Roger Williams, believed that since the medieval apostasy all church forms had ceased. Preaching to the New Model Army in 1648, he declared that the apostasy had left the church in mystical Babylon, "since all the glory of the Gospel is gone, and all the gifts of the spirit constituting a Gospel Church are ceased." [131] As this suggests, he shared Williams's opinion that contemporary Christians lacked proper authority to found churches and administer ordinances, and Erbery warned the English Baptist congregations that "you are not in a capacity to *baptize or be baptized,* there being no *true Administrator,* nor a *man sent of God with power from on high to baptize:* First, because you have not *the faith of the Gospel.* Secondly, you are *fallen from your first love,* therefore the

Apostacy is compleat and perfect and appears most visible in your Churches."[132]

The saints had been "scattered" by the persecution of Antichrist and now formed, in Erbery's view, a *"Church in the Wilderness."*[133] Like Williams, he believed that the task of this wilderness church was to destroy all that was false in present forms of Christianity. He stated that the Holy Spirit was "coming forth, and visibly come already as *Fire in the scattered Saints,"* and predicted that this spiritual fire "shall burn up the Churches, who because they would not, as the Primitive Saints did, wait for the Spirit to build them, the Spirit shall come to burn and consume them at last."[134] Thus Erbery and Williams agreed that the church's latter-day witnesses, by abstaining from ordinances and refuting religious error, were preparing the way for the church's millennial glory.

But for Erbery the millennium would not bring the restoration of apostolic piety and practice which Williams so much desired. Instead, Erbery was convinced that the new Zion would be within the saints. He spiritualized the millennium by interpreting it as the mystical presence of God in the saints:

> *Mount Sion* is not an outward Church-state, as the Churches now imagine, and call themselves, though they be indeed the *daughter of Babylon;* but *Zion is* the *state of all the Saints in the Spirit as they are in God, and God in them:* For as *Zion* was the place where God dwelt; so all the Saints from the beginning of the world have been still waiting for this, for the full discoverie of God in them.[135]

Just as there had been dispensations of law and then of gospel in preceding ages, Erbery now believed that a third, spiritual dispensation was breaking forth in the world.[136] Within this new age, "all *religious formes* shall fall, that the *power of righteousness* may rise and appear in all: *The new Heaven and new Earth, where dwelleth Righteousnesse,* hath no form of Religion there."[137]

In agreement with Erbery and Williams, Henry Vane believed that the visible church had been destroyed by the apostasy, during which persecution had scattered the *"Spiritual part of the Church"* and forced it to exist *"in a wilderness* condition, for 1260 years, now near expired."[138] Vane therefore found no authority for the practices of the visible churches, and advocated that he and other "spiritual" Christians withdraw from them:

> Untill that [millennial] season, this sort of beleevers, instead of being found within the pale of the visible church, do follow Gods invitation of them into the secret chambers of his presence, and do dwell in his house, (a building not made with hands, in the person and spirit of Christ) where they behold his beauty, shutting the doors about them, as to any visible entercourse with the worldly Church.[139]

But Vane was much closer to Erbery than to Williams in his opinions about the shape of the millennium; the focus of his piety was mystical and he anticipated that the "glorious day of Christs 2d appearance" would consummate a new "dispensation in Spirit."[140]

Thus the mystical dimension so prominent in the piety of Erbery and Henry Vane marked a definite difference from the convictions of Roger Williams. For them the immediate spiritual communication of God with his wilderness church was the inauguration of a new age of the spirit; they dispensed with the formal aspects of Christian worship because they felt they were no longer necessary. Vane prophesied that through the ministry of the witnesses "Heaven shall be opened, and a fuller and more excellent discovery of Christ in Spirit ministred, than ever yet hath been," will usher in 1,000 years of bliss.[141] Erbery concurred with this prophecy of a new dispensation and added that "the Spirit which the Apostles were drunk with at first, was but the first fruits, but a taste of that which shall be more fully drawn forth in the last dayes."[142]

Williams viewed the wilderness condition of the church quite differently. To be sure, all three men envisioned themselves, like ancient Israel, embarked upon a wilderness "pilgrimage into the land of promise." And Williams further agreed with Erbery and Vane that during this time God stirred up his saints through immediate action of his spirit and not through the mediation of the church's ministry and sacraments. But he did not believe, as they did, that this spiritual ministry would become the defining characteristic of the millennial age. Instead, he interpreted the era of the wilderness as a transitional state between the apostolic churches and their approaching restoration.

Within this epoch of pilgrimage he had a definite task to perform as one of Christ's witnesses, but he had no authority to convert the natives or minister to churches. The wilderness in which he lived with the Indians and which he depicted in the *Key into the Language of America* was not simply the American frontier; more significantly for him, it was the long age of faithful wandering in which he worked and waited for the church's revival.

6

Spiritual Ministry, 1645–54

Roger Williams returned to New England in early autumn 1644, having successfully completed his mission of obtaining a charter for Providence Plantations. In many respects it was a return to familiar employments; he seems to have devoted considerable energy to operating the trading post which, prior to the trip to England, he had established with Richard Wilcox. And, once again, he involved himself in diplomatic relations between English and Indians. But the new legal status granted by the parliamentary charter brought with it the considerable political problems inherent in attempting to unify the four separate and contentious towns of Providence Plantations: Newport, Portsmouth, Providence, and Warwick. Soon after his arrival in Providence, Williams was elected "chiefe officer" of the colony and spent much of his three-year tenure in that post encouraging the towns to accept the charter and make provision for union under its authority, a step which was not taken until 18 May 1647. In all, rivalries among the leaders of the towns and continuing conflicts over jurisdiction with the surrounding colonies made these early years of "democratical" government in Providence Plantations a difficult experiment.

The instability of the colonial government was such, in fact, that in November 1651, Roger Williams embarked upon a second journey to England to secure confirmation of the colony's charter. The trip was necessitated by the political maneuvers of William Coddington, who had succeeded Williams as president of the colony. Coddington had departed Rhode Island for England in 1649 in order to obtain a charter which would place a major parcel of territory in his own name; in August 1651, Williams learned that Coddington had obtained this commission and had been "made Governor of this colony for his life."[1] The freemen of Providence Plantations quickly organized to protect their interests, and three months later Roger Williams sailed for England as their ambassador to Parliament. He was to be absent more than two years, and, once again, he used the opportunity to publish a considerable body of devotional and polemical material.

Despite his political responsibilities and secular employment during the years from 1644 to 1651, Williams had continued to ponder matters of piety and to involve himself in religious controversy. This period was thus one important source for the material which he published in 1652. For example, while traveling among the Indians about the year 1650, Williams had received word of the serious illness and subsequent recovery of his wife, Mary. He composed and delivered to her a letter of consolation, directing her attention to the lessons of spiritual health to be learned from physical sickness. Not many months before, Williams had received a "large and pious letter" from the wife of Sir Henry Vane in which she recounted her own and her husband's religious opinions.[2] Recalling this correspondence, Williams published his letter to his wife as a devotional manual entitled *Experiments of Spiritual Life & Health* (1652), and prefaced it with a dedication to Lady Vane.

He had also pursued the debate over religious liberty during the years prior to his second trip to England. In 1647, John Cotton had responded to *The Bloudy Tenent* with a careful justification of the godly commonwealth entitled *The Bloudy Tenent, Washed, and Made White in the Bloud of the Lambe.* In the same volume, Cotton also continued the debate over Williams's separation from the Massachusetts churches by publishing *A Reply to Mr. Williams His Examination.* Incensed that Cotton had not adequately replied to the typological argument for separation of church and state, Williams began work on his own rejoinder, *The Bloody Tenent Yet More Bloody* (1652), and was "deeply engaged" in its composition by the summer of 1650.[3] He also hoped to respond to Cotton's *Reply to Mr. Williams*, but "the streights of time" delayed this project, and it was apparently never completed.[4]

Prolongation of the controversy over liberty of conscience attained particular relevance through an event which occurred only a few months prior to Williams's departure to England. In July 1651, three Baptist residents of Rhode Island—John Clarke, the physician mentioned earlier and leader of the group, Obadiah Holmes, and John Crandall—entered Massachusetts on a business visit. During their visit to Lynn, Massachusetts, the three Baptists were apprehended in the home of one William Witter, where they were holding a private religious service at which Clarke was prophesying. For this offense, they were briefly imprisoned and fined, and Holmes was whipped. Clarke accompanied Roger Williams to England in November and gave full account of the episode in *Ill Newes from New-England* (1652).

Williams quickly took up the cause of his Baptist friends. His old associate in dissent, John Endecott, was then governor of Massachusetts, and Williams wrote him in protest regarding the legal action against the Baptists: "Sir, I must be humbly bold to say, that 'tis impossible for any Man or Men to maintain their *Christ* by their *Sword*, and to worship a true Christ! to fight against all *Consciences* opposite to theirs, and not to fight against *God* in some of them."[5] In addition, after arriving in England, Williams appended to *The Bloody Tenent Yet More Bloody* a copy of his letter to Endecott, in order that it might serve "as a Testimony to Mr. Clarks Narrative."[6]

Finally, certain theological issues should also be considered as part of the New Engalnd background to Roger Williams's publications in 1652. The first of these was his growing concern that millenarian speculation, although it took various specific forms, generally focused on expectations of a godly commonwealth, a temporal kingdom of the saints. He observed this tendency in Cotton's *Bloudy Tenent, Washed* and in the preaching of Rhode Island Baptists such as John Clarke.[7] In 1652, he responded skeptically from his own perspective, which restricted millennial expectations to a hope for the restoration of the church.

A second theological development was the disagreement within the Baptists churches of the colony concerning whether or not the practice of laying on of hands was a "foundation" of the Christian religion and therefore "necessary to church communion and fellowship" (cf. Heb. 6:1–3).[8] This and similar disputes confirmed Williams in his opinion that the saints remained a wilderness people who could not yet discern the shape of the true apostolic church. As he had written John Winthrop, Jr. in 1650, regarding affairs in Connecticut, the religious disagreements of the era gave him cause to "rejoice and mourn: rejoice that the Lord Jesus his name is more sounded, and mourn that not after the first pattern, in which I find no churches extant framed, but all (by a dreadful fate) opposing, dissolving, &c."[9]

These various controversial themes which received Roger Williams's attention in New England from 1645 to 1651—liberty of conscience, frredom for lay preachers, the shape of the true church, and the nature of the millennium—were also the topics of debate among the godly in England when he disembarked there in early 1652. Further, the English situation was such that Williams explicated his views on these themes in reference to the single, broad issue of the church's ministry, its forms, authority, maintenance, and qualifications.

A Ministry for the Wilderness

Events in England during the years between Roger Williams's two visits had wrought considerable political change. The civil wars had ended in 1648, but their conclusion by no means marked the end of upheaval. In December of that year, the troops of Colonel Thomas Pride purged the Long Parliament of those members who opposed a trial of the king. Following this dramatic intervention by the army, the remaining members of Parliament, known as the Rump, moved quickly forward with the trial, and Charles I was executed in January 1649. It was to this Rump Parliament, which continued to sit until 1653, that Roger Williams was sent as an emissary to protect the Rhode Island charter.

As recent scholarship has demonstrated, the Rump was a complex body faced with an exceptionally difficult political task.[10] Its members did not share a common viewpoint, and they were soon assailed by both those who abhorred the execution of the king and those who interpreted that act as the prelude to further reform. The former group of opponents included ousted members of Parliament and numerous Presbyterian ministers among its leading spokesmen, while the latter group had its political base among the Levellers and sectaries of the army. The very real power of these two groups, together with the continuing presence of royalist sentiment in Ireland and Scotland, quickly placed the Rump in a defensive position. Thus, although it had been brought into being by a revolutionary series of events, the Rump possessed neither the internal consensus nor the external support to pursue a revolutionary course. Instead, it adopted a conciliatory and moderate posture, attempting to consolidate support and establish a widely acceptable political and religious settlement.

During the four years of the Rump's existence, various proposals for a religious settlement provoked extensive controversy both in Parliament and among the public, and one broad phrase came to refer to the whole of the numerous issues involved: *the propagation of the gospel.* In some cases, the phrase primarily meant missionary activity. In July 1649, for example, legislation was enacted for advancing the gospel in New England and for incorporating a Society for the Propagation of the Gospel whose object was Indian missions. And in 1650 various acts were passed for the propagation of the gospel in Wales, Ireland, and the northern counties of England. Since the summer of 1650, however, a bill in various stages of refinement had given the phrase *propagation of the gospel* a much broader connotation. When this proposal emerged from committee in early 1652, *propagation of the gospel* had come to mean the state regulation and maintenance by tithes of the ministry throughout the nation.[11]

The proposal for the regulation and maintenance of the ministry was largely the work of some Independent ministers, including John Owen, Thomas Goodwin, Philip Nye, Sidrach Simpson, and John Goodwin, who had petitioned Parliament on the subject on 11 February 1652. A Committee for the Propagation of the Gospel was then appointed, with Oliver Cromwell and several of the ministers among its members, in order to consider the matter; by the end of March, they had prepared fifteen proposals "for the Furtherance and Propagation of the *Gospel* in this Nation."[12]

The basic purpose of these proposals was to develop a procedure for insuring the "Piety and Soundness in the Faith" of the nation's preachers. To this end, they recommended that no person be allowed to preach who had not gathered personal testimonies from six godly ministers and laymen and presented these credentials to a board of triers, "appointed to sit in every County; to examine, judge and approve" all such applicants.[13] An additional group of parliamentary appointees, they suggested, should be assigned to travel circuits through the nation ejecting unfit ministers and teachers.[14] Some toleration would be extended to scrupulous consciences, and well-ordered separate assemblies would be allowed, provided the locations of such churches were registered with the magistrate. But no preaching would be permitted which violated what the authors of the proposals referred to as the "Principles of Christian Religion, without acknowledgement whereof the Scriptures do clearly and plainly affirm that Salvation is not to be obtained."[15]

This church establishment, based upon boards of triers and ejectors and limited toleration of differing consciences, was for the present to be supported by the traditional means of public payment of tithes. On 29 April 1652, Parliament directed that the tithe system would continue to be enforced until the Committee for the Propagation of the Gospel could develop a suitable alternative means of ministerial maintenance.[16]

Both as evangelism and as a scheme for ministerial regulation and maintenance, the propagation of the gospel was perceived by the Rump Parliament and the Independent ministers as a means for securing and establishing the government. The common wisdom asserted that Protestant piety was the foundation of loyal citizenship, and, hence, the acts for evangelism were directed against the surviving strongholds of royalism in Wales and the northern counties.[17] Similarly, the fifteen proposals advocated the removal of any ministers or schoolmasters who were "Disturbers of the Publike peace . . . Popish, Scandalous, or disaffected to the Government of the Commonwealth."[18]

Thus the established church proposed by John Owen and his associates during the early months of 1652 was consistent with the general principles of godly reformation advocated by the Independents since the *Apologeticall Nar-*

ration (1643). Reform was to be an orderly process directed by the church's "nursing fathers," the magistrates, with the advice of the ordained ministry. The limits of tolerable religious opinion had been extended somewhat in the intervening years, but, just as John Cotton had written in the 1630s, those opinions which were judged clearly erroneous were impediments to reformation which could not be allowed.

These proposals for the propagation of the gospel provoked angry responses from the spokesmen for religious radicalism in England, and Roger Williams wrote important contributions to this sectarian polemic against the suggested religious settlement. Two of his publications, *The Fourth Paper, Presented by Major Butler* and *The Hireling Ministry None of Christs,* were dashed off in the spring of 1652 in direct response to the fifteen proposals of the Committee for the Propagation of the Gospel. As has been noted, *The Bloody Tenent Yet More Bloody* was composed in New England, but Williams published it in April 1652, in the midst of the debate over church establishment, and he appended material to it which emphasized the relevance of its arguments to the present controversy. Finally, in September 1652 he published anonymously *The Examiner Defended,* which retraced many of these same issues.

The concerns of the Baptists and sectarians associated with the army were summarized in the four points of a paper which Major William Butler presented to the Committee for the Propagation of the Gospel. In late March 1652, Roger Williams included this petition, a letter to Butler from Christopher Goad, and his own "Testimony . . . By way of Explanation" of the petition in the brief tract entitled *The Fourth Paper, Presented by Major Butler.* Among the persons who provided funds for publication of the pamphlet were Sir Henry Vane's brother, Charles Vane, and the Baptist millenarian Colonel Henry Danvers.[19] Since Butler's four points indicated the primary areas of sectarian dissatisfaction with the Independent proposals for a religious settlement, an examination of them provides a means for setting Roger Williams's controversial writings of 1652 in their proper historical context.

Major Butler's first proposition queried "whether Christ Jesus, the Lord of the Harvest, doth not send forth Labourers into his Vineyard, furnishing them by his Spirit, and bearing witness to their Labours, without the Testimony, and Reward of men?"[20] It should be recalled that the leaders of the radical sects were laymen like John Bunyan elevated to the ministry by divine calling and congregational approval, or exclergymen like Roger Williams, "who had renounced their ordination and succumbed to piety."[21] On behalf of such laborers in Christ's "Vineyard," Butler was proposing that the preparation and guidance of the true ministry came from the Holy Spirit rather than from the universities or from state-appointed boards of ordained clergymen. In opposition to the Independent plan for nominating triers and ejectors to evaluate the nation's ministry, Butler was asserting that the spirit furnished the preacher with the credentials and qualifications for his task.

This reliance on the spirit to call and direct the ministry was a prominent tradition in sectarian piety. It had been quite clearly presented by the Baptist lay preacher Samuel How in *The Sufficiency of the Spirit's Teaching, without Human Learning* (1639), a sermon occasioned by a dispute between How and John Goodwin, the London Independent, over the necessity of a learned ministry.[22] In his sermon How argued that "only such that are taught by the Spirit, are capable of true discerning of Spiritual Things."[23] For this reason, university learning was neither a proper nor necessary preparation for authentic preaching of the gospel. The spirit of God converting the heart and enlightening the mind was the only true guide to sound doctrine and the right comprehension of Scripture:

> To me it appears plain, that Men destitute of the Spirit of God, be they as learned as may be in Men's learning; yet do they pervert all Scriptures to their own destruction, when as the unlearned one, simple Men and Women, having the Spirit of Truth in them, shall rightly know them and God's Mind in them for their great Comfort.[24]

Human learning, said How, is useful in its proper realm, "Human and Worldly Imployments," but its use in interpreting and proclaiming the gospel is a usurpation of the role of the spirit.[25]

The same arguments were later utilized by the army chaplains John Saltmarsh and William Dell. Like How, William Dell had no objection to human learning in its proper, secular sphere, but he did *"oppose* it as it is made another *John Baptist,* to prepare the *way* of *Christ* into the *world,* or to prepare the *worlds* way to *Christ:* And also, as men make it *necessary, for the true knowledge of the Scriptures;* Yea, the *very Unction for the Ministry."*[26] In this manner, both Dell and Saltmarsh rejected their own university training for the ministry and instead based the validity of their callings upon the inward presence of the spirit. Writing in 1647, Saltmarsh interpreted this change as part of a historical process by which a new form of ministry was replacing the old. Present ministers, he stated, speak less by the spirit than by "Arts and Sciences and Languages Required."[27] But a ministry set apart from other Christians by such worldly attainments and knowledge demonstrated by that very fact its bondage to the Catholic Antichrist. A new ministry was therefore arising which was set apart not by its outward works but by the gracious gift of the spirit: "This Ministry is a Ministry of *Jesus Christ* in *all his Saints* or *people,* according to his administration of *light* and *glory* and *truth* in them."[28]

Thus any Christian, from whatever background, might be called by the spirit to the task of preaching. This point was forcefully argued by William Dell in *The Tryal of Spirits both in Teachers & Hearers* (1653), a book which Roger Williams carried home to Providence in 1654.[29] "The proof of a mans sending from God is this," Dell asserted, "to be annointed with the Spirit: as John 20. 22 . . . . and he that saith, The Unction of the Spirit alone is not sufficient for the Ministry of the New Testament, he denyes Christ and his Apostles to have been sufficient Ministers, and he perverts the Scripture, and seduces the people."[30] The critical question, then, was how to evaluate the spirit by which a preacher spoke. Was it God's spirit or merely his own human spirit? One must "try" the spirits. The Independent ministers had proposed that this be done through appointed boards of clerics and godly laymen who would examine all prospective preachers, but Dell disagreed. He declared that only those "who can try spirits by the Spirit of God, and doctrines by the Word of God, written in their hearts by the Spirit, are fit to commend Ministers to the work of God: that is, the Congregations of the faithfull."[31] The effect of the sectarian argument for the "sufficiency" of the spirit's teaching was thus two-fold. First, it opened the ranks of the preachers to laymen by denying that university learning was a prerequisite for the ministry. Second, it located responsibility for the regulation of the ministry solely with the individual churches rather than with the state.

This conviction that ministers should be spiritual men selected from among the members of their individual congregations was, of course, interrelated with the widespread sectarian opposition to mandatory support by tithes of the ordained parish clergy. As Major Butler's first proposition had stated, the ministry of Christ required from men neither approbation *nor reward*. Ministers should be supported by their own secular work or by the free contributions of their congregations, and, when William Erbery saw the people oppressed by tithes, he said, "the Lord God Almighty began to *roar like a man of War, and to cry like a woman in travel* within me."[32] Throughout the 1650s, this "refusal of the whole radical wing to compromise on the subject of tithes" would remain a constant source of political turmoil.[33]

In summary, the sectarian ministers were usually men who based their callings upon religious experience and the encouragement of the churches they served. They lacked or had rejected the religious value of formal education, and they often supported their preaching vocation by pursuing a manual trade. Known contemptuously as "mechanicks," it became a convention among them that a lowly social station constituted a mark of calling; "they decried learning as an impediment to inspiration, and they made of social obscurity a virtue; for the Almighty, as Scripture affirms, had chosen not the proud and the noble but the poor and the low."[34] Thus they confidently declared that Christ and the apostles had been mechanics, and the educated in their number even purposely adopted mechanic trades.[35] William York Tindall, in his study of John Bunyan, has therefore observed that Bunyan's "emphasis upon his lowliness appears to be the product of an exaggerated modesty until its adherence to the practice of the devout makes it evident that, far from being modest, it was at once boastful, in its implication of divine preference, and defiant, in reaction against worldly disdain."[36]

Roger Williams's polemical tracts of 1652 clearly exhibited the major features of this sectarian interpretation of

ministry. His understanding of himself and others as
apocalyptic witnesses laid great emphasis upon the special, immediate spiritual calling to the prophetic vocation,
and his writings of 1652 gave even greater prominence to
this conviction than had his pamphlets of 1644 and 1645.[37]
Williams also gave considerable attention and praise to the
lay preachers who, like that "despised and yet beloved
Samuel How," were proclaiming the gospel without benefit
of ordination:

> Sure it is that there have been and are many *excellent
> Prophets* and *Witnesses* of *Christ Jesus*, who never entred
> (as they say) into the *Ministry*, to wit, *Lawyers*, *Physitians*,
> *Souldiers*, *Tradesmen*, and others of higher and lower *rank*,
> who by *Gods holy Spirit* (breathing on their *meditations* of
> the *holy Scriptures*, and other private helps) have attained
> and much improved, an excellent *Spirit* of *knowledge*, and
> *Utterance* in the holy things of Jesus Christ.[38]

Finally, he shared the sectarian belief that "it is one of the
grand *Designes* of the most *High*, to breake downe the
Hireling Ministry," and he therefore directed his pen
against all those who turned preaching into a "Trade" by
accepting tithes.[39]

In his preface to *The Hireling Ministry None of Christs*,
Roger Williams took some pains to present his own credentials as one whom piety had compelled to adopt the life of
the mechanic prophet:

> Since I have not been altogether a stranger to the Learn-
> ing of the Aegyptians, and have trod the hopefullest
> paths to Worldly preferments, which for Christ's sake I
> have forsaken[,] since I know what it is to Study, to
> Preach, to be an Elder, to be applauded; and yet also
> what it is also to tug at the Oar, to dig with the Spade,
> and Plow, and to labour and travel day and night
> amongst English, amongst Barbarians! . . . why should I
> not be humbly bold to give my witness faithfully, to give
> my counsel effectually, and to perswade with some truly
> pious and conscientious spirits, rather to turn to Law, to
> Physic, to Souldiery, to Educating of Children, to Dig-
> ging (and yet not cease from Prophecying) rather then to
> live under the slavery, yea and the censure (from Christ
> Jesus and his Saints, and others also) of a mercenary and
> Hireling Ministry?[40]

Having thus "trod the hopefullest paths" of the ordained and learned clergy and having then forsaken them, Williams felt himself unusually qualified to enlist "pious and conscientious spirits" for the ranks of the lay preachers. For, after all, had not the first, apostolic ministry been composed of men who counted their mission above their maintenance and who by "their owne hands day and night, supplied their owne and others *Necessities?*"[41]

Insofar, then, as Major Butler and other sectarians opposed the parliamentary plan for regulation and maintenance of the clergy, Roger Williams shared their opposition. Likewise, he identified himself with their plea for the liberty of the lay preachers. Butler's second and third propositions had asserted that God, not the state, dealt the proper punishment to heretical ministers, and that civil powers had no authority to "assume a Judgement" in spiritual matters.[42] These, of course, were among the most prominent contentions of Williams's *Bloudy Tenent,* and he applauded their application to the present controversy over liberty of preaching. He was confident that throughout "the last Will and Testament of *Christ* Jesus, we find not the least title of *Commission* to the *Civil Magistrate* (as *Civil*) to *judge* and *act* in the matters of his *Spiritual Kingdom.*"[43]

On this issue of liberty, however, a difference existed between Roger Williams and many of the sectarian saints. As in his disagreements with the Independents regarding liberty, this present difference was interrelated with differing millenarian expectations. Following the execution of the king in 1649, both the army enthusiasts and the sectarian churches anticipated the millennial rule of the saints with a heightened zeal and made proposals to Cromwell for the furtherance of Christ's kingdom. In general, the enthusiasts expected the establishment of a temporal kingdom of the saints, a "fifth monarchy," which would supplant the crumbling fourth monarchy of world history, the Roman empire now perpetuated in the papacy and the various European kingdoms. Expecting as they did to dominate the ungodly of the world, they therefore restricted their pleas for liberty to liberty *for the saints.* In some, but not all, interpretations godly rule was to be established by physical force. Thus John Canne, whose views on separation Williams had approved in 1644, had by 1653 become an ardent fifth monarchist:

> About the yeere 1655. the righteous alone shall flourish and be exalted. A two-edged sword is in their hand, to execute vengence upon the Heathen, and punishment upon the people: to bind their Kings with chaines, and their Nobles with fetters of iron. To execute upon them the judgement written. And this Supream Power shall abide with them four or five yeares without interruption, untill they have broken in pieces the fourth Monarch.[44]

Such convictions ran counter, of course, to Williams's entire argument for the purposes and extent of religious liberty. *The Bloody Tenent Yet More Bloody* reiterated his position of the preceding decade that ungodly men were to be left alone in the "field" of the world, while Christ's witnesses concentrated their efforts upon preparations for the restoration of the church. And in that "restoration work," the only sword which Williams advocated was the sword of Christ's spirit in the testimony of his prophets.

Roger Williams feared that the saints were "too secure" and optimistic in their belief that the millennial advent was presently occurring, and he therefore remarked of Major General Thomas Harrison, one of the fifth monarchy enthusiasts, that he was "a very gallant, most deserving, heavenly man, but most high flown for the kingdom of the saints, and the fifth monarchy now risen, and their sun never to set again, &c." He numbered with himself such men as Oliver Cromwell and Henry Vane, who were "not so full of that faith of miracles, but still imagine changes and persecutions and the very slaughter of the witnesses, before that glorious morning so much desired of a worldly kingdom, if ever such a kingdom (as literally it is by so many expounded) be to arise in this present world and dispensation."[45] He placed the source of the saints' misguided optimism in their too narrow application of prophecy to events in England; these prophecies had a "more *generall* and *universall concernment*" and required the completion of the witnesses' testimony throughout the world for their fulfillment.[46] Contrasting his own views with hopes for the establishment of a temporal monarchy, Williams therefore stated that one purpose for writing *The Bloody Tenent Yet More Bloody* was to prepare the witnesses of Jesus for the apocalyptic slaughter of the witnesses, which he feared was "near *approaching,* and will be *Ushered* in, *provoak'd* and *hastned* by the *proud security, worldly pomp, fleshly confidence,* and *bloudy violences* of *Gods* own children, wofully exercised each against other, and so rendred wofully *ripe* for such an *Universal* and *dreadfull Storm* and *Tempest!*"[47]

Meanwhile, Williams articulated the positive aspects of his millenarian theory through consideration of the nature and function of the ministry during the apocalyptic age in which he lived. Previous chapters have examined Williams's conviction that the 1260 year reign of Antichrist had destroyed the visible church and its ordinances; these chapters have particularly stressed his further belief that the church would only be restored through the millennial appearance of new apostles. In the long historical interim between the dissolution of the church and its revival, Williams was convinced, the "secret motion" of the Holy Spirit was stirring up individual witnesses to wage verbal battle against antichristian errors and thereby to prepare the way for the millennial church. As has been noted, the term *propagation of the gospel* referred not only to governmental supervision of the preaching ministry but also to evangelism, and his millenarian interpretation of church history was the core around which Williams molded his contribution to that aspect of the controversy. In so doing, he differed not only from the proposals of the Independents but also from the developing practice of the Baptist churches.

The Baptist congregations in this period had begun to develop their own institutions of evangelization which were not dependent upon the support of the commonwealth. Observing that the early churches had commissioned men for special evangelistic journeys, as with Silas or Barnabas, the Baptists began to appoint men with aptitude for itinerant preaching to travel out to form new churches, settle disputes, or discuss matters of common concern. These men were given the title of *messenger* and were supported by the contributions of the congregations;

in this manner the messenger came to be considered a regular office, not of an individual church, but of a group of churches.[48] Both John Bunyan and the fifth monarchist Baptist Vavasor Powell held this itinerant evangelistic office.[49]

Another aspect of sectarian evangelistic concern was an interest in conversion of the Jews, arising out of the belief that this occurrence would immediately precede the millennium. The fourth of Major William Butler's proposals had therefore asked "whether it be not the duty of the Magistrate to permit the Jews, whose conversion we look for, to live freely and peaceably amongst us?"[50] This appeal for toleration of the Jewish people, based upon the millenarian hope for their conversion to Christianity, had been one of the arguments for religious liberty employed by the early General Baptist congregation pastored by Thomas Helwys and John Murton.[51] And by the 1650s this same millennialist concern had spread among the Independents, resulting in petitions to the Rump Parliament requesting that the Jews, who had been expelled from England in 1290, be readmitted and tolerated in the Commonwealth.[52]

Roger Williams responded to these evangelistic interests by, first, agreeing with the Baptists that there was a "twofold *Ministry* of *Christ Jesus*," pastors and teachers for nurturing the converted, and messengers or apostles sent out to preach for the conversion of the unregenerate. But he went on to observe that proper sending out of messengers required both "*Apostolical Gifts* and *Abilities* in the Men *sent*" and a true "*spiritual power* in the *Senders*." No one, Williams declared, had satisfactorily demonstrated that these qualities existed in present-day churches.[53] Williams considered this same problem in *The Hireling Ministry None of Christs* and concluded that he could not "bring in the Result of a satisfying discovery, that either the Begetting Ministry of the Apostles or Messengers to the Nations, or the Feeding and Nourishing Ministry of Pastors and Teachers, according to the first Institution of the Lord Jesus, are yet restored and extant."[54] The true church and its ministry having been destroyed by the apostasy, Williams therefore advocated readmission of the Jews in the hope of their future conversion, but he doubted the present possibility of that occurrence.[55] Until Christianity had been purified of its antichristian pollutions, the Jews, like the American Indians, would not be converted:

> We may see a great mistake as touching that great point of *Conversion:* There is a great breathing in the *souls* of *Gods* people after the *Conversion* of the *English, Irish, Jewes, Indians,* and blessed be *God* for those Breathings. Yet doubtlesse the first great *worke* is the bringing of the *Saints* out of *Babel,* or *confused worships,* and the *downefall* of the *Papacie,* after the *witnesses slaughtered.* Hence it is probably conceived by some upon *Revel.* 15. that untill the *Vyals* be powred forth upon *Antichrist,* the smoak so filleth the Temple, that no man, that is (few of the *Jewes* or Gentiles) shall by conversion enter in.[56]

The purgative testimony of Williams and the other witnesses must be concluded before the church's restoration and expansion could begin.

As he had in 1644 and 1645, Williams continued to emphasize that the only ministry available to the church in the wilderness was the ministry of Christ's "*Martyrs or Witnesses,* standing before the *Lord,* and testifying his holy *Truth* during all the *Reign* of the *Beast.*"[57] This preparative ministry of purification did not depend upon formal powers of ordination in the churches; rather, it was empowered by the immediate calling of the Holy Spirit. But in the millennial church, the temporary ministry of the witnesses would be replaced by a ministry of the apostolic form, ordained by laying on of hands. Williams therefore declared, "I prejudice not an Externall *Test* and *Call,* which was at first and shall be againe in force at the *Resurrection* of the *Churches.* . . . But in the present *State* of things, I cannot but be humbly bold to say, that I know no other *true Sender,* but the most *Holy Spirit,*" which sends out the witnesses by its "gracious *Inspiration* and *Instigation.*"[58]

Once again, Roger Williams's opinions should be distinguished from the convictions of Puritan spiritualists such as Sir Henry Vane, William Dell, William Erbery, or John Saltmarsh. Whereas Williams considered the prophetic ministry directed by the Holy Spirit to be an abnormal state of affairs brought about by the church's apostasy, Henry Vane, for example, considered it the harbinger of a new age of the spirit in which Christians would pass beyond the use of outward forms to "the knowledg of Christ in Spirit."

Vane therefore believed that this spiritual or "angellicall ministry" was bringing into the world "a more excellent way of preaching, hearing, and obeying the gospel."[59] From this perspective, Vane spoke of two phases of the spiritual ministry of the witnesses. In the first they were speaking against false worships, as Williams interpreted their task. But following the apocalyptic slaughter of the witnesses, they would rise again and begin "the second part of their Prophetical Ministry" in which "Heaven shall be opened, and a fuller and more excellent discovery of Christ in Spirit ministered, than ever yet hath been."[60]

John Saltmarsh specifically rejected the position of those like Roger Williams who awaited the restoration of the apostolic form of ministry. That first ministry, said Saltmarsh, had been destroyed by the medieval apostasy and would never be restored. The true restoration, instead, would be the revelation of Christ in spirit "in the *Saints,* or all true *Christians.*"[61] To the Seekers, who believed themselves to be in the wilderness awaiting the revival of outward ordinances and ministries, Saltmarsh announced that their expectations were indeed a *"wildernesse-condition,"* since they would prove *"waste* and *barren* as to spiritual* things."[62]

As the comments of John Saltmarsh suggest, there did exist in England scattered groups of Seekers whose opinions were similar to Williams's beliefs. One hears, for example, of the "chaos of confusion" created in the Baptist church at Bristol by persons who argued that "while the church of Christ was in her wilderness state they should not use [ordinances], and so took liberty to forbear them."[63] It is not known whether Williams actively associated himself with any of these Seeker groups during his trips to England. But the Scot Robert Baillie noted in 1644 that Williams had some influence upon them:

> Sundrie of the Independent partie are stepped out of the Church, and follows my good acquaintance Mr. Roger Williams; who sayes, there is no church, no sacraments, no pastors, no church-officers, or ordinance in the world, nor has been since a few years after the Apostles.[64]

But whatever the relationship between Williams and the Seekers, his opinions should be differentiated from those of the Puritan spiritualists such as Vane and Saltmarsh, if Williams's piety is to be understood in all its dimensions.[65]

The Dimensions of Williams's Piety

Although his public career had been a long jeremiad, lamenting the expiration of the true church and attacking the errors which impeded its rebirth, Williams had by no means ignored the personal devotional life which sustained his "wilderness" piety. Indeed, the conviction had arisen from his background in the Separatist tradition that desire for the true church order was itself a product of, and evidence for, the inward spirit of regeneration. Personal conversion to God remained for him the foundation of the Christian life, and he explained in 1652 that "there is an absolute necessity (not so of a true order of ministry, baptism, &c., but) of a true regeneration and new birth, without which it is impossible to enter into or to see the kingdom of God."[66] In April of 1652 he published *Experiments of Spiritual Life & Health* as a guide to the religious experiences which gave evidence of this "personall union and communion with the Father of Spirits."[67] In so doing, Williams announced that he would not controvert matters of liberty and reformation but only examine the nature and course of the godly life:

> At other times I have been drawne to consider of the little flock of Jesus, his Army, his body, his building, that for these many hundred years have been scattered, routed and laid wast and desolat: At present, I onely examine who are the personall and particular Sheep of Jesus Christ, his Souldiers, his living materials, though scattered, divided, and not compos'd and ordered at their souls desire.[68]

Composed as a letter to his wife on the occasion of her recovery from serious illness, Williams's consideration of "spiritual life and health" was organized under three main heads. In the first he asked what evidences for the presence of true spiritual life could be discerned within the individual self. The second division examined those experiences which argued not only for the presence of a converted spirit but also for the "strength and vigour" of that spirit. Finally, under a third heading, Williams proposed the means or methods, such as prayer, meditation, fasting, or the study of Scripture, by which "the Spirit of God usually breatheth for the preserving and maintaining of a truly spirituall and Christian Health and Chearfullnesse."[69] He hoped that the observations of his treatise would thereby serve as a "handfull of *flowers*" presented to his wife and other Christians for their enjoyment and encouragement, and he promised that each of these flowers would contain "some choice *example*, or *speech* of some *son* or *daughter* of *God*, pickt out from the *Garden* of the holy *Scriptures* for our spiritually *refreshing* and *consolation*."[70]

In instructing and encouraging the saints in their personal religious life and discipline, *Experiments of Spiritual Life & Health* was not, of course, opening a new literary frontier. The broad concerns of Williams's pamphlet—the *evidences* for the presence of spiritual life within the individual and the *means* by which this spiritual life might be strengthened—had been the topics of numerous Puritan devotional tracts prior to his own.[71] The first concern had been particularly emphasized by the influential Puritan divine Richard Sibbes in *The Bruised Reed and Smoking Flax* (1630).

The text for *The Bruised Reed and Smoking Flax*, Matt. 12:20, was rendered by Sibbes as "A bruised reed shall he not break, and smoking flax shall he not quench, till he send forth judgment unto victory."[72] As it appeared in Matthew, the text was part of a quotation drawn from Isaiah which Matthew had used to indicate that Jesus fulfilled the prophecy of the divine servant who would come healing and proclaiming the justice of God. Sibbes exposited the passage as a description of the work of Christ's healing mercy in the conversion of the soul. He began by observing that quite often in Scripture "the church is compared to weak things," and thus the "bruised reed" signified a person in the feeble first stages of conversion.[73] The interior life of such a person hinged upon a feeling of misery and upon the recognition that sin was the cause of that misery. Sibbes argued that this "bruised" and miserable condition was necessary in order to focus the individual's attention on the mercy of God in Christ, and he therefore interpreted these discomforts of the soul positively, as the first step in the growth of the Christian conscience.[74]

The "smoking flax," said Sibbes, represented the small

spark of grace mixed with corruption now present in the Christian. This spark was a "new creature" which "groweth up by degrees" and which, in these early stages of the conversion process, often gave off more smoke than light. Once again, Sibbes reassured his readers that this mixture of grace and nature was a proper and useful condition for the soul. It protected the person from the danger of "security," a term which in Puritan parlance meant over-confidence about one's spiritual state and a concomitant lack of self-examination.[75] He urged the sincere Christian to take comfort during his introspective struggles from the promise that, despite its small beginnings, Christ would not "quench" the smoking flax of the soul's rebirth. The more mature Christian, in turn, should follow Christ's example and encourage godly desires in the hearts of weaker brethren.

At this point Sibbes turned to consider how a person could recognize that the soul was in fact being turned toward God, and he proceeded to set down the "trials" by which this could be ascertained. He prefaced these remarks with warnings to the overly zealous: they should have "two eyes" in order to see inward good as well as imperfection, and they should remember that in the covenant of grace sincerity and the "truth of grace" counted for more than the particular amount.[76] For Sibbes, a critical test for this "truth of grace" was the impetus of the genuinely godly soul to express itself through the active working of godly desires and deeds. A "heavenly light," Sibbes declared, has been kindled in the soul which enables man to discern the word and will of God and which inclines the human will, by a "spirit of power," to do that divine will. If, therefore, the individual found himself experiencing a new and personal comprehension of Scripture, a deep and active desire to reform his life, and a grief and sensitivity to his own lapses of piety, these experiences argued for the converting presence of the Holy Spirit.[77] Throughout a truly Christian life, this "gracious frame of holiness set up in our hearts by the Spirit of Christ" would gradually increase in strength and power of expression.[78] Sibbes therefore urged saints at every level of spiritual growth to practice the introspective disciplines which were a fruit of conversion, thereby to "keep the soul open for the entertainment of the Holy Ghost."[79]

In urging the saints to disciplined spiritual growth, Sibbes touched upon Roger Williams's second major concern in *Experiments of Spiritual Life & Health,* the presentation of methods for encouraging the growth of faith. This matter of personal devotional life had long been a prominent topic in Puritan literature, and had been most thoroughly examined in Lewis Bayly's famous devotional manual, *The Practise of Pietie* (1613). Of wide and lasting influence throughout the English Puritan community, this work went through more than thirty editions in the twenty years following its publication. In it, Bayly emphasized a point made by Sibbes, that a truly saving faith expresses itself through godly works.[80] He appealed to his readers to let their practice of religion issue from their hearts and urged them to "get forthwith (like a *wise Virgin*) the *Oyle* of *Piety* in the *Lampe* of thy *conversation:* that thou maist be in *a continuall readinesse* to *meete* the *Bridegroom,* whether hee commeth by Death, or by Judgement."[81] To assist in this preparation of the godly heart, *The Practise of Pietie* gave an account of the "daily practice" by which the pious might maintain their spiritual readiness: morning and evening Scripture reading, prayers, family devotions, and preparation for the sabbath. It also suggested prayers for particular occasions (the morning, illness, death) and presented meditations to prepare the spirit for devotion and worship.

Bayly's directions regarding the reading of Scripture give apt illustration of the manner in which Puritan devotional manuals inculcated a strict religious discipline and at the same time focused the efforts of that discipline upon the personal religious experience of the individual. He explained how the entire Bible might be read through once each year by studying chapters each morning and evening, and he emphasized that this reading must include careful reflection if it was to be profitable to the soul. Bayly urged his reader, "Apply these things to thine owne heart, and reade not these Chapters as matters of *Historicall* discourse; but as if they were so many *Letters* or *Epistles* sent down from God out of *heaven* unto thee."[82]

Just as Richard Sibbes, in *The Bruised Reed,* had applied Scripture to the subjective state of the Christian during the process of conversion, so Bayly admonished the saint to peruse each Bible passage with an eye to its message for his soul. This insistence upon the interaction between the objective word of God in Scripture and the individual soul grew out of the central place given to the conversion experience in Puritan faith; God's purpose in acting through the preached or written word was not merely "to teach us, but (the spirit going with it) to work grace, necessary to strengthen the inward man."[83] As the Puritan pastor William Gouge explained, the word is the outward means of God's action in the process of conversion, while "the inward meanes (or rather cause) is the sanctifying Spirit of God, who softneth, quickneth, openeth our hearts, and maketh them as good ground."[84] Throughout Puritanism there appeared this emphasis upon the conjunction of spirit and word in which the Holy Spirit was understood both to have inspired the writers of Scripture and to act as the agent of conversion within the reader or hearer.[85]

It was the presence of this new spirit, what Roger Williams described as the "holy, heavenly *inner* man . . . born of an immortall seed," which enabled the godly man to "experience," to know and be convinced by, the objective word of God in Scripture or preaching.[86] Richard Sibbes therefore asserted that the reality of spiritual experience provided the only possible validation for the truths which man found presented objectively in the Bible:

> Principles are proved, you know, from experience, for they have nothing above them. There is no other principle to prove the word, but experience from the working of it. How know you the light to be the light, but by itself? . . . There is no child of God but can say by experience, that the word is the word.[87]

Similarly, William Gouge, although he advocated the use of reason, knowledge, comparison, and languages as aids in "searching" Scripture, was quick to admit that

> howsoever many arguments may be brought to convict a mans judgement thereof, so as in his judgement he cannot gainsay it, yet it is only the inward testimonie of the Spirit, which is able to perswade mans heart thereof, and so make it willingly embrace and entertaine the Scripture as Gods word.[88]

Conversely, the spiritual experience which convinced the saint of Scripture's truth enabled him to use that new comprehension of Scripture as a guide for evaluating and directing his own behavior. From this perspective, the Cambridge divine John Preston remarked that "there is a sagacitie given to the Saints, a certaine new qualitie, that others want, by which they are able to finde out the steppes of Gods way."[89]

Thus the self-examination counseled by Richard Sibbes in *The Bruised Reed* or by Roger Williams in *Experiments of Spiritual Life & Health* presupposed the active working of the Holy Spirit upon the hearts of their readers. Only the spiritual man was convinced of the truth of Scripture and could comprehend its import for his own inner life. Likewise, the advice offered by Bayly and Williams for strengthening the life of faith would be effeciive only for those whose wills were being "softened" and redirected by the spirit. For persons thus embarked upon the Christian life, Roger Williams's manual of piety, like those which had preceded and would follow it, provided an encouraging guide to aid in evaluating and advancing personal godliness.

Following his own dictum that "deep and frequent *examination* of our *spirituall* condition is an excellent means of *Christian health*,"[90] Williams proposed various "trialls" by which his readers could test whether the true spirit of God was present and active in their hearts. In each of these tests, he contrasted the motivations for the godly person's actions with the motives which prompted the natural or hypocritical man to perform those same acts. Thus, although it was true that the hypocrite might say prayers, he did so out of regard for the opinion of others or out of fear of divine judgment. *"Gods children,"* on the other hand, prayed because they, "like true *lovers,* delight to be private, and fervent with their heavenly *Father* and *Husband.*"[91] The life of Paul, said Williams, illustrated this difference between the prayers of unregenerate men and the true prayer of the saints:

> True prayer is the pouring out of the heart to God, the true breathing of the *soul* to God, arising as *Incense* and *perfume* unto God: Hence (no doubt) although *Paul* before his conversion prayed much unto *God*, (for he was a Pharasie) yet he never praid *indeed*, untill his great *change*, and the descending of the holy *Spirit* of prayer upon him.[92]

In light of this biblical witness, Williams's readers must examine their own experience and judge whether their prayers were such as would arise "as Incense and perfume unto God."

Like Richard Sibbes, Williams emphasized the spiritual value of the recognition that each Christian's life was a mixture of grace and nature in which struggle with sin was an ever-present reality. This recognition meant, first, that the saints were humble and sensitive to their own errors and insufficiencies. They depended upon God, not their own abilities, because they recognized "the evill *inclination* of their own *spirits*, and the *excellency*, and *sufficiency* of *Gods* most holy *Spirit*."[93] It was therefore an argument for spiritual health when the godly person felt contrition for sinful desires or sins committed: "A *contrite*, and broken heart is an *House* wherein *God* dwells, an House well ordered, *swept*, and *garnished*."[94] Second, the recognition that the Christian was "smoking flax" in which spiritual and human affections were intermixed led to a view of the Christian life as gradual growth in the faith. Thus, in the broad format of his tract, Williams dealt first with the evidences for spiritual life and then with the evidences for the healthy and vigorous soul which were the marks of a mature Christian. The desire for such spiritual growth was itself a mark of true godliness:

> It must needs argue a life of grace, when we can view the lives and deaths of the blessed martyrs, or witnesses of Christ Jesus, (either in the holy Scriptures, or other Records), I say can view them with a liking and true affecting of their graces, with an humble acknowledgement of our own wants and poverties, and a mourning desire of attaining to such beauteous profession of Christ Jesus.[95]

But if in these various ways *Experiments of Spiritual Life & Health* stood in continuity with the expositions of godliness in other manuals of Puritan piety, it nevertheless showed the influence of the distinctive dimensions of Roger Williams's own religious orientation. His belief that the church presently existed in a scattered, wilderness state while awaiting its millennial restoration made its impression upon several of the "experiments" by which he tested spiritual life and health. He emphasized, for example, that it was a sign of true godliness to "mourne and lament" the lost possibility of participation in the communion of saints. The healthy soul possessed a "holy vehement longing,

after the *enjoyment of God,* and of *Christ,* in a *visible,* and
open profession of his own holy *worship* and *Ordinances,*
separate from all false *worships, Gods,* and *Christs.*"[96] But
such participation in the society of the saints, said Williams, would only be "with *hardship* and *difficulty* attained
unto," since, as he had earlier informed the colonists of
Massachusetts Bay, the saints might be "awake" in matters
of personal godliness but "asleep" in their knowledge of
the true church of Christ.[97]

This longing for participation in true Christian community, which for Williams was a major mark of spiritual
vigor, was in fact a central point of continuity and of
paradox in his entire career. On both sides of the Atlantic
he had made his name on his willingness to stand alone on
the issues he deemed important, and he had publicly characterized himself as an individual, even solitary, witness
unassociated with the churches of the world. In so doing,
Williams had devoted himself to publishing works of controversy, written in opposition to the prevailing opinions
of his day. But this career of opposition was not the product of a cantankerous spirit. He made friends easily, and
most people who met him liked him.[98] Nor did it arise
from a principle of individualism. The goals which he en-
visaged for Christianity and for civil society were preemi-
nently communal in character: the communion of saints in
a true church and the unified participation of citizens in an
orderly and peaceful state. Throughout his life "holy vehement longing" for community in its purity had set him
apart from its imitations in this world.

7 Controversy with the Quakers

The preceding chapters have traced, through a variety of situations, Roger Williams's developing interpretation of personal piety and the Christian community. Throughout his career, it has been noted, he laid great stress upon the distinction between the church and the world, the godly and the unregenerate. At the same time, his millenarian theology placed major emphasis upon the imperfection of the saints and the church during the present historical dispensation. No true church, he believed, was extant in the world, and the saints were therefore a "scattered" people, a church in the wilderness, awaiting the new age in which they would once again commune with their Lord through the ordinances of Christian worship.

Given this orientation of Williams's piety, the rise of a movement of spiritualist perfectionism which, moreover, stressed the potentially sanctifying presence of divine light within every man seemed ordained to excite his controversial instincts. But his opportunity to debate the Quakers did not come for twenty years, until, in the summer of 1672, George Fox and his twelve Quaker associates traveled through Rhode Island. Although thwarted in his attempt to debate Fox himself, Williams prepared fourteen propositions by which he hoped to refute the Quakers and debated three of their missionaries, John Burnyeat, William Edmundson, and John Stubbs, at a series of four public meetings.[1] In 1676, Williams published the substance of these debates, together with supplementary material which he had not then had time to present; he entitled the work *George Fox Digg'd out of His Burrowes,* a pun utilizing the name of another Quaker patriarch, Edward Burrough.

The Rise of Quakerism

At several points this study has noted the presence of Puritan enthusiasts, such as Williams's friend Sir Henry Vane, whose faith emphasized the indwelling of Christ or the Holy Spirit in the elect. Such persons refrained, like Roger Williams, from participation in chuch ordinances; but *unlike* him they did so because they believed such external aids to communion with God were no longer necessary. The ordinances of worship had been replaced by the immediate presence of the spirit. Thus William Dell observed that "by the true Baptism of the New Testament we doe actually put on Christ, and are made one with Christ, and this is not done by any water washing, but by the spirit."[2] As Dell's comment implied, the same spirit which had informed the New Testament churches was now present with the contemporary saints. The Welsh army chaplain William Erbery made the similar observation that the spirit which had motivated the apostles was being "more fully drawn forth" in the present age, and he complained that Independent and Baptist preachers knew no more of the gospel than "what is written in the letter of Scripture." Did they not realize that the apostles had preached the gospel to the world without written texts by the movement of the spirit within them?[3]

These spiritualists often interpreted their religious experience as part of the advent of a new age of the spirit. The medieval apostasy, they believed, had supplanted apostolic spirituality with a legalistic formalism, but the coming days would witness a revival of that spirit, and Christ would reign in and through his saints. This sense of the indwelling spirit was actively expressed as millenarian enthusiasm for the establishment of Christ's kingdom. Thomas Collier preached to the New Model Army on this theme in 1647: "Christ will come in the Spirit, and have a glorious Kingdome in the spirits of his people, and they shall by the power of Christ in them, raign over the world, and this is the new heavens and the new earth."[4]

It was in the context of this spiritualist enthusiasm

among England's religious radicals that early Quakerism developed.[5] As with the spiritualists, Fox and the early Quakers asserted that the spirit which had been in the apostles was now also in the "Children of Light." They went further to make this spirit the "Judg and Toutch-stone" by which to try contemporary society, their own lives, and Scripture itself. As Geoffrey Nuttall has observed, this differed from the central emphasis in Puritanism: "Hitherto, God's Word in Scripture has been treated as the criterion by which to test faith and experience. Now, the Holy Spirit is introduced as the touchstone by which all else is to be tried, including the Bible itself. A contrast, though not necessarily an opposition, is thus created between them."[6] The consequence of this was that the spirit became the authority to which the Quakers appealed in religious or social controversy. George Fox, for example, explained to Oliver Cromwell that the Quaker prophets were under divine compulsion to oppose the established clergy; "they yt [that] have ye same spiritt yt [that]Christ & ye prophetts & Apostles had could not but declare against all such" hireling ministers.[7]

This conviction regarding the continuity of the spirit from the apostles to themselves led the Quakers to perceive their community as the veritable recapitulation of apostolic Christianity. This perception could lead to extremes of behavior. Acting out his unity with Christ, James Nayler attempted to fast for forty days and, in 1656, mounted himself upon a mule and made triumphal entry into Bristol.[8] In milder form, the same principle permeates Thomas Holme's description of his imprisonment, which should be compared with Paul singing in prison at midnight (Acts 16:25–34):

> A little before midnight, the power of the Lord came upon me, and sweet melody was within me. And about midnight I was compelled to sing; and the power was so great, it made all my fellow-prisoners amazed, and some were shaken, for the power was exceeding great. And I scarcely know whether I was in the body, yea or no. And there appeared light in the prison and astonished me. And I was afraid, and trembled at the appearance of the light; my legs shook under me. And my fellow-prisoners beheld the light, and wondered. And the light was so glorious, it dazzled my eyes.[9]

The recurrence of the words *light* and *power* in this and other Quaker writings suggests much of the religious experience involved, an "astonished" sense of the new and active spirit within.

As with the spiritualists, the Quakers interpreted this "light within" through millenarian language. For them, the sense of completion became an internalized apocalypse in which Christ's reign was established within the individual.[10] Through this millenarian interpretation inward experience was turned outward toward society, and nothing became more typical of early Quakerism than prophetic "testimony" against the evils of English society and tireless missionary travel throughout Christendom. The millennium, said George Fox, was made present through Quaker testimony; and by his preaching "ye everlastinge day" was announced and God's "son sett over all" who would make profession and thereby receive the light.[11]

The well-known opinion of the early Quakers that the divine light was within every man seems to have developed in relation to this apocalyptic sense that the battles and judgments of the last days were even now occurring within the saints. Finality demanded choice, according to the Quaker missionaries, and they pressed their audiences to recognize the potential for moral rectitude already present in their hearts. In this tone, Edward Burrough announced in 1656 that

> God is light, and has lightened every one of you with the true light of life eternal, if you love it and be guided by it; or of death everlasting, if you hate it, and disobey it, and walk contrary to it. That is the light which convinces you of sin, of lying, of swearing, and cursed-speakings, and drunkenness, which are the fruits of the cursed tree, which burdens the ground of the Lord, which the ax is now laid to the root of, to cut it down and cast it into everlasting burning.[12]

Although the Quakers shared a good many opinions with Puritan sectarians such as Roger Williams, the abnormal behavior connected with their spiritualist enthusiasm made them the objects of fear and derision. Like various of the sectarians, and like Roger Williams himself, they abstained from ordinances, opposed tithes and oaths, and upheld lay preaching against the hireling ministry of the established clergy. But both their theology and their piety provoked a massive Puritan polemic against them. Not only stalwarts of the Puritan mainstream such as John Owen and Richard Baxter but also sectarians such as the Baptist John Bunyan or the Seeker John Jackson printed attacks upon the Foxians. In 1659 George Fox himself rebutted the works of these and numerous other detractors in a massive book entitled *The Great Mystery of the Great Whore Unfolded*. In his *George Fox Digg'd out of His Burrowes* Roger Williams made a rather belated contribution to this prolonged and bitter controversy.

Williams Debates the Foxians

Roger Williams's second trip to England, although undertaken in the public service, severely strained his personal finances. Not only did he sell his trading post in order to meet the costs of the journey, but he also tutored the children of several members of Parliament in order to maintain himself while in England. Nevertheless, upon his return to Providence in 1654, he agreed to serve as president of the colony. The centrality of agriculture, especially the raising of livestock, in the Rhode Island economy meant that much of his time in office and for many years afterward would be expended in arbitrating land disputes involving the fertile pasturage on the Narragansett Bay islands and in the Narragansett lands to the west.[13]

Despite these domestic political responsibilities, Williams kept abreast of the political situation in England throughout the 1650s. What he heard profoundly disturbed him, and, following the death of Cromwell and the collapse of the Puritan commonwealth, he wrote John Winthrop, Jr., that "great ulcers" had arisen in his thoughts regarding the declining Protestant cause in England and Europe. He often referred to the opinion of John Archer in *The Personall Reigne of Christ upon Earth* (1642) that the papacy, before its downfall, would reconquer the Protestant nations.[14] He confided to Winthrop his fear of "Popish invasions" in England and his further "fear (as long I have feared, and long since told Oliver [Cromwell], to which he much inclined,) the bloody whore is not yet drunk enough with the blood of the saints and witnesses of Jesus."[15]

Williams's pessimism apparently revised his millennial timetable without fundamentally altering the structure of his millennial thought. His characteristic ideas regarding the testimony of the witnesses, the suspension of the ordinances, and the eventual restoration of the church would appear in *George Fox Digg'd out of His Burrowes.* What changed in the interim between his letters to the younger Winthrop and his debate with the Quakers was Williams's sense of the immediacy of the millennial renewal. He continued to abstain from the ordinances, for example, but now projected his hope for their restitution into a more distant future.

In retaining this chastened millennial hope, Williams was not unique. Among English Baptists such as Hanserd Knollys, Henry Danvers, and John Bunyan, millenarian reflection and writing continued into the last decade of the century.[16] In Rhode Island at the time of Williams's controversy with the Quakers, this Baptist millenarianism appeared in debate regarding whether the sabbath should be celebrated on the first or seventh day of the week. The so-called Seventh Day Baptists in England and Rhode Island depicted their Saturday observance as an important harbinger of " 'the kingdom of our Lord, which is now hastening upon us.' " Williams briefly involved himself in this debate but doubted that the sabbatarian Baptists were correct in their opinions.[17]

His ruminations on the sabbath were typical of Williams's religious life in the years between his return from England and the debate with the Quakers in 1672. Despite this long hiatus in his publishing, he continued to exercise his vocation as a witness in the "wilderness" through public preaching and religious controversy. He preached monthly at meetings in the home of Richard Smith, Jr., to whose father Williams had sold his trading post; and only a year before his death Williams was laying plans to publish a collection of these "discourses."[18] Nor did Williams shrink from controversy. He drafted papers disputing millenarian speculation about the American Indian and probing the religious significance of King Philip's War. And in 1670 he challenged Major John Mason and others "to discuss by disputation, writing or printing" the relationship between religious liberty and the preservation of civil peace.[19] Even in Williams's mid-seventies, the continued presence of religious intolerance in New England was still capable of arousing his indignation. "I pray your patience to suffer me to say," he wrote Thomas Hinckley in 1679, "that, above these forty years in a barbarous wilderness, driven out on pain of death, I have, (as I believe) been the Eternal his poor witness in sackcloth against your churches, and ministries, as being but State politics and a mixture of golden images, unto which (were your carnal sword so long) you would musically persuade, or by fiery torments compel, to bow down as many as (that great type of inventors and persecutors) Nebuchadnezzar did."[20]

Thus, when he decided to debate the Quaker missionaries in 1672, Williams did not consider himself to be emerging from retirement. Although the Quakers derided the "doting spirit" of the "old priest," Williams himself saw the controversy as simply another in the long series of spiritual battles which had engaged him for more than forty years.

The Quakers had first entered Rhode Island in 1657, finding safety there from the considerable and sometimes severe persecution encountered in the other colonies. Since the variety of religious opinions already present in the colony included a good many inclinations toward spiritualist piety, the Quakers soon reaped a large harvest of converts, including such persons as William Coddington, Nicholas Easton, and Williams's old mentor in the Baptist faith, Katherine Scott. By 1672 Nicholas Easton was governor, and Quakers held considerable political and economic power throughout the colony. Hence, Williams had broad experience with Quaker life and thought long before the debate with Burnyeat, Edmundson, and Stubbs. In addition, during his visit to England from 1652 to 1654 he had spoken with "some of their Chief then in *London*," and he therefore had personal recollections of the earliest days of the Quaker movement.[21] But although these experiences were significant for Williams's formulation of his position against the Quakers, another factor was of particular importance. Williams intended, both in the debate and in his subsequent book, to refute George Fox's work *The Great Mystery of the Great Whore*.[22] This rambling treatise by Fox was a justification and reassertion of the Friends' doctrine and practice in reaction to the numerous

Puritan polemics against them. In the book, Fox quoted from various Puritan tracts, repudiated them, and then leveled his own countercharges. For this reason, the book represented an extreme statement of the Quaker position, and, in replying to it, Williams adopted the opposite set of extremes. This polarization of views means that *George Fox Digg'd out of His Burrowes* should not be considered in isolation or used as a simple guide to Roger Williams's doctrinal position; rather, it must be carefully related to the whole range of his thought.

As the focus for debate between himself and the Quakers, Roger Williams had composed fourteen propositions repudiating Quakerism. These were argued in sequence during the three days of the disputation and may be grouped under two major headings. First, Williams charged that the Quakers were possessed of "proud" spirits which rejected all of God's spiritual and natural guides to pious and civil behavior. In place of divine guidance, declared Williams, the Quakers placed their reliance only upon themselves. He therefore warned the Quaker readers of his tract that "I have proved, and will prove (if God please) that spiritual Pride, that is Pride about spiritual matters, is the Root and Branch of your whole Religion, and that the King Eternal, who did cast out proud Angels out of his Palace, will hardly open his Gates to proud and scornful Dust and Ashes."[23] Williams sought to demonstrate this charge by examining the Quaker theological positions on the nature of Christ, the place of Scripture, the forms of worship, and eschatology.

These Quakers are *"Rebellious Traitors,"* Williams stated, who, by asserting the presence of Christ within them, "bear Arms against the *Mediator* between God and Man, the Man Christ Jesus."[24] The true Christian, as Williams had argued in *Experiments of Spiritual Life & Health,* is humble and deeply conscious of his personal failings; he is sustained by the promise of Christ that he is redeemed despite imperfection. But Williams was convinced that the Quaker interpretation of Christ led away from Christian humility to a belief in the perfection of the individual based upon union with Christ. By preaching the "Christ within" and ignoring the historical Christ, he stated, Quakerism did nothing more than exalt the individual self.[25] By confusing Christ's spirit with their own sinful spirit, "they preached not *Christ Jesus* but *Themselves*, yea they preached the *Lord Jesus* to be *Themselves*." [26]

Williams further charged that Quaker belief in the "immediate and infallible" divine light within made them unwilling to test the spirit by which they acted; he urged John Burnyeat to try his religion by comparison with Scripture, "the outward and external *Light* . . . by which God witnesseth himself and his Truth in the World." [27] It was by this written word that the spiritual word was communicated to the reader or hearer. As Williams had written to John Winthrop, Jr., this "word literal is sweet, as it is the field where the mystical word or treasure, Christ Jesus, lies hid." [28] Once again, Williams was sounding a note which had been prominent in *Experiments of Spiritual Life & Health:* the saint must evaluate his experience by the objective rule and example of the Bible. In response to a statement by William Edmundson that the spirit was "above" the Scriptures and was the source of the Scriptures, Williams therefore insisted upon the interconnection of word and spirit:

> It is easie to boast of the *Spirit,* but the *true Spirit* (in a Sense) and the holy *Scriptures* are one, as the *Father* and *Son* are one, and therefore can not but be willing to be examined by the holy *Records.* [29]

It has already been observed that the Quakers interpreted their religious experience of spiritual completion or perfection not only through the idea of the indwelling Christ but also through an eschatology which described that experience as part of "a new age in the Spirit, with fresh light and with freedom for new practice." [30] Just as the former idea contrasted with Roger Williams's sense of the Christian's personal imperfection, so the latter conflicted with his eschatology of the church's imperfection. This difference between Williams and the Quakers was particularly marked with regard to their opposing reasons for abstaining from the ordinances. When Williams attacked the Quaker spokesmen for interpreting the ordinances as inward experience and discontinuing their external practice, John Stubbs replied that Williams had no right to chastise them since he too was "not living in *Church Ordinances.*" But Williams replied to this that it was one thing to be in Arms against the *King of Kings* and his *visible Kingdome* and *Administration of it*, & to turn off all to *Notions* and *Fancies* of an invisible Kingdome, and invisible Officers and Worships as the *Quakers* did: Another thing among so many pretenders to be the true *Christian Army* and *Officers* of Christ Jesus to be in doubt unto which to associate and to lift our selves.[31]

Since Williams hoped that these visible officers and ordinances would be regained "at the time of the *Restitution*, and Christs return the second time," he rejected the Quaker declaration that the ordinances had been superseded by the second coming of Christ within.[32]

Quaker reliance upon the presence of the Holy Spirit to direct their actions led at times to abnormal behavior which "testified" to the spirit's power and authority. Williams utilized the most extreme examples of this—excessive fasting, bodily quakings, or public nudity—to stress that Quaker confidence in the immediate stirrings of the spirit was foolish, misguided, and uncivilized.[33] Such "brutish" and irrational reaction to inward whims, he declared, could lead them to civil violence or to *"fiery* Persecutions" of persons who opposed their doctrines.[34] And even if Quakerism did not lead so far, it nonetheless reduced its practitioners to a rude barbarism lacking "Courteous Speech, Courteous Salutation, and respective Behaviour" to social superiors, which in many cases made them inferior to the Indians in their civility.[35]

In sum, Quaker expression of the spirit's power eventuated in a form of piety which offended both Williams's vision of the church and his conservative interpretation of the social order. In *The Bloody Tenent Yet More Bloody*, Williams had argued that God directed human life according to three orders of law:

> The true and living God, is the God of order, spiritual, civil and natural: Natural is the same ever and perpetual; civil alters according to the constitutions of peoples and nations; spiritual he hath changed from the national in one figurative land of Canaan, to particular and congregational churches all the world over; which order spiritual, natural or civil, to confound and abrogate, is to exalt mans folly against the most holy and incomprehensible wisdom of God.[36]

In Williams's opinion, the Quaker piety both neglected the proper spiritual order and offended the natural or social order; it did so because it followed the "proud imaginings" of its supposed inner light rather than the outward and visible guides of social custom and Scripture.

In the context of this attack upon the Quaker emphasis on the inner spirit, Roger Williams's own views on the role of the spirit were deemphasized. For example, he had earlier given full support to lay preachers who asserted that they were sufficiently informed by the Holy Spirit and did not require the aid of formal education. But these "mechanick" preachers had received that inspiration during study and meditation upon Scripture.[37] Now, the Quaker prophets seemed to Williams to be declaring that the spirit was sufficient not only without human learning but also without the divine learning of holy writ. To redress that balance between God's internal and objective teachings, Williams therefore asserted the value of "Schools of Learning" and the knowledge of Greek and Hebrew in a way that he had not done in earlier decades and different settings. He now announced that "the right and regular propagation of natural, of civil, and expecially of *Divine Knowledge* scatters the thick Fogs of the *Quakers* affected hellish ignorance."[38]

Similarly, Williams had consistently stressed that during the antichristian centuries it was the immediate stirring of the Holy Spirit which had motivated the ministry of the witnesses, a ministry in which he included himself. But in the present controversy he attacked the Quaker concept of the immediate action of the spirit as both ridiculous and dangerous. A point which he constantly reiterated was that God reveals his will through means, that man's knowledge of God is mediated knowledge. A closer examination of his writing suggests, however, that this did not represent a shift in his thought but was instead his attempt to place clear limits upon the doctrine of the Holy Spirit. Thus, among the "means" by which God spoke to man Williams included not only providence, the ordinances, or preaching, but also dreams, meditations, or private fasts. He added that "sometimes it pleaseth God by the Ministration of his *Ministring Spirits* (the invisible Angels) to work by unknown and unseen ways to us." He found that "the immediate Teachings of God by *Dreams,* by *Vision,* by *Voices"* were often mentioned in Scripture both before and after the time of Christ.[39] This fact, said Williams, was not at issue. What was at issue was the Quaker "pretence of Spirit" by which they refused to be judged or guided by the examples and rules of Scripture. They were thus unable to differentiate between the revelations of God and the "Devils whisperings," because they lacked an objective *"Rule* or *Touchstone"* by which to evaluate religious experience.[40]

This assertion that the Quakers were unable to distinguish between divine and satanic spirits was interconnected with the second major point which Williams argued in his fourteen propositions. The "main ground," he said, of his controversy with the Quakers was that, at the same time that they exalted "their Illuminations in themselves," they glorified "Cursed, rotten Nature" by their doctrine of the inner light.[41] The Quakers, in other words, had *never actually experienced conversion.* The spirit by which they acted, according to Roger Williams, was not the true spirit of God: "Till a spirit of Regeneration and Conversion change the heart of a man, there is no other *Christ* nor *Spirit* within, but the *spirit of Sathan,* which is the spirit by which the *Quakers* are acted, and is the arrantest *Jugler* & *Cheater* in the world."[42] The Quaker belief that there existed divine light within every man, awaiting his recognition, did not correspond to the Puritan experience and interpretation of the conversion process. The structure of that conversion experience had been the subject of innumerable sermons and of manuals of piety such as Williams's own *Experiments of Spiritual Life & Health.* Among congregationalists a recounting of that experience had come to be required of persons seeking admission to church membership. The emphasis upon the availability of salvation present in the doctrine of the inner light proposed a radically new interpretation of the salient features of Puritan conversions: repentance for a sinful nature, meditation on experience in light of Scripture, or sense of being chosen and acted upon by God. Williams therefore suggested that the Quakers, like the Catholics, did not "seem to know *Experimentally* what *true* and *saving grace is.*"[43]

His view was shared by Sir Henry Vane, whose spiritualist piety otherwise had a number of similarities to that of the Quakers. Vane believed that the Quaker inner

light was only the light of nature, man's Adamic birthright.
More charitable than Williams at this point, he conceded
that the Quakers might live as good natural men by the aid
of this inner light, but he went on to deny that they had
any part in the covenant of grace. They were witnesses, he
said, only to the covenant of nature.[44]

In Quakerism, then, Williams was presented with a disturbing sight, one aspect of his own piety expanded into a
seeming rejection of the other aspect. Throughout his
career he had used Scripture to evaluate and direct personal and communal experience. Both the conversion of
the individual and the reformation of the church, themes
which ran throughout his published writings, were understood or criticized from his perspective upon, and meditation on, the Bible. Following his departure from the
ordained ministry, it was the scriptural concept of the
eschatological witness which he used to provide an interpretation for his own sense of religious duty and mission.
Finally, it was the restitution of what he believed to be the
church forms revealed in the Bible which provided the goal
toward which he worked and on behalf of which he wrote.
By reversing the priorities of Williams's piety, the Quakers
profoundly threatened his sense of order and purpose;
their emphasis upon the spirit as the arbiter, rather than
Scripture, appeared to remove the framework within
which his own deep sense of the spirit's power had been
interpreted.

Williams therefore rejected the Quaker claim that Fox
and his associates were "Apostles and Messengers of
Christ Jesus."[45] Men who advocated novelty in religion
and who did not appear to have experienced true conversion were not, to Williams's mind, the apostles who would
bring about the "Great Conversion of Jews and Gentiles
yet expected" and prophesied in Revelation.[46]

> Surely the true Messengers of Jesus will say no other
> than what *Moses* and the *Prophets* foretold and wrought,
> Act. 26. therefore *Fox* and his *Foxians* that tells us they
> have all by the Spirit and need no Record, are Theives
> and Robbers, whom, *Moses*, and the *Prophets*, and the
> *Apostles* abhor'd to think of.[47]

Champlin Burrage has suggested that Williams and
many of the Seekers were disappointed that the Quaker

apostles did not reinstitute the ordinances and that for this reason they found it "impossible to recognize in Fox and other Quaker leaders the specially inspired prophets and apostles whom some had taken them to be."[48] This is in part correct; one reason that Williams decided to give "testimonie against the uncleane spirit of ye Quakers" was that he had "ever sought after ye Restauration of ye Ordinances of Christ Jesus in Puritie."[49] But the question of outward ordinances was really only symptomatic of the larger differences between the piety of Roger Williams and that of the Quakers. His firm emphasis upon the interconnection between the inner and the objective testimonies of the spirit of God ran counter to their perspective at almost every point. Although in his seventies, he therefore strove once more to act as a witness for Christ, and even gave serious thought to sailing for London in order to see his anti-Quaker polemic through the press. It was, he declared, "heavily incumbent upon my Spirit to be as zealous for my Lord Jesus as they are for Sathan."[50]

Conclusion

Few statements so neatly summarize the central concerns of Roger Williams's piety as a comment by the British sociologist Mary Douglas:

> Ideas about separating, purifying, demarcating and punishing transgressions have as their main function to impose system on an inherently untidy experience. It is only by exaggerating the difference between within and without, above and below, male and female, with and against, that a semblance of order is created.[51]

The recurrent themes of Williams's thought were indeed the concern for order and disorder, the distinction between within and without, the desire for purification. His spiritual pilgrimage in quest of "lost Zion," the true church, was marked time and again by the implications of these concerns. His strictly Separatist concept of the church while in Massachusetts, the distinction between church and state on which he based his appeal for religious liberty, and his attack upon the "satanic" spirit of the Quakers present various formulations of these central concerns. The precise character of each formulation, as has been seen, depended upon the historical influences of the moment.

But this study has attempted to demonstrate that the critical point at which these themes of order, purity, and belonging came together was not in ideas which he held about the church, the state, or religious liberty. Rather, the crucial focus of these concerns was in his idea of himself and of his personal religious duty in the world; as it has been described here, his millenarian piety provided the continuities, both logical and historical, among the various aspects and developments of his thought. Williams's conviction that he was among the eschatological witnesses commissioned by God to purify Christianity in preparation for its millennial restoration enabled him to place his individual activities within a meaningful framework. The impurity and disorder which he deplored in the present were never dissociated in his mind from the golden ages of past and future; the present might lack order or purity but it never lacked meaning, because one was passing through it on the way to lost Zion. To his credit, Roger Williams maintained that sense of religious vocation throughout his mature life.

Notes

Chapter One

1 John Milton, *Areopagitica*, in *John Milton: Complete Poems and Major Prose*, ed. Merritt Y. Hughes (New York: Odyssey Press, 1957), p. 720.

2 Daniel Featley, *The Dippers Dipt*, 5th ed. (London: For N. B. and Richard Royston, 1647), p. A4 recto.

3 For the Puritan background of Roger Williams's thought see Mauro Calamandrei, "Neglected Aspects of Roger Williams' Thought," *Church History* 21 (1952): 239–58; Perry Miller, *Roger Williams: His Contribution to the American Tradition* (Indianapolis: Bobbs-Merrill, 1953); Edmund S. Morgan, *Roger Williams: The Church and the State* (New York: Harcourt, Brace and World, 1967).

4 For descriptions of the historical, theological, and social development of Puritanism from approximately 1560 to 1640, see Patrick Collinson, *The Elizabethan Puritan Movement* (Berkeley: University of California Press, 1967); William Haller, *The Rise of Puritanism* (New York: Columbia University Press, 1938); Christopher Hill, *Society and Puritanism in Pre-Revolutionary England* (New York: Schocken Books, 1964); Marshall M. Knappen, *Tudor Puritanism* (Chicago: University of Chicago Press, Phoenix Books, 1966); Alan Simpson, *Puritanism in Old and New England* (Chicago: University of Chicago Press, 1955).

5 Cf. A. S. P. Woodhouse, ed., *Puritanism and Liberty*, 2d ed. (Chicago: University of Chicago Press, 1951), Introduction, p. 37.

6 In the nineteenth century the majority of Roger Williams's published works appeared in a 6 vol. edition by the Narragansett Club. In 1963 these volumes were reprinted by Russell & Russell, and a seventh volume was added containing Williams's other known publications. Williams will be cited from these editions; his published works, listed in order of their original date of publication, are as follows: Roger Williams, *A Key into the Language of America* (1643), ed. James Hammond Trumbull, Publications of the Narragansett Club, 1st ser., 1:77–282 (1866); Roger Williams,

Mr. Cottons Letter Lately Printed, Examined and Answered (1644), ed. Reuben Aldridge Guild, Publications of the Narragansett Club, 1st ser., 1:313–96 (1866); [Roger Williams], *Queries of Highest Consideration* (1644), ed. Reuben Aldridge Guild, Publications of the Narragansett Club, 1st ser., 2:251–75 (1867); [Roger Williams], *The Bloudy Tenent, of Persecution, for Cause of Conscience, Discussed, in a Conference between Truth and Peace* (1644), ed. Samuel L. Caldwell, Publications of the Narragansett Club, 1st ser., 3:1–425 (1867); Roger Williams, *Christenings Make Not Christians* (1645), in *The Complete Writings of Roger Williams*, ed. Perry Miller, 7 vols. (New York: Russell & Russell, 1963), 7:29–41; R[oger] W[illiams], *The Fourth Paper, Presented by Major Butler . . . with a Testimony to the Said Fourth Paper* (1652), in Miller, ed., *Complete Writings*, 7:119–41; Roger Williams, *Experiments of Spiritual Life & Health* (1652), in Miller, ed., *Complete Writings*, 7:45–114; Roger Williams, *The Hireling Ministry None of Christs* (1652), in Miller, ed., *Complete Writings*, 7:147–91; Roger Williams, *The Bloody Tenent Yet More Bloody* (1652), ed. Samuel L. Caldwell, Publications of the Narragansett Club, 1st ser., 4:1–547 (1870); [Roger Williams], *The Examiner Defended* (1652), in Miller, ed., *Complete Writings*, 7:195–279; Roger Williams, *George Fox Digg'd out of His Burrowes* (1676), ed. J. Lewis Diman, Publications of the Narragansett Club, 1st ser. 5:1–503 (1872).

The great majority of Williams's surviving letters are collected in *Letters of Roger Williams, 1632–1682*, ed. John Russell Bartlett, Publications of the Narragansett Club, 1st ser. 6:1–418 (1874) (hereafter cited as *Letters of RW*).

7   John Bunyan, *Grace Abounding to the Chief of Sinners* (London: J. M. Dent, 1928); John Winthrop, "Relation of His Religious Experience," in *Winthrop Papers*, ed. Allyn Bailey Forbes and Stewart Mitchell, 5 vols. (Boston: Massachusetts Historical Society, 1929–47), 3:338–44; Thomas Goodwin, "Memoir of Thomas Goodwin, D.D., Composed out of His Own Papers and Memoirs, by His Son," in *The Works of Thomas Goodwin*, 9 vols. (Edinburgh: James Nichol, 1861), 2:lxi–lxxv.

8   Winthrop, "Relation," p. 339; Bunyan, *Grace Abounding*, p. 8.

9   Goodwin, "Memoir," pp. lii–liii; Bunyan, *Grace Abounding*, p. 10; Winthrop, "Relation," p. 339.

10 Bunyan, *Grace Abounding*, pp. 14–16.

11 Goodwin, "Memoir," p. lv.

12 Ibid., p. liv; Winthrop, "Relation," p. 340; Bunyan, *Grace Abounding*, pp. 16–17.

13 Bunyan, *Grace Abounding*, p. 23.

14 Ibid., pp. 14, 18.

15 Goodwin, "Memoir," p. lxiii.

16 Bunyan, *Grace Abounding*, p. 61.

17 Ibid., p. 73; Winthrop, "Relation," pp. 342–43.

18 Cf. Owen C. Watkins, *The Puritan Experience: Studies in Spiritual Autobiography* (New York: Schocken Books, 1972), pp. 61–63.

19 William James, *The Varieties of Religious Experience: A Study in Human Nature* (New York: Longmans, Green, 1902), p. 196.

20 Williams, *Cottons Letter . . . Examined*, p. 342.

21   Rupert Taylor, *The Political Prophecy in England* (New York: Columbia University Press, 1911), pp. 82–103, 121–23; Harry Rusche, "Merlini Anglici: Astrology and Propaganda from 1644 to 1651," *English Historical Review* 80 (1965): 322–33; Harry Rusche, "Prophecies and Propaganda, 1641–1651," *English Historical Review* 84 (1969): 752–70.

22   B. S. Capp, *The Fifth Monarchy Men: A Study in Seventeenth-Century English Millenarianism* (London: Faber and Faber, 1972), pp. 13–22; Christopher Hill, *Antichrist in Seventeenth-Century England* (London: Oxford University Press, 1971), p. 149; Hugh R. Trevor-Roper, *Religion, the Reformation and Social Change* (London: Macmillan, 1967), pp. 237–93; Charles Webster, *The Great Instauration: Science, Medicine and Reform, 1626–1660* (London: Duckworth Press, 1975).

23   See Geoffrey F. Nuttall, *Visible Saints: The Congregational Way, 1640–1660* (Oxford: Basil Blackwell, 1957), p. 158.

24   Thomas Brightman, *A Revelation of the Apocalypse,* in *The Works of That Famous, Reverend, and Learned Divine, Mr. Tho: Brightman* (London: By John Field for Samuel Cartwright, 1644), pp. 380–82, 824. Brightman died in 1607, and his guide to Revelation was first published in Amsterdam in 1615.

25   Ibid., p. 380; see also pp. 701, 824.

26   Ibid., pp. 381–82.

27   Brightman's views have been characterized as a form of postmillennialism by Peter Toon, "The Latter-Day Glory," in *Puritans, the Millennium and the Future of Israel: Puritan Eschatology 1600 to 1660,* ed. Peter Toon (Cambridge: James Clarke, 1970), p. 31.

28   Brightman, *Revelation of the Apocalypse,* p. 607.

29   Ibid., p. 162.

30   Toon, "Latter-Day Glory," pp. 32–39; John F. Wilson, *Pulpit in Parliament: Puritanism during the English Civil Wars, 1640–1648* (Princeton: Princeton University Press, 1969), pp. 192–94.

31   William Haller, *Foxe's Book of Martyrs and the Elect Nation* (London: Jonathan Cape, 1963). Similar convictions that their nations had been elected to a position of millennial leadership had been advanced by Savonarola at Florence and by Scottish divines since the time of John Knox; see Donald Weinstein, "Millenarianism in a Civic Setting: The Savonarola Movement in Florence," In *Millennial Dreams in Action: Studies in Revolutionary Religious Movements,* ed. Sylvia L. Thrupp (New York: Schocken Books, 1970), pp. 194–95; Sidney A. Burrell, "The Apocalyptic Vision of the Early Covenanters," *Scottish Historical Review* 43 (April 1964): 8–15.

32   Joseph Mede, *The Key of the Revelation, Searched and Demonstrated out of the Naturall and Proper Characters of the Visions,* trans. Richard More, 2d ed., 2 vols. (London: By J. L. for Philemon Stephens, 1650), 1:27.

33   Ibid., 1:12–13

34   Ibid., 1:38.

35   Ibid., 2:13.

Chapter Two   1   Winthrop's words appear in "A Modell of Christian Charity," a sermon he preached aboard the Arabella as it sailed for New England in 1630; see *Winthrop Papers,* ed. Allyn Bailey Forbes and

Stewart Mitchell, 5 vols. (Boston: Massachusetts Historical Society, 1929–47), 2:293.

2   Ibid., 2:166; 3:54

3   Ibid., 2:91, 111 (emphasis added). For a similar view that, in 1629, New England provided a "resting place" in which to avoid the Lord's scourge of England, see William Bradford, *Of Plimoth Plantation* (Boston: Commonwealth of Massachusetts, 1900), p. 295.

4   George L. Haskins, *Law and Authority in Early Massachusetts* (New York: Macmillan, 1960).

5   Francis Rose-Troup, *John White* (New York: G. P. Putnam, 1930), pp. 12–23, 63; Charles M. Andrews, *The Colonial Period of American History*, 5 vols. (New Haven: Yale University Press, 1934), 1:352.

6   Andrews, *Colonial Period*, 1:354–55; S. F. Haven, Introduction to "Records of the Company of the Massachusetts Bay," *Transactions of the American Antiquarian Society* 3(1850): lxi–lxii, cxxxvi.

7   Andrews, *Colonial Period*, 1:365–67.

8   Ibid., 1:321–23, 326, 365–67,

9   "Records of the Council for New England," ed. Charles Deane, *Proceedings of the American Antiquarian Society* (April 1867), pp. 124–25.

10 Andrews, *Colonial Period*, 1:339–42.

11 [John White], *The Planters Plea*, in *Tracts and Other Papers, Relating to the Origin, Settlement, and Progress of the Colonies in North America, from the Discovery of the Country to the Year 1776*, comp. Peter Force, 4 vols. (1837; reprint ed., Gloucester, Mass.: Peter Smith, 1963), 2:38–42.

12 Ibid., p. 9.

13 *Records of the Governor and Company of the Massachusetts Bay in New England (1628–86)*, ed. Nathaniel Bradstreet Shurtleff, 5 vols. (Boston: Commonwealth of Massachusetts, 1853–54), 1:384 (hereafter cited as *Records of Mass.*).

14 *Winthrop Papers*, 2:126, 133, 148; John Cotton, *Gods Promise to His Plantations*, Old South Leaflets, vol. 3, no. 53, p. 14.

15 *Winthrop Papers*, 2:152.

16 Cotton, *Gods Promise to His Plantations*, p. 12.

17 *Winthrop Papers*, 2:121.

18 Ibid., 2:126.

19 Ibid., 2:161.

20 Ibid., 2:166.

21 Ibid., 2:199.

22 Ibid., 2:163–64.

23 Ibid., 2:164–65, 178, 180, 336; *Records of Mass.*, 1:37, 63, 385.

24 *The Humble Request of His Majesties Loyall Subjects, the Governour and the Company Late Gone for New England*, in *Winthrop Papers*, 2:231–33.

25 [White], *Planters Plea*, p. 44.

26 Ibid., pp. 32–37.

27 *Records of Mass.*, 1:387.

28 Bradford, *Of Plimoth Plantation*, p. 317; John Cotton, "John Cotton's Letter to Samuel Skelton," ed. David D. Hall, *William and Mary Quarterly*, 3d ser., 22 (1965): 481.

29 *Records of Mass.*, 1:37, 386–87; W. P. Upham, "Papers Relating to the Rev. Samuel Skelton," *Essex Institute Historical Collections* 13 (1875): 143–44.
30 Bradford, *Of Plimoth Plantation*, p. 317.
31 John Smyth, *Principles and Inferences concerning the Visible Church*, in *The Works of John Smyth*, ed. W. T. Whitley, 2 vols. (Cambridge: Cambridge University Press, 1915), 1:252, 256–57. For a useful account of Separatist conceptions of the church, see B. R. White, *The English Separatist Tradition* (London: Oxford University Press, 1971).
32 Henry Barrow, *A Plaine Refutation of M. G. Giffardes Reprochful Booke*, in *The Writings of Henry Barrow, 1590–91*, ed. Leland H. Carlson (London: George Allen and Unwin, 1966), p. 36.
33 Ibid., p. 338.
34 John Robinson, *A Treatise of the Lawfulness of Hearing of the Ministers in the Church of England*, in *The Works of John Robinson, Pastor of the Pilgrim Fathers*, ed. Robert Ashton, 3 vols. (London: John Snow, 1851), 3:362–63. See also George D. Langdon, *Pilgrim Colony: A History of New Plymouth, 1620–1691* (New Haven: Yale University Press, 1966), pp. 102–5.
35 Edward Winslow, *Hypocrisie Unmasked by a True Relation of the Proceedings of the Governour and Company of the Massachusets against Samuel Gorton* (1646; reprint ed., Providence: Club for Colonial Reprints, 1916), p. 99.
36 The classic exposition of the distinction between Separatism and nonseparating congregationalism appears in Perry Miller, *Orthodoxy in Massachusetts, 1630–1650* (Cambridge: Harvard University Press, 1933), pp. 73–101.
37 Cited in Champlin Burrage, *The Early English Dissenters in the Light of Recent Research (1550–1641)*, 2 vols. (Cambridge: Cambridge University Press, 1912), 2:157.
38 Ibid., 2:294.
39 Ibid., 1:281–335; 2:292–305.
40 Bradford, *Of Plimoth Plantation*, pp. 315–16; Miller, *Orthodoxy in Massachusetts*, pp. 127–31; Langdon, *Pilgrim Colony*, pp. 108–11.
41 "Records of the Company of the Massachusetts Bay," pp. 30c–30e.
42 James Duncan Phillips, *Salem in the Seventeenth Century* (Boston: Houghton Mifflin, 1933), p. 193.
43 Bradford, *Of Plimoth Plantation*, p. 316.
44 *Records of Mass.*, 1:407–9.
45 Ibid., 1:52–53, 407–8.
46 Cotton, "Letter to Samuel Skelton," p. 480. It was also the practice of John Robinson and the Pilgrims to refuse public communion to members of the Church of England; see Langdon, *Pilgrim Colony*, pp. 110–11.
47 Cotton, "Letter to Samuel Skelton," p. 481.
48 *Winthrop Papers*, 2:332–33, 335–36.
49 Ibid., p. 333.
50 Cotton, "Letter to Samuel Skelton," p. 481.
51 Bradford, *Of Plimoth Plantation*, pp. 331–32; *Winthrop Papers*, 2:308; John Winthrop, *Journal: History of New England, 1630–1649*, ed.

James Kendall Hosmer, 2 vols. (New York: Charles Scribner's Sons, 1908), 1:51–52.

52 Cotton, "Letter to Samuel Skelton," pp. 482–84.

53 Ibid., pp. 482–83.

54 "Letters of Roger Williams to Lady Barrington," *New England Historical and Genealogical Register* 43 (1889): 317. For a plausible reconstruction of the early life of Roger Williams, consult Samuel Hugh Brockunier, *The Irrepressible Democrat, Roger Williams* (New York: Ronald Press, 1940).

55 James E. Ernst, "New Light on Roger Williams' Life in England," *Collections of the Rhode Island Historical Society* 22 (1929): 98–99.

56 Williams, *Cottons Letter...Examined*, p. 342.

57 Brockunier, *Irrepressible Democrat*, pp. 22–23.

58 Williams, *Bloody Tenent Yet More Bloody*, p. 65.

59 Henry Barrow, *A Brief Discoverie of the False Church*, in *The Writings of Henry Barrow, 1587–1590*, ed. Leland H. Carlson (London: George Allen and Unwin, 1962), p. 366. Subsequently, Cotton and Hooker would agree with Williams and the Separatists on this point. By the 1640s opposition to read prayers had become fairly common among the various English congregational groups, according to Geoffrey F. Nuttall, *The Holy Spirit in Puritan Faith and Experience* (Oxford: Basil Blackwell, 1946), pp. 66–67.

60 "Letters to Lady Barrington," p. 319.

61 Edmund S. Morgan, *Visible Saints: The History of a Puritan Idea* (New York: New York University Press, 1963), pp. 65–105.

62 *Winthrop Papers*, 3:316–18; Williams, *Cottons Letter...Examined*, pp. 325, 335, 352–53, 361, 363.

63 Williams, *Cottons Letter...Examined*, p. 355; cf. pp. 358, 360, 363.

64 John Cotton, *A Letter of Mr. John Cottons Teacher of the Church in Boston, in New England, to Mr. Williams a Preacher There*, ed. Reuben Aldridge Guild, Publications of the Narragansett Club, 1st ser., 1:305 (1866).

65 John Cotton, *A Coppy of a Letter of Mr. Cotton of Boston, in New England, Sent in Answer of Certaine Objections Made against Their Discipline and Orders There* (n.p., 1641), p. 1; John Cotton, *A Reply to Mr. Williams His Examination*, ed. J. Lewis Diman, Publications of the Narragansett Club, 1st ser., 2:62 (1867).

66 Williams, *Cottons Letter...Examined*, p. 381.

67 John Canne, *A Necessitie of Separation from the Church of England, Proved by the Nonconformists Principles*, ed. Charles Stovel (London: Hanserd Knollys Society, 1849), pp. 131–32; Barrow, *Brief Discoverie of the False Church*, p. 570.

68 Canne, *Necessitie of Separation*, pp. 28, 195, 95–96. Compare Williams's statement, above, that communion with "spiritual societie...is the fayrest evidence of Adoption." In the minds of many Separatist saints fear of communion in false worship was connected with the warning of Rev. 14:9–11 that such persons would receive the "mark of the beast." So, for example, consideration of these verses by one godly woman "struck such terror into her soul" that she dreaded to hear common prayer and began "to look about, and scrutinously to make search after the primitive, scriptural, and instituted worship of the Lord;" *The Records of a*

Church of Christ, Meeting in Broadmead, Bristol, 1640–1687, ed. Edward Bean Underhill (London: Hanserd Knollys Society, 1847), pp. 16–17.

69 Cited in Burrage, *Early English Dissenters,* 2:375.
70 Williams, *Cottons Letter. . .Examined,* p. 350 (emphasis added).
71 Winthrop, *Journal,* 1:61–62; *Letters of RW,* p. 356.
72 Winthrop, *Journal,* 1:61–62.
73 *Letters of RW,* pp. 2–3, 356. Williams's first child, Mary, was born in August 1633, only shortly before his return to Salem.
74 Winthrop, *Journal,* 1:92–94; Bradford, *Of Plimoth Plantation,* p. 370.
75 *Records of Mass.,* 1:87; Thomas Hutchinson, *The History of the Colony and Province of Massachusetts-Bay,* ed. Lawrence Shaw Mayo, 2 vols. (Cambridge: Harvard University Press, 1936), 1:413.
76 Winthrop, *Journal,* 1:83; *Letters of RW,* p. 3. At Plymouth the decision for "our beloved Mr. Nowell to surrender up one sword" greatly pleased Roger Williams, who, like Henry Barrow, deplored the "confusion" of sacred and secular offices. For Barrow, see above, p. 24
77 John Cotton, "A Copy of a Letter from Mr. Cotton to Lord Say and Seal in the Year 1636," in Hutchinson, *History of the Colony,* 1:414–15.
78 Edmund S. Morgan, *Roger Williams: The Church and the State* (New York: Harcourt, Brace and World, 1967), p. 71.
79 Cotton, "Cotton to Lord Say and Seal," pp. 414–15.
80 *Records of Mass.,* 1:88, 91, 94; Winthrop, *Journal,* 1:67.
81 *Winthrop Papers,* 3:117.
82 Winthrop, *Journal,* 1:101.
83 William Hubbard, *A General History of New England, from the Discovery to MDCLXXX,* ed. William Thaddeus Harris, Collections of the Massachusetts Historical Society, 2d ser., 5:117, 204–5 (1815).
84 Winthrop, *Journal,* 1:120.
85 B. Richard Burg, ed., "A Letter of Richard Mather to a Cleric in Old England," *William and Mary Quarterly,* 3d ser., 29 (1972): 86, 94.
86 *Letters of RW,* p. 104.
87 Winthrop, *Journal,* 1:112–13; Miller, *Orthodoxy in Massachusetts,* p. 58.
88 Winthrop, *Journal,* 1:113.
89 Ibid., 1:116–17; *Winthrop Papers,* 3:147–48. The scriptural passages applied to Charles I were Rev. 16:13–14; 17:12–13; 18:19.
90 Robert Gray, *A Good Speed to Virginia,* ed. Wesley F. Craven (1609; reprint ed., New York: Scholars' Facsimiles and Reprints, 1937).
91 *Winthrop Papers,* 2:140–41.
92 Ibid., 3:149.
93 Ibid., 3:148; Morgan, *Roger Williams,* p. 122.
94 Ola Elizabeth Winslow, *Master Roger Williams* (New York: Macmillan, 1957), pp. 112–13.
95 [Williams], *Bloudy Tenent,* p. 400.
96 Ibid., pp. 400–401; Williams, *Christenings,* pp. 31–34.
97 Williams, *Christenings,* pp. 33–35.
98 *Winthrop Papers,* 3:147; Winthrop, *Journal,* 1:117–19. Although Wil-

liams's tract may have given hope to those opposed to the stockholders' control of land disbursement, the magistrates seem to
have objected to its direct attack upon the crown and not to have
regarded it as an attack upon the land system. Cf. Francis Jen-
nings, "Virgin Land and Savage People," *American Quarterly* 23
(1971): 532–36.

99 Winthrop, *Journal*, 1:127–29, 135.

100 Ibid., 1:142.

101 Cotton, *Reply to Mr. Williams*, p. 62.

102 Ibid., pp. 44–47.

103 Winthrop, *Journal*, 1:137.

104 *Winthrop Papers*, 3:175; *Records of Mass.*, 1:146; Winthrop, *Journal*,
1:145; Israel Stoughton, "A Letter of Israel Stoughton, 1635," *Proceedings of the Massachusetts Historical Society* 58 (1925): 450.

105 Stoughton, "Letter of Israel Stoughton," p. 457; *Winthrop Papers*,
3:200. A similar act of iconoclasm had occurred at John Cotton's
English parish in 1621, when a cross was removed from the
mayor's ceremonial mace. For a discussion of this incident, which
led to Cotton's suspension for nonconformity, see Larzer Ziff, *The
Career of John Cotton: Puritanism and the American Experience*
(Princeton: Princeton University Press, 1962), pp. 51–52.

106 Winthrop, *Journal*, 1:151.

107 Stoughton, "Letter of Israel Stoughton," pp. 450–51; [Thomas
Hooker], "Touchinge Ye Crosse in Ye Banners," ed. Worthington
C. Ford, *Proceedings of the Massachusetts Historical Society* 42 (1909):
272–80. See also Howard Millar Chapin, *Roger Williams and the
King's Colors* (Providence: Society of Colonial Wars in the State of
Rhode Island and Providence Plantations, 1928), pp. 21–22.

108 Winthrop, *Journal*, 1:149; see also Williams, *Cottons Letter . . .
Examined*, p. 325.

109 Cotton, *Reply to Mr. Williams*, p. 13.

110 Winthrop, *Journal*, 1:149.

111 Brockunier, *Irrepressible Democrat*, pp. 141, 152; Williams, *Hireling
Ministry*, p. 188.

112 Winthrop, *Journal*, 1:154.

113 Ibid.

114 Cotton, *Reply to Mr. Williams*, p. 76.

115 Winthrop, *Journal*, 1:155.

116 Ibid., 1:157, 162–63.

117 Ibid., 1:168.

118 Ibid., 1:192–94.

119 *Winthrop Papers*, 3:241.

120 John Cotton, *A Sermon Preached . . . at Salem, 1636* (Boston: n.p.,
1713), p. 19.

121 Ibid., pp. 24–25.

122 *Winthrop Papers*, 3:315–16.

123 Ibid., 3:316–17.

**Chapter
Three**

1 John Smyth, "The Differences of the Churches of the Separation," in *The Works of John Smyth*, ed. W. T. Whitley, 2 vols.
(Cambridge: Cambridge University Press, 1915), 1:271.

2 John Garrett, *Roger Williams: Witness beyond Christendom,
1603–1683* (New York: Macmillan, 1970), p. 243.

sembly: Its History and Standards, 2d ed. (Philadelphia: Presbyterian Board of Publication and Sabbath-School Work, 1897), pp. 180–81.

4   C. G. Bolam, Jeremy Goring, H. L. Short, and Roger Thomas, *The English Presbyterians: From Elizabethan Puritanism to Modern Unitarianism* (London: George Allen and Unwin, 1968), pp. 20–21, 36–38; Ethyn Williams Kirby, "The English Presbyterians in the Westminster Assembly," *Church History* 33 (1964): 418–28; Mitchell, *Westminster Assembly*, pp. 150, 160–61, 167, 209–10.

5   John F. Wilson, *Pulpit in Parliament: Puritanism during the English Civil Wars, 1640–1648* (Princeton: Princeton University Press, 1969), pp. 260–62.

6   Raymond Phineas Stearns, "The Weld-Peter Mission to England," *Publications of the Colonial Society of Massachusetts* 32 (1934): 188–246.

7   John Spencer, "A Short Treatise concerning the Lawfulnesse of Every Mans Exercising His Gift as God Shall Call Him Thereunto," *Transactions of the Congregational Historical Society* 4 (1909–10): 367.

8   Robert Baillie, *The Letters and Journals of Robert Baillie*, ed. David Laing, 3 vols. (Edinburgh: Bannatyne Club, 1841–42), 2:212.

9   John Cotton, *A Reply to Mr. Williams His Examinations*, ed. J. Lewis Diman, Publications of the Narragansett Club, 1st ser. 2:10 (1867). For biographic information on Staresmore, see John Robinson, *The Works of John Robinson, Pastor of the Pilgrim Fathers*, ed. Robert Ashton, 3 vols. (London: John Snow, 1851), 3:381–85; Champlin Burrage, *The Early English Dissenters in the Light of Recent Research (1550–1641)*, 2 vols. (Cambridge: Cambridge University Press, 1912), 1:171–77, 182.

10 *Letters of RW*, pp. 188, 235–36; Burrage, *Early English Dissenters*, 2:296, 299, 302–4, 316; John Callender, *An Historical Discourse, on the Civil and Religious Affairs of the Colony of Rhode-Island*, ed. Romeo Elton, *Collections of the Rhode Island Historical Society* 4 (1838): 97, 117.

11 [Williams], *Bloudy Tenent*, p. 8.

12 Gardiner, *Civil War*, 1:262–67; Baillie, *Letters and Journals*, 2:117, 123; Thomas Goodwin et al., *An Apologeticall Narration* (London: For Robert Dawlman, 1643), pp. 25–26.

13 Lawrence Kaplan, "Presbyterians and Independents in 1643," *English Historical Review* 84 (1969): 247–48, 250–52; Baillie, *Letters and Journals*, 2:118; Gardiner, *Civil War*, 1:268.

14 Bertha Meriton Gardiner, ed., "A Secret Negotiation with Charles the First, 1643–1644," *Camden Miscellany* 8 (1883): 5–6.

15 Ibid.

16 John Lightfoot, *The Journal of the Proceedings of the Assembly of Divines*, ed. John Rogers Pitman (London: J. F. Dove, 1824), p. 163; Baillie, *Letters and Journals*, 2:121.

17 Baillie, *Letters and Journals*, 2:121; Lightfoot, *Journal*, p. 93.

18 Goodwin et al., *Apologeticall Narration*, pp. 8, 9, 11–12, 23, 26, 30–31.

19 Ibid., p. 2.

20 Ibid., p. 3.

21 Ibid., p. 4.
22 Ibid., pp. 4–5.
23 Ibid., pp. 9–11.
24 Ibid., p. 24.
25 Ibid., p. 23.
26 *Reformation of Church-Government in Scotland, Cleered from Some Prejudices, by the Commissioners of the Generall Assembly of the Church of Scotland* (London: For Robert Bostock, 1644), pp. 5, 11–13.
27 Ibid., pp. 3–20.
28 Ibid., p. 4 (emphasis added).
29 Ibid., pp. 2–3.
30 Ibid., pp. 6–7.
31 Ibid., pp. 14, 17.
32 Thomas Goodwin, *Zerubbabels Encouragement to Finish the Temple* (London: For R. D., 1642), pp. 12–13. This theme of a gradual, progressive movement toward a millennial age is discussed in William Bridge, *Christs Coming Opened in a Sermon before the Honourable House of Commons* (London: For Peter Cole, 1648), pp. 4–5; Jeremiah Burroughes, *Sions Joy* (London: By T. P. and M. S. for R. Dawlman, 1641), p. 44; *A Glimpse of Sions Glory* (London: For William Larnar, 1641), pp. E1 recto–E2 recto; R. G. Clouse, "The Rebirth of Millenarianism," in *Puritans, the Millennium and the Future of Israel: Puritan Eschatology 1600 to 1660*, ed. Peter Toon (Cambridge: James Clarke, 1970), p. 64; Wilson, *Pulpit in Parliament*, p. 192.
33 John F. Wilson, "A Glimpse of Syons Glory," *Church History* 21 (1962): 66–73.
34 *Glimpse of Sions Glory*, pp. E1 verso, A4 recto–B1 recto.
35 Ibid., pp. C3 verso–D3 verso.
36 John Archer, *The Personall Reigne of Christ upon Earth* (London: Benjamin Allen, 1642), pp. 4–5, 21–25, 49–53.
37 Ibid., p. 44; cf. Goodwin, *Zerubbabels Encouragement*, p. 55.
38 *Glimpse of Sions Glory*, p. E1 recto; see also Burroughes, *Sions Joy*, pp. 33–34, 44.
39 Burroughes, *Sions Joy*, p. 2; see also William Bridge, *Babylon's Downfall*, in *The Works of the Rev. William Bridge*, 5 vols. (London: E. Palmer & Son, 1845), 4:297–98, 300, 306; William Bridge, *On Zechariah I. 18–21, II. 1.*, in *Works*, 4:338; Sidrach Simpson, *A Sermon Preached at Westminster before Sundry of the House of Commons* (London: For Peter Cole, 1643), pp. 7, 24, 27, 38.
40 William Bridge, *The Truth of the Times Vindicated*, in *Works*, 5:269–77; Jeremiah Burroughes, *The Glorious Name of God, the Lord of Hosts* (London: For R. Dawlman, 1643); John Goodwin, *Anti-Cavalierisme* (London: By G. B. and R. W. for Henry Overton, [1642]).
41 Burroughes, *Glorious Name of God*, pp. 105–6; see also Burroughes, *Sions Joy*, p. 25.
42 Sidney A. Burrell, "The Apocalyptic Vision of the Early Covenanters," *Scottish Historical Review* 43 (April 1964): 5–6, 16–18, 20–21.
43 Ibid., pp. 19–21.
44 George Gillespie, *A Sermon Preached before the Honourable House of*

Commons at Their Late Solemn Fast (London: For Robert Bostock, 1644), pp. 6–8.

45   Ibid., p. 9.
46   Ibid., pp. 37–38.
47   Ibid., p. 36.
48   Ibid., p. 41.
49   [Williams], *Queries,* p. 254 (emphasis deleted).
50   *Catalogue of the Pamphlets . . . Collected by George Thomason, 1640–1661,* ed. G. K. Fortescue, 2 vols. (London: British Museum, 1908), 1:304, 306, 309.
51   Cotton, *Reply to Mr. Williams,* p. 10; *A Reply of Two of the Brethren to A[dam] S[teuart],* 2d ed. (London: By M. Simmons for H. Overton, 1644), pp. 6–7.
52   [Williams], *Queries,* pp. 259–60.
53   Ibid., p. 254 (emphasis deleted).
54   Ibid., pp. 257–58.
55   Ibid., p. 258.
56   Ibid., p. 261.
57   Ibid., pp. 261–62.
58   Ibid., pp. 264–66.
59   Ibid., pp. 266–69.
60   Ibid., pp. 269–70, 273.
61   Williams, *Bloody Tenent Yet More Bloody,* p. 383; see also pp. 191, 358; [Williams], *Queries,* pp. 269–70.
62   Williams, *Bloody Tenent Yet More Bloody,* pp. 293, 385.
63   Williams, *Hireling Ministry,* p. 158.
64   Williams, *Cottons Letter . . . Examined,* p. 386; [Williams], *Queries,* pp. 262–63; [Williams], *Bloudy Tenent,* p. 409; Williams, *Hireling Ministry,* pp. 160–61, 167. For Williams's use of John Foxe, see *Bloody Tenent Yet More Bloody,* pp. 114, 115, 177–78, 206–7, 380, 464.
65   Williams, *Cottons Letter . . . Examined,* p. 386; Williams, *Bloody Tenent Yet More Bloody,* p. 383. In the Geneva Bible (1560 ed.) the marginal note to Rev. 11:3 identifies the two witnesses as "all the preachers that shulde buylde up Gods Church."
66   Williams, *Hireling Ministry,* p. 161.
67   [Williams], *Queries,* p. 269; see also Williams, *Christenings,* pp. 40–41; Williams, *Hireling Ministry,* pp. 168–69, 178–79.
68   Williams, *Hireling Ministry,* p. 159.
69   [Williams], *Queries,* p. 273.
70   Ibid., p. 253 (emphasis deleted). The ordinance for censorship and licensing of the press had been passed on 14 June 1643; see Gardiner, *Civil War,* 1:149.
71   Cotton, *Letter of Mr. John Cottons,* p. 299.
72   Ibid., pp. 309–11.
73   Masson, *John Milton,* 3:19.
74   Williams, *Cottons Letter . . . Examined,* p. 316; responsibility for publication was also denied by Cotton, *Reply to Mr. Williams,* pp. 9–10.
75   Williams, *Cottons Letter . . . Examined,* p. 316 (emphasis deleted).
76   Williams suggested in his preface that he had written the reply shortly after originally receiving Cotton's epistle, but internal evidence demonstrates that its final composition did not occur

until after Williams arrived in England in 1643. For example, references appear in the body of the text to speeches made in Parliament and to books printed in the period from 1639 to 1643. In addition, Williams interjected explanations directed to an English audience; see *Cottons Letter...Examined*, pp. 315, 316, 319, 324, 328, 337, 349, 386.

77 Ibid., pp. 315–19.
78 Cotton, *Reply to Mr. Williams*, pp. 46, 67.
79 Williams, *Cottons Letter...Examined*, p. 321; see also pp. 324–25.
80 Ibid., p. 325; the ram's horn, or trumpet, is the instrument associated with announcement of the millennium throughout Revelation.
81 Ibid., p. 326.
82 Ibid., pp. 315, 338; cf. 2 Cor. 11:26–27.
83 Ibid., p. 315.
84 Ibid., pp. 338, 339–40.
85 Ibid., p. 325.
86 Williams, *Bloody Tenent Yet More Bloody*, pp. 191–92; see also p. 394; Williams, *Cottons Letter...Examined*, pp. 352–53; Williams, *Major Butler*, p. 131; Williams, *Hireling Ministry*, pp. 155–56, 160, 166–67.
   Winthrop Papers, ed Allyn Bailey Forbes and Stewart Mitchell, 5 vols. (Boston: Massachusetts Historical Society, 1929–47), 3:315.
88 Ibid.
89 See above, p. 89
90 *Winthrop Papers*, 3:316.
91 William York Tindall, *John Bunyan, Mechanick Preacher* (New York: Columbia University Press, 1934), p. 13. Although most of the enthusiastic prophets were Puritan radicals, Arise Evans was a royalist recipient of revelations throughout this period. In 1643, for example, he received a divine inspiration to defend infant baptism and the apostolic succession of the English bishops; see Robert Barclay, *The Inner Life of the Religious Societies of the Commonwealth* (London: Hodder and Stoughton, 1876), pp. 216–17.
92 Marshall M. Knappen, *Tudor Puritanism* (Chicago: University of Chicago Press, Phoenix Books, 1966), p. 297.
93 Samuel Rawson Gardiner, *History of the Commonwealth and Protectorate, 1649–1660*, 4 vols. (London: Longmans, Green, 1894), 2:24.
94 Edmond Jessop, *Discovery of the Errors of the English Anabaptists* (London: By W. Jones for Robert Bird, 1623), p. 77.
95 Ibid.; Burrage, *Early English Dissenters*, 1:193–94. For Wilkinson's views on church membership, see above, p. 34.
96 John Winthrop, *Journal: History of New England, 1630–1649*, ed. James Kendall Hosmer, 2 vols. (New York: Charles Scribner's Sons, 1908), 1:309; cf. Cotton, *Reply to Mr. Williams*, p. 11.
97 Anna Trapnel, *The Cry of a Stone* (London: n.p., 1654), pp. 1–7, 15, 29, 57–58. The experiences of a similar London prophetess, Sarah Wight, were recounted by Henry Jessey, *The Exceeding Riches of Grace Advanced by the Spirit of Grace to an Empty Nothing Creature*,

Viz., Mrs. Sarah Wight (London: By Matthew Simmons for Henry Overton and Hannah Allen, 1647).

98   Trapnel, *Cry of a Stone,* pp. 9–10, 35–38; Louise Fargo Brown, *The Political Activities of the Baptists and Fifth Monarchy Men in England during the Interregnum* (Washington: American Historical Association, 1912), p. 49.

99   Trapnel, *Cry of a Stone,* p. 36.

100 *A Short Story of the Rise, Reign, and Ruin of the Antinomians, Familists & Libertines, That Infected the Churches of New-England* (London: For Ralph Smith, 1644), pp. 38–39.

101 *Letters of RW,* pp. 91–92; Winthrop, *Journal,* 1:297.

102 For an analysis of the careers of Saltmarsh and the other New Model Army chaplains, see Leo Frank Solt, *Saints in Arms* (Stanford: Stanford University Press, 1959).

103 *Wonderful Predictions Declared in a Message, as from the Lord, to His Excellency Sr. Thomas Fairfax and the Councell of His Army* (London: By Robert Ibbitson, 1648), p. 2.

104 Ibid., p. 1.

105 Ibid., pp. 4–6; similar warnings comprised the substance of three letters to the army officers in October 1647 by John Saltmarsh, *Englands Friend Raised from the Grave* (London: For Giles Calvert, 1649).

106 John Canne, *A Voice from the Temple to the Higher Powers* (London: By Matthew Simmons, 1653), pp. 1–10; Canne is referred to by Williams, *Cottons Letter . . . Examined,* pp. 381, 386, 393. Canne's belief that he had the gift of prophecy was shared by the Welsh Fifth Monarchist Vavasor Powell; see Champlin Burrage, "The Fifth Monarchy Insurrections," *English Historical Review* 25 (1910): 723.

107 [Williams], *Bloudy Tenent,* p. 307; cf. p. 371.

108 Henry Vane, *A Pilgrimage into the Land of Promise, by the Light of the Vision of Jacobs Ladder and Faith* (n.p., 1664), p. 91.

109 John Lilburne, "A Worke of the Beast," in *Tracts on Liberty in the Puritan Revolution, 1638–1647,* ed. William Haller, 3 vols. (New York: Columbia University Press, 1933), 2:7, 12–14.

110 Ibid., p. 22.

111 Ibid., p. 24.

112 Ibid., p. 10; cf. Williams's statement to John Winthrop, above, p. 89.

113 This letter was published by John Clarke, *Ill Newes from New-England,* Collections of the Massachusetts Historical Society, 4th ser., 2:45–52 (1854); the quotation appears on p. 50.

114 Williams, *Cottons Letter . . . Examined,* p. 342. Williams makes a similar statement on p. 344: "Christs consolations are so sweet, that the soule that tasteth them in truth, in suffering for any truth of his, will not easily part with them, though thousands are deceiv'd and deluded with counterfeits."

115 Ibid., p. 355; see also pp. 347–48, 358, 360, 363.

116 Ibid., pp. 380–84.

117 Ibid., pp. 317–18, 333, 352–53, 388.

Chapter   1   Williams, *Bloody Tenent Yet More Bloody*, p. 103.
Five   2   Ibid., p. 104.
              3   John Cotton, *A Reply to Mr. Williams His Examination*, ed. J. Lewis
                  Diman, Publications of the Narragansett Club, 1st ser., 2:8,
                  43 (1867).
              4   Williams, *Bloody Tenent Yet More Bloody*, p. 54. Cotton did not
                  recall receiving the arguments from Hall and said, in 1647, that
                  they had been sent to him by Williams himself; see John Cotton,
                  The Bloudy Tenent, Washed, and Made White in the Bloud of the Lambe
                  (London: By Matthew Symmons for Hannah Allen, 1647), p. 15.
              5   *A Most Humble Supplication of Many of the King's Majesty's Loyal
                  Subjects*, in *Tracts on Liberty of Conscience and Persecution,
                  1614–1661*, ed. Edward Bean Underhill (London: Hanserd Knol-
                  lys Society, 1846), pp. 214–225. This edition is based upon a 1646
                  edition of the tract; Champlin Burrage has suggested that, when
                  the pamphlet originally appeared in 1620, it circulated only in
                  manuscript (*The Early English Dissenters in the Light of Recent Re-
                  search* [*1550–1641*], 2 vols. [Cambridge: Cambridge University
                  Press, 1912], 1:264–65). John Hall's copy was in manuscript, "in
                  writing," according to Williams, *Bloody Tenent Yet More Bloody*, p.
                  54.
              6   Williams cited Cotton as the major author, *Bloudy Tenent*, p. 221;
                  but Cotton stated that he had no hand in writing the "Model";
                  Bloudy Tenent, Washed, pp. 150, 192.
              7   "A Model of Church and Civil Power," quoted in [Williams],
                  Bloudy Tenent, pp. 232–33, 259–61.
              8   Williams, *Bloody Tenent Yet More Bloody*, p. 483.
              9   *Letters of RW*, pp. 50–51; the Williams manuscript is not extant.
             10   A. S. P. Woodhouse, *Puritanism and Liberty*, 2d ed. (Chicago:
                  University of Chicago Press, 1951), Introduction, p. 44.
             11   Cotton, *Bloudy Tenent, Washed*, p. 92.
             12   Ibid., pp. 42–43; see also pp. 51, 53.
             13   Cotton's answer to the Baptist arguments, as cited in [Williams],
                  Bloudy Tenent, pp. 41–44, 53.
             14   Ibid., pp. 41–42.
             15   Ibid., p. 50.
             16   Ibid., p. 53; see also pp. 50–51.
             17   "A Model of Church and Civil Power," quoted in [Williams],
                  Bloudy Tenent, p. 261.
             18   Four important examples of these congregational apologies were
                  A Reply of Two of the Brethren to A[dam] S[teuart], 2d ed. (London:
                  By M. Simmons for H. Overton, 1644); John Goodwin, *Theomachia*
                  (London: For Henry Overton, 1644); *A Paraenetick or Humble Ad-
                  dresse to the Parliament and Assembly for (Not Loose, but) Christian
                  Libertie* (London: By Matthew Simmons for Henry Overton, 1644);
                  The Ancient Bounds (London: By M. S. for Henry Overton, 1645).
             19   *Ancient Bounds*, pp. 27–28.
             20   *Paraenetick*, p. 14.
             21   *Two of the Brethren to A. S.*, pp. 24–26.
             22   *Ancient Bounds*, pp. 4, 7.
             23   *Paraenetick*, pp. 5–7, 13–14.
             24   John Goodwin, *Theomachia*, p. 12.

25 Ibid., p. 52; see also p. 18.
26 Woodhouse, *Puritanism and Liberty*, Introduction, pp. 46–47; Leo F. Solt, *Saints in Arms* (Stanford: Stanford University Press, 1959), p. 64. In the main, this broadening of the Independent argument for toleration did not occur until after publication of Williams's *Bloudy Tenent*.
27 *Winthrop Papers*, ed. Allyn Bailey Forbes and Stewart Mitchell, 5 vols. (Boston: Massachusetts Historical Society, 1929–47), 5:23–25; see also pp. 142, 147. The colony had passed a law against Anabaptists in 1644.
28 John Spencer, *A Short Treatise concerning the Lawfulnesse of Every Mans Exercising His Gift as God Shall Call Him Thereunto*, *Transactions of the Congregational Historical Society* 4 (1909–10): 367.
29 John Lightfoot, *The Journal of the Proceedings of the Assembly of Divines*, ed. John Rogers Pitman (London: J. F. Dove, 1824), p. 93.
30 *The Compassionate Samaritane Unbinding the Conscience, and Pouring Oyle into the Wounds Which Have Been Made upon the Separation*, in *Tracts on Liberty in the Puritan Revolution, 1638–1647*, ed. William Haller, 3 vols. (New York: Columbia University Press, 1934), 3:71. See also *Liberty of Conscience*, in Haller, *Tracts on Liberty*, 3:119, 121; *The Power of Love*, in Haller, *Tracts on Liberty*, 2:285, 295–96.
31 *Power of Love*, p. 300; see also *Compassionate Samaritane*, pp. 65–66.
32 [Williams], *Bloudy Tenent*, p. 56.
33 Ibid., p. 58.
34 Ibid., p. 62.
35 Ibid. Williams has here played upon his own prior statement that the Baptist's arguments actually had been written in milk in order to smuggle them out of Newgate prison, where he was being held; the milk was invisible until heated by a flame.
36 Roger Williams's use of typology is carefully examined by Perry Miller, *Roger Williams: His Contribution to the American Tradition* (Indianapolis: Bobbs-Merrill, 1953). Unfortunately, Miller's hypothesis that the use of typology was distinctive to Williams, and is therefore a key to his thought, is completely erroneous. For revisions of Miller which take into account the widespread use of typology among the Puritans, see Sacvan Bercovitch, "Typology in Puritan New England: The Williams-Cotton Controversy Reassessed," *American Quarterly* 19 (1967): 166–91; Thomas M. Davis, "The Exegetical Traditions of Puritan Typology," *Early American Literature* 5 (1970): 11–50; Jesper Rosenmeier, "The Teacher and the Witness: John Cotton and Roger Williams," *William and Mary Quarterly*, 3d ser., 25 (1968): 408–31.
37 [Williams], *Bloudy Tenent*, pp. 200, 316, 338–45, 347; see also *A Most Humble Supplication*, p. 226.
38 Williams, *Bloody Tenent Yet More Bloody*, p. 131; see also [Williams], *Bloudy Tenent*, p. 239.
39 [Williams], *Bloudy Tenent*, p. 322.
40 Thomas Helwys, *A Short Declaration of the Mistery of Iniquity* (1612; reprint ed., London: Baptist Historical Society, 1935), p. 78. For a similar typological comparison of material and spiritual Israel, see [Williams], *Bloudy Tenent*, pp. 316–30.
41 [Williams], *Bloudy Tenent*, p. 347.

42 *A Most Humble Supplication*, pp. 226–30 (quotation appears on p. 229); see also Helwys, *Mistery of Iniquity*, pp. 42, 48–49, 71, 77–79.
43 [Williams], *Bloudy Tenent*, pp. 209–10 (emphasis deleted).
44 Ibid., p. 127.
45 Ibid., pp. 174–75, 233–34, 367; see also Leonard Busher, *Religions Peace*, in Underhill, *Liberty of Conscience and Persecution*, p. 23.
46 [Williams], *Bloudy Tenent*, pp. 147, 199–200; Busher, *Religions Peace*, p. 53; *Objections Answered by Way of Dialogue . . .*, in Underhill, *Liberty of Conscience and Persecution*, pp. 121–22.
47 [Williams], *Bloudy Tenent*, p. 363.
48 Ibid., pp. 73, 111.
49 Thomas Goodwin, *The Great Interest of States & Kingdomes* (London: For R. Dawlman, 1646), p. 8 (emphasis deleted).
50 [Williams], *Bloudy Tenent*, p. 251; see also pp. 72–73, 246, 287, 331, 388.
51 Ibid., pp. 79–80.
52 Ibid., pp. 80–81.
53 Ibid., pp. 109–12; see also Busher, *Religions Peace*, p. 24; *Objections*, pp. 121–22; *A Most Humble Supplication*, pp. 214–15.
54 [Williams], *Bloudy Tenent*, p. 89.
55 Ibid., pp. 371–72.
56 Ibid., p. 369.
57 Ibid., p. 184; see also pp. 174–75, 320, 365.
58 Ibid., p. 234.
59 Ibid., p. 187.
60 Ibid., pp. 65–67.
61 Ibid., p. 338.
62 Ibid.; see also p. 114.
63 Ibid., p. 338.
64 Busher, *Religions Peace*, p. 42; see also p. 45.
65 Ibid., pp. 16–17, 51, 53.
66 Ibid., p. 49.
67 Burrage, *Early English Dissenters*, 1:279.
68 [Williams], *Bloudy Tenent*, p. 190.
69 Ibid., p. 11.
70 Williams, *Key*, p. 79.
71 Ibid., p. 80.
72 Ibid., p. 77.
73 George R. Potter, "Roger Williams and John Milton," *Collections of the Rhode Island Historical Society* 13 (1920): 123.
74 *Catalogue of Pamphlets . . . Collected by George Thomason, 1640–1661*, ed. G. K. Fortescue, 2 vols. (London: British Museum, 1908), 1:416.
75 Williams, *Christenings*, pp. 31–35.
76 Ibid., pp. 35–41.
77 Donald Wing, *A Short-Title Catalogue of Books Printed in England . . . 1641–1700*, 3 vols. (New York: Columbia University Press, 1948), 2:302; 3:40; Paul G. Morrison, *Index of Printers, Publishers, and Booksellers in Donald Wing's Short-Title Catalogue* (Charlottesville: University of Virginia Press, 1955), p. 56.
78 Williams, *Key*, pp. 87, 180, 281; Williams, *Christenings*, p. 36.
79 *Letters of RW*, p. 317.

80   Ibid., p. 2.
81   Howard M. Chapin, ed., *Documentary History of Rhode Island*, 2 vols. (Providence: Preston and Rounds, 1916), 1:1–2.
82   *Winthrop Papers*, 3:177.
83   John Winthrop, *Journal: History of New England, 1630–1649*, ed. James Kendall Hosmer, 2 vols. (New York: Charles Scribner's Sons, 1908), 1:183–84.
84   *Letters of RW*, p. 338.
85   Ibid., pp. 231–32.
86   *Winthrop Papers*, 3:392.
87   *Letters of RW*, pp. 21, 24.
88   Ibid., p. 17.
89   John Mason, *A Brief History of the Pequot Wars*, Collections of the Massachusetts Historical Society, 2d ser., 8:135–45 (1826).
90   "Some Letters Written by Roger Williams," *Rhode Island Historical Tracts* 14 (1881): 27.
91   *Letters of RW*, pp. 38–39; see also pp. 98, 101–2.
92   Ibid., p. 305.
93   "Ten Letters of Roger Williams, 1654–1678," ed. Clarence S. Brigham, *Publications of the Rhode Island Historical Society*, n.s. 8 (1900): 157.
94   *Letters of RW*, p. 48.
95   Ibid., p. 88; see also Williams, *Key*, p. 212.
96   A recent interpretation has pointed out that there is also a parallel to the "emblem books" which were popular during the period and which made edifying religious and moral observations upon pictures or engravings; see John J. Teunissen and Evelyn J. Hinz, in Roger Williams, *A Key into the Language of America* (Detroit: Wayne State University Press, 1973), Introduction, pp. 52–67. The point, of course, remains the same, that Williams's interpretation of Indian society was proceeding upon two levels, literal and symbolic.
97   Williams, *Key*, pp. 169–70 (emphasis deleted from poem).
98   Ibid., p. 106.
99   Ibid., pp. 133, 162.
100   Ibid., p. 137.
101   Ibid., p. 106.
102   Ibid., p. 141.
103   Jack L. Davis, "Roger Williams among the Narragansett Indians," *New England Quarterly* 43 (1970): 601.
104   Williams, *Key*, p. 222.
105   [Williams], *Bloudy Tenent*, p. 250.
106   Williams, *Key*, p. 268 (emphasis added).
107   Williams, *Christenings*, p. 32.
108   Ibid., p. 34; see also [Williams], *Bloudy Tenent*, pp. 320–21, 365.
109   Williams, *Christenings*, p. 34.
110   Ibid., p. 32.
111   Ibid., p. 36.
112   Ibid., p. 39.
113   Ibid., pp. 36, 39.
114   Ibid., p. 37.
115   Ibid., pp. 39, 40–41; see also [Williams], *Bloudy Tenent*, pp. 294–95.

116 Williams, *Christenings*, pp. 39, 40–41; see also [Williams], *Bloudy Tenent*, p. 295.

117 Thomas Thorowgood, *Jewes in America, or, Probabilities That the Americans Are of That Race* (London: By W. H. for Tho. Slater, 1650), pp. 5–6, 81; Williams, *Key*, pp. 83–84.

118 Williams, *Christenings*, p. 40; see also Williams, *Hireling Ministry*, p. 168.

119 Davis, "Williams among the Narragansett," p. 602.

120 Williams, *Christenings*, p. 40.

121 Williams, *Key*, pp. 85–87; see also Williams, *Christenings*, p. 35.

122 *Letters of RW*, p. 188.

123 *New Englands First Fruits* (London: By R. O. and G. D. for Henry Overton, 1643), pp. 10–11 (misnumbered 18–19).

124 *The Glorious Progress of the Gospel, amongst the Indians in New England*, Collections of the Massachusetts Historical Society, 3d ser., 4:95 (1834); see also pp. 93–94.

125 *The Light Appearing More and More towards the Perfect Day*, Collections of the Massachusetts Historical Society, 3d ser., 4:127–28 (1834).

126 John Eliot, *The Christian Commonwealth: Or, the Civil Policy of the Rising Kingdom of Jesus Christ*, Collections of the Massachusetts Historical Society, 3d ser., 9:133–36, 143–64 (1846).

127 *The Light Appearing*, p. 131.

128 Cotton, *Bloudy Tenent, Washed*, p. 148.

129 Raymond Phineas Stearns, "The Weld-Peter Mission to England," *Publications of the Colonial Society of Massachusetts* 32 (1934): 242–43.

130 Thomas Shepard, *The Clear Sun-shine of the Gospel Breaking forth upon the Indians in New-England*, Collections of the Massachusetts Historical Society, 3d ser. 4:61 (1834).

131 William Erbery, *The Lord of Hosts* (London: By Tho. Newcomb for Giles Calvert, 1648), p. 30; see also William Erbery, *The General Epistle to the Hebrews* (London: n.p., 1652), pp. 1–4.

132 William Erbery, *A Call to the Churches* (London: n.p., 1653), p. 3; see also pp. 10–11.

133 Erbery, *Epistle to the Hebrews*, pp. 1, 3.

134 Ibid., p. 3; see also p. 5; William Erbery, *The Sword Doubled to Cut off Both the Righteous and the Wicked* (London: By G. D. for Giles Calvert, 1652), p. 33.

135 Erbery, *Sword Doubled*, p. 29.

136 Erbery, *Call to the Churches*, pp. 24–28.

137 Erbery, *Sword Doubled*, p. 38.

138 Henry Vane, *Two Treatises* (n.p., 1662), pp. 1–2, 45.

139 Henry Vane, *A Pilgrimage into the Land of Promise, by the Light of the Vision of Jacobs Ladder and Faith* (n.p., 1664), p. 69.

140 Ibid., pp. 21–23.

141 Vane, *Two Treatises*, pp. 72–73.

142 Erbery, *Sword Doubled*, p. 58.

Chapter   1 *Letters of RW*, p. 212.
Six   2 Ibid., p. 187.
          3 Ibid., p. 198.
          4 Williams, *Bloody Tenent Yet More Bloody*, pp. 40–41.

5   Ibid., p. 515.

6   Ibid., pp. 1, 502–18.

7   John Cotton, *The Bloudy Tenent, Washed, and Made White in the Bloud of the Lambe* (London: By Matthew Symmons for Hannah Allen, 1647), pp. 42–43, 51, 53, 92; Williams, *Bloody Tenent Yet More Bloody*, pp. 125–29, 251–53, 278, 353–54; *Letters of RW*, p. 188.

8   John Callender, *An Historical Discourse, on the Civil and Religious Affairs of the Colony of Rhode-Island*, ed. Romeo Elton, *Collections of the Rhode Island Historical Society* 4 (1838): 114–15, 118.

9   *Letters of RW*, p. 199.

10 The following generalizations are primarily based upon the work of Blair Worden, *The Rump Parliament, 1648–1653* (Cambridge: Cambridge University Press, 1974). See also David Underdown, *Pride's Purge: Politics in the Puritan Revolution* (Oxford: Clarendon Press, 1971).

11 David Masson, *The Life of John Milton*, new ed., 4 vols. (London: Macmillan, 1896), 4:387–88.

12 Ibid., 4:390–92. The fifteen proposals were first printed by Roger Williams as an appendix to *The Fourth Paper, Presented by Major Butler*, pp. 138–41; they were subsequently printed separately.

13 The proposals of the ministers printed in Williams, *Fourth Paper, Presented by Major Butler*, p. 138 (emphasis deleted).

14 Ibid., p. 139.

15 Ibid., pp. 140–41 (emphasis deleted).

16 Samuel Rawson Gardiner, *History of the Commonwealth and Protectorate, 1649–1660*, 4 vols. (London: Longmans, Green, 1894–1901), 2:32.

17 Worden, *Rump Parliament*, pp. 234–36, 240–42.

18 The proposals of the ministers printed in Williams, *Fourth Paper, Presented by Major Butler*, p. 139 (emphasis deleted).

19 Ibid., p. 119.

20 Ibid., p. 124.

21 William York Tindall, *John Bunyan, Mechanick Preacher* (New York: Columbia University Press, 1934), p. 5.

22 Samuel How, *The Sufficiency of the Spirit's Teaching, without Human Learning*, 5th ed. (London: n.p., n.d.), pp. v–vi.

23 Ibid., p. 4.

24 Ibid., p. 29.

25 Ibid., pp. 11–12.

26 William Dell, *A Plain and Necessary Confutation of Divers Gross and Antichristian Errors, Delivered . . . by Mr. Sydrach Simpson* (London: By Robert White for Giles Calvert, 1654), Apologie to the Reader.

27 John Saltmarsh, *Sparkles of Glory* (London: For Giles Calvert, 1647), p. 47.

28 Ibid., p. 50.

29 *Letters of RW*, p. 286.

30 William Dell, *The Tryal of Spirits both in Teachers & Hearers* (London: For Giles Calvert, 1653), p. 23 (emphasis deleted).

31 Ibid., p. 10 (emphasis deleted).

32 William Erbery, *The Sword Doubled to Cut off Both the Righteous and the Wicked* (London: By G. D. for Giles Calvert, 1652), p. 1.

33 Louise Fargo Brown, *The Political Activities of the Baptists and Fifth*

Monarchy Men in England during the Interregnum (Washington: American Historical Association, 1912), p. 201.

34 Tindall, *John Bunyan*, p. 71.
35 Ibid., pp. 74, 78–79, 82, 83, 87.
36 Ibid., pp. 87–88.
37 Williams, *Fourth Paper, Presented by Major Butler*, pp. 130–31; Williams, *Hireling Ministry*, pp. 155–62; Williams, *Bloody Tenent Yet More Bloody*, pp. 191–92, 383, 394.
38 Williams, *Hireling Ministry*, pp. 166–67.
39 Ibid., p. 163.
40 Ibid., p. 153 (emphasis deleted).
41 Ibid., p. 165.
42 Williams, *Fourth Paper, Presented by Major Butler*, pp. 124–25.
43 Ibid., p. 193.
44 John Canne, *A Voice from the Temple to the Higher Powers* (London: Matthew Simmons, 1653), p. 30 (emphasis deleted).
45 *Letters of RW*, pp. 236, 260.
46 Williams, *Hireling Ministry*, p. 162.
47 Williams, *Bloody Tenent Yet More Bloody*, p. 26.
48 J. F. V. Nicholson, "The Office of 'Messenger' amongst British Baptists in the Seventeenth and Eighteenth Centuries," *Baptist Quarterly* 17 (1958): 207–11; W. T. Whitley, *A History of British Baptists* (London: Kingsgate Press, 1932), pp. 87–88.
49 Tindall, *John Bunyan*, p. 12.
50 Williams, *Fourth Paper, Presented by Major Butler*, p. 125.
51 *Objections: Answered by Way of Dialogue . . .*, in Edward Bean Underhill, ed., *Tracts on Liberty of Conscience and Persecution, 1614–1661* (London: Hanserd Knollys Society, 1846), pp. 120–21.
52 Peter Toon, "The Question of Jewish Immigration," in *Puritans, the Millennium and the Future of Israel: Puritan Eschatology 1600 to 1660*, ed. Peter Toon (Cambridge: James Clarke, 1970), pp. 115–25. Toon fails to see the role of eschatology in the desires of the early General Baptists and Roger Williams for readmission of the Jews; they are, rather, for him "large hearted Englishmen" with "advanced views of religious toleration" (pp. 116–17).
53 Williams, *Fourth Paper, Presented by Major Butler*, pp. 130–31.
54 Williams, *Hireling Ministry*, p. 160 (emphasis deleted).
55 Williams, *Fourth Paper, Presented by Major Butler*, p. 136.
56 Williams, *Hireling Ministry*, p. 168.
57 Williams, *Bloody Tenent Yet More Bloody*, p. 383; see also pp. 191–92.
58 Williams, *Hireling Ministry*, p. 160. For the assertion that a true apostolic ministry is ordained by laying on of hands, see Williams, *Bloody Tenent Yet More Bloody*, p. 64.
59 Henry Vane, *A Pilgrimage into the Land of Promise, by the Light of the Vision of Jacobs Ladder and Faith* (n.p., 1664), pp. 90–91.
60 Henry Vane, *Two Treatises* (n.p., 1662), pp. 72–73.
61 Saltmarsh, *Sparkles of Glory*, pp. 116–21, 289–98.
62 Ibid., pp. 294–95. ·
63 *The Records of a Church of Christ, Meeting in Broadmead, Bristol, 1640–1687*, ed. Edward Bean Underhill (London: Hanserd Knollys Society, 1847), p. 31.

64   Robert Baillie, *The Letters and Journals of Robert Baillie,* ed. David Laing, 3 vols. (Edinburgh: Bannatyne Club, 1841–42), 2:211–12; see also pp. 191–92.

65   This distinction is not made in Christopher Hill, *The World Turned Upside Down: Radical Ideas during the English Revolution* (New York: Viking Press, 1972), pp. 148–58; see also above, pp. 61–62.

66   *Letters of RW,* p. 248.

67   Williams, *Experiments,* p. 47 (emphasis deleted).

68   Ibid., p. 48 (emphasis deleted).

69   Ibid., pp. 54, 59 (emphasis deleted).

70   Ibid., pp. 52, 56, 59.

71   The place of Williams's tract in the tradition of Puritan devotional manuals has been pointed out by Winthrop S. Hudson, in *Roger Williams, Experiments of Spiritual Life and Health,* ed. Winthrop S. Hudson (Philadelphia: Westminster Press, 1951), Introduction, p. 23.

72   Richard Sibbes, *The Bruised Reed and Smoking Flax,* in *The Complete Works of Richard Sibbes,* ed. Alexander Balloch Grosart, 7 vols. (Edinburgh: James Nichol, 1862–67), 1:42.

73   Ibid., p. 43.

74   Ibid., pp. 46–47.

75   Ibid., p. 50; M. van Beek, *An Inquiry into Puritan Vocabulary* (Groningen, The Netherlands: Wolters-Noordhoff, 1969), pp. 65, 117. Cf. Williams's accusation that the millenarian saints were "too secure," above, p. 147.

76   Sibbes, *Bruised Reed,* p. 58.

77   Ibid., pp. 59–65.

78   Ibid., p. 78.

79   Ibid., p. 75.

80   Lewis Bayly, *The Practise of Pietie, Directing a Christian How to Walk That He May Please God,* 12th ed. (London: For John Hodgetts, 1620), pp. 175–200.

81   Ibid., p. 235.

82   Ibid., pp. 245–46.

83   Richard Sibbes, *The Fountain Opened,* in *The Works of the Reverend Richard Sibbs,* 3 vols. (Aberdeen: Chalmers, 1812), 1:196.

84   William Gouge, *The Whole-Armour of God* (London: John Beale, 1639), p. 219.

85   Geoffrey F. Nuttall, *The Holy Spirit in Puritan Faith and Experience* (Oxford: Basil Blackwell, 1946), pp. 22–26.

86   Williams, *Experiments,* p. 57.

87   Richard Sibbes, *The Glorious Feast of the Gospel,* in *Complete Works of Richard Sibbs,* 2:495.

88   Gouge, *Whole-Armour of God,* p. 329.

89   John Preston, *The New Covenant,* 3d ed. (London: By I. D. for Nicholas Bourne, 1629), p. 192.

90   Williams, *Experiments,* p. 100.

91   Ibid., p. 76.

92   Ibid., p. 75.

93   Ibid., p. 85.

94   Ibid.

95   Ibid., p. 69 (emphasis deleted).

96 Ibid., pp. 52–53, 82.

97 Ibid., pp. 66–67.

98 Cf. Edmund S. Morgan, *Roger Williams: The Church and the State* (New York: Harcourt, Brace and World, 1967).

Chapter
Seven

1 Williams, *George Fox*, pp. 1–7.

2 [William Dell], *Baptismon Didache* (London: For Giles Calvert, 1648), p. 21.

3 William Erbery, *A Call to the Churches* (London: n.p., 1653), pp. 4–7.

4 Thomas Collier, *A Discovery of the New Creation* (London: For Giles Calvert, 1647), p. 8.

5 Prominent scholarly studies which place Quakerism in the milieu of radical Puritanism include, chronologically, William Charles Braithwaite, *The Beginnings of Quakerism* (London: Macmillan, 1912); Geoffrey F. Nuttall, *The Holy Spirit in Puritan Faith and Experience* (Oxford: Basil Blackwell, 1946); Hugh Barbour, *The Quakers in Puritan England* (New Haven: Yale Unviersity Press, 1964). Nuttall's book, pp. 91–92 and 134–37, makes the strongest assertion of this relationship, namely, that the Puritan movement as a whole was a "movement towards immediacy in relation to God."

6 Nuttall, *Holy Spirit in Puritan Faith*, p. 28.

7 George Fox, *The Journal of George Fox*, ed. Norman Penney, 2 vols. (Cambridge: Cambridge University Press, 1911), 1:167.

8 Geoffrey F. Nuttall, *James Naylor, a Fresh Approach* (London: Friends' Historical Society, 1954).

9 Cited in Geoffrey F. Nuttall, *Studies in Christian Enthusiasm: Illustrated from Early Quakerism* (Wallingford, Pa.: Pendle Hill, 1948), p. 55.

10 T. L. Underwood, "Early Quaker Eschatology," in *Puritans, the Millennium and the Future of Israel: Puritan Eschatology 1600 to 1660,* ed. Peter Toon (Cambridge: James Clarke, 1970), pp. 91–103.

11 Fox, *Journal*, 1:136.

12 Edward Burrough, *The Visitation of the Rebellious Nation of Ireland,* in *Early Quaker Writings, 1650–1700,* ed. Hugh Barbour and Arthur O. Roberts (Grand Rapids, Mich.: William B. Eerdmans, 1973), p. 92.

13 For the role of agriculture in seventeenth century Rhode Island, see Carl Bridenbaugh, *Fat Mutton and Liberty of Conscience: Society in Rhode Island, 1636–1690* (New York: Atheneum, 1976).

14 *Letters of RW*, pp. 299, 307–8, 310–11; see also Williams, *Bloody Tenent Yet More Bloody*, pp. 220–21; John Archer, *The Personall Reigne of Christ upon Earth* (London: Benjamin Allen, 1642), pp. 51–53.

15 *Letters of RW*, p. 311.

16 See, for example, Hanserd Knollys, *Apocalyptical Mysteries* (London: n.p., 1667); Hanserd Knollys, *The Parable of the Kingdom of Heaven Expounded* (London: For Benjamin Harris, 1674).

17 Ernest A. Payne, "More about the Sabbatarian Baptists," *Baptist Quarterly* 14 (1951): 161–63; *Letters of RW*, pp. 361–62.

18 Samuel Hugh Brockunier, *The Irrepressible Democrat, Roger Williams* (New York: Ronald Press, 1940), p. 268; *Letters of RW*, p. 404.

19   *Letters of RW,* pp. 286, 313, 347, 354; "Some Letters Written by Roger Williams," *Rhode Island Historical Tracts* 14(1881): 61–62.
20   *Letters of RW,* pp. 396–97.
21   Williams, *George Fox,* p. 43.
22   Ibid., pp. 1–3.
23   Ibid., "To the People Called Quakers"; Williams's fourteen propositions appear on pp. 4–5.
24   Ibid., p. 91.
25   Ibid., pp. 69–72, 78.
26   Ibid., p. 72.
27   Ibid., pp. 140–41.
28   *Letters of RW,* p. 212.
29   Williams, *George Fox,* pp. 136–37.
30   Nuttall, *Holy Spirit in Puritan Faith,* p. 101.
31   Williams, *George Fox,* pp. 102–3.
32   Ibid., p. 95.
33   Ibid., pp. 50, 56, 59–62, 99, 134, 210–12, 314.
34   Ibid., p. 5.
35   Ibid., pp. 308–10.
36   Williams, *Bloody Tenent Yet More Bloody,* p. 80.
37   See above, pp. 142–45.
38   Williams, *George Fox,* pp. 146–47; see also p. 390.
39   Ibid., pp. 290–91.
40   Ibid., pp. 291–92.
41   Ibid., p. 343.
42   Ibid., p. 132; see also pp. 58, 189–90.
43   Ibid., p. 199.
44   Henry Vane, *The Retired Mans Meditations* (London: Robert White, 1655), pp. 184–85; Henry Vane, *Two Treatises* (n.p., 1662), pp. 20–38.
45   Williams, *George Fox,* p. 3 (emphasis deleted).
46   Ibid., p. 350.
47   Ibid., p. 351.
48   Champlin Burrage, "The Antecedents of Quakerism," *English Historical Review* 30 (1915): 90.
49   Roger Williams, "Roger Williams to the Commissioners of the United Colonies," ed. Robert C. Winthrop, Jr., *Proceedings of the Massachusetts Historical Society,* 2d ser., 3: 258–59 (1887).
50   Ibid., p. 259. Williams also mentioned, in a letter to Samuel Hubbard, plans to travel to England; see *Letters of RW,* p. 362.
51   Mary Douglas, *Purity and Danger: An Analysis of Concepts of Pollution and Taboo* (New York: F. A. Praeger, 1966), p. 4.

Selected Bibliography

Primary Sources

Ainsworth, Henry. *The Communion of Saincts*. Amsterdam: N.p., 1642.

The Ancient Bounds. London: By M. S. for Henry Overton, 1645.

Archer, John. *The Personall Reigne of Christ upon Earth*. London: Benjamin Allen, 1642.

Baillie, Robert. *The Letters and Journals of Robert Baillie*. Edited by David Laing. 3 vols. Edinburgh: Bannatyne Club, 1841–42.

Barrow, Henry. *The Writings of Henry Barrow, 1587–1590*. Edited by Leland H. Carlson. London: George Allen and Unwin, 1962.

―――. *The Writings of Henry Barrow, 1590–1591*. Edited by Leland H. Carlson. London: George Allen and Unwin, 1966.

Bayly, Lewis. *The Practise of Pietie, Directing a Christian How to Walke That He May Please God*. 12th ed. London: For John Hodgetts, 1620.

Bradford, William. *Of Plimoth Plantation*. Boston: Commonwealth of Massachusetts, 1900.

Bridge, William. *Christs Coming Opened in a Sermon before the Honourable House of Commons*. London: For Peter Cole, 1648.

Brightman, Thomas. *The Works of That Famous, Reverend, and Learned Divine, Mr. Tho: Brightman*. London: By John Field for Samuel Cartwright, 1644.

Bunyan, John. *Grace Abounding to the Chief of Sinners*. Introduction by G. B. Harrison. London: J. M. Dent, 1928.

Burroughes, Jeremiah. *The Glorious Name of God, the Lord of Hosts.* London: For R. Dawlman, 1643.

———. *Sions Joy.* London: For R. Dawlman, 1641.

Canne, John. *A Necessitie of Separation from the Church of England.* Edited by Charles Stovel. London: Hanserd Knollys Society, 1849.

———. *A Voice from the Temple to the Higher Powers.* London: By Matthew Simmons, 1653.

Clarke, John. *Ill Newes from New England.* Collections of the Massachusetts Historical Society, 4th ser., 2:1–113 (1854).

Collier, Thomas. *A Discovery of the New Creation.* London: For Giles Calvert, 1647.

Cotton, John. *The Bloudy Tenent, Washed, and Made White in the Bloud of the Lambe.* London: By Matthew Symmons for Hannah Allen, 1647.

———. *A Letter of Mr. John Cottons Teacher of the Church in Boston, in New England, to Mr. Williams a Preacher There.* Edited by Reuben Aldridge Guild. Publications of the Narragansett Club, 1st ser., 1:295–311 (1866).

———. *A Reply to Mr. Williams His Examination.* Edited by J. Lewis Diman. Publications of the Narragansett Club, 1st ser., 2:9–237 (1867).

Dell, William. *The Tryal of Spirits Both in Teachers & Hearers.* London: For Giles Calvert, 1653.

Eliot, John. *The Christian Commonwealth.* Collections of the Massachusetts Historical Society, 3d ser., 9:127–64 (1846).

Erbery, William. *A Call to the Churches.* London: N.p., 1653.

———. *The General Epistle to the Hebrews.* London: N.p., 1652.

———. *The Sword Doubled to Cut Off Both the Righteous and the Wicked.* London: By G. D. for Giles Calvert, 1652.

Fox, George. *The Journal of George Fox.* Edited by Norman Penney. 2 vols. Cambridge: Cambridge University Press, 1911.

———. *The Works of George Fox.* 8 vols. Philadelphia: Marcus T. C. Gould, 1831.

Fox, George, and Burnyeat, John. *A New-England Fire-Brand Quenched.* N.p., 1678.

Gillespie, George. *A Sermon Preached before the Honourable House of Commons at Their Late Solemne Fast.* London: For Robert Bostock, 1644.

A Glimpse of Sions Glory. London: For William Larnar, 1641.

Goodwin, Thomas. *The Great Interest of States & Kingdoms.* London: For R. Dawlman, 1643.

———. *Zerubbabels Encouragement to Finish the Temple.* London: For R. D., 1642.

Goodwin, Thomas; Nye, Philip; Simpson, Sidrach; Burroughes, Jeremiah; and Bridge, William. *An Apologeticall Narration, Humbly Submitted to the Honourable Houses of Parliament.* London: For R. Dawlman, 1643.

Gouge, William. *The Whole-Armour of God.* London: By John Beale, 1639.

Helwys, Thomas. *A Short Declaration of the Mistery of Iniquity.* 1612. Reprint. London: Baptist Historical Society, 1935.

How, Samuel. *The Sufficiency of the Spirit's Teaching, without Human Learning.* 5th ed. London: N.p., n.d.

Hubbard, William. *A General History of New England, from the Discovery to MDCLXXX.* Edited by William Thaddeus Harris. Collections of the Massachusetts Historical Society, 2d ser., vols. 5–6 (1815).

[Mather, Richard]. *Church-Government and Church-Covenant Discussed.* London: By R. O. and G. D. for Benjamin Allen, 1643.

Mede, Joseph. *The Key of the Revelation, Searched and Demonstarted out of the Naturall and Proper Characters of the Visions.* Translated by Richard More. 2d ed. 2 vols. London: For Philemon Stephens, 1650.

New Englands First Fruits. London: By R. O. and G. D. for Henry Overton, 1644.

A Paraenetick or Humble Addresse to the Parliament and Assembly for (Not Loose, but) Christian Libertie. London: By Matthew Simmons for Henry Overton, 1644.

Preston, John. *The New Covenant.* 3d ed. London: By I. D. for Nicolas Bourne, 1629.

Records of the Governor and Company of the Massachusetts Bay in New England (1628–86). Edited by Nathaniel Bradstreet Shurtleff. 5 vols. Boston: Commonwealth of Massachusetts, 1853–54.

Reformation of Church-Government in Scotland, Cleered from Some Prejudices, by the Commissioners of the Generall Assembly of the Church of Scotland. London: For Robert Bostock, 1644.

A Reply of Two of the Brethren to A[dam] S[teuart]. 2d ed. London: By M. Simmons for H. Overton, 1644.

Robinson, John. *The Works of John Robinson, Pastor of the Pilgrim Fathers.* Edited by Robert Ashton. 3 vols. London: John Snow, 1851.

Saltmarsh, John. *Free Grace.* London: For Giles Calvert, 1645.

———. *Sparkles of Glory.* London: For Giles Calvert, 1647.

Sibbes, Richard. *The Complete Works of Richard Sibbes.* Edited by Alexander Balloch Grosart. 7 vols. Edinburgh:

James Nichol, 1862–67.

Smyth, John. *The Works of John Smyth.* Edited by W. T. Whitley. 2 vols. Cambridge: Cambridge University Press, 1915.

Thorowgood, Thomas. *Jewes in America, or, Probabilities That the Americans Are of That Race.* London: By W. H. for Tho. Slater, 1650.

Trapnel, Anna. *The Cry of a Stone.* London: N.p., 1654.

Vane, Henry. *A Pilgrimage into the Land of Promise, by the Light of the Vision of Jacobs Ladder and Faith.* N.p., 1664.

———. *The Retired Mans Meditations.* London: Robert White, 1655.

———. *Two Treatises.* N.p., 1662.

Williams, Roger. *An Answer to a Letter Sent from Mr. Coddington of Rode-Island, to Governour Leveret of Boston in What Concerns R. W. of Providence.* Providence: Society of Colonial Wars in the State of Rhode Island and Providence Plantations, 1946.

———. *An Answer to a Scandalous Papr Which Came to My Hand from Ye Massachusetts Clamouring against Ye Purchase & Slandering Ye Purchasers of Qunnunnagut Iland, & Subscribed by John Easton.* Providence: Society of Colonial Wars in the State of Rhode Island and Providence Plantations, 1945.

———. *The Bloody Tenent Yet More Bloody.* Edited by Samuel L. Caldwell. Publications of the Narragansett Club, 1st ser., 4:1–547 (1870).

[Roger Williams]. *The Bloudy Tenent, of Persecution, for Cause of Conscience, Discussed, in a Conference betweene Truth and Peace.* Edited by Samuel L. Caldwell. Publications of the Narragansett Club, 1st ser., 3:1–425 (1867).

———. *Christenings Make Not Christians.* In *The Complete Writings of Roger Williams,* edited by Perry Miller, vol. 7. New York: Russell & Russell, 1963.

[Williams, Roger]. *The Examiner Defended.* In *The Complete Writings of Roger Williams,* edited by Perry Miller, vol. 7. New York: Russell & Russell, 1963.

———. *Experiments of Spiritual Life & Health.* In *The Complete Writings of Roger Williams,* edited by Perry Miller, vol. 7. New York: Russell & Russell, 1963.

———. *The Fourth Paper, Presented by Major Butler . . . with a Testimony to the Said Fourth Paper.* In *The Complete Writings of Roger Williams,* edited by Perry Miller, vol. 7. New York: Russell & Russell, 1963.

———. *George Fox Digg'd out of His Burrowes.* Edited by J. Lewis Diman. Publications of the Narragansett Club, 1st ser., 5:1–503 (1872).

————. *The Hireling Ministry None of Christs.* In *The Complete Writings of Roger Williams,* edited by Perry Miller, vol. 7. New York: Russell & Russell, 1963.

————. *A Key into the Language of America.* Edited by James Hammond Trumbull. Publications of the Narragansett Club, 1st ser., 1:77–282 (1866).

————. *Letters of Roger Williams, 1632–1682.* Edited by John Russell Bartlett. Publications of the Narragansett Club, 1st ser., 6:1–418 (1874).

————. "Letters to Lady Barrington." *New England Historical and Genealogical Register* 43 (1889): 315–20.

————. *Mr. Cottons Letter Lately Printed, Examined and Answered.* Edited by Reuben Aldridge Guild. Publications of the Narragansett Club, 1st ser., 1:313–96 (1866).

[Williams, Roger]. *Queries of Highest Consideration.* Edited by Reuben Aldridge Guild. Publications of the Narragansett Club, 1st ser., 2:251–75 (1867).

————. "Some Letters Written by Roger Williams." *Rhode Island Historical Tracts* 14 (1881): 23–62.

————. "Ten Letters of Roger Williams, 1654–1678." Edited by Clarence S. Brigham. *Publications of the Rhode Island Historical Society,* n.s., 8 (1900): 141–61.

Winthrop, John. *Journal: History of New England, 1630–1649.* Edited by James Kendall Hosmer. 2 vols. New York: Charles Scribner's Sons, 1908.

————. *Winthrop Papers.* Edited by Allyn Bailey Forbes and Stewart Mitchell. 5 vols. Boston: Massachusetts Historical Society, 1929–47.

Zeal Examined: Or, a Discourse for Liberty of Conscience in Matters of Religion. London: By G. D. for Giles Calvert, 1652.

Source Collections

Barbour, Hugh, and Roberts, Arthur O., eds. *Early Quaker Writings, 1650–1700.* Grand Rapids, Mich.: William B. Eerdmans, 1973.

Chapin, Howard M., ed. *Documentary History of Rhode Island.* 2 vols. Providence: Preston and Rounds, 1916.

Haller, William, ed. *Tracts on Liberty in the Puritan Revolution, 1638–1647.* 3 vols. New York: Columbia University Press, 1934.

Underhill, Edward Bean, ed. *Tracts on Liberty of Conscience and Persecution, 1614–1661.* London: Hanserd Knollys Society, 1846.

Woodhouse, A. S. P., ed. *Puritanism and Liberty.* 2d ed. Chicago: University of Chicago Press, 1951.

Secondary Sources

Andrews, Charles McLean. *The Colonial Period of American History.* 4 vols. New Haven: Yale University Press, 1934.

Backus, Isaac. *A History of New England with Particular Reference to the Denomination of Christians Called Baptists.* 2d ed. 2 vols. Newton, Mass.: Backus Historical Society, 1871.

Bailyn, Bernard. *The New England Merchants in the Seventeenth Century.* Cambridge: Harvard University Press, 1955.

Barbour, Hugh. *The Quakers in Puritan England.* New Haven: Yale University Press, 1964.

Barclay, Robert. *The Inner Life of the Religious Societies of the Commonwealth.* London: Hodder and Stoughton, 1876.

Bercovitch, Sacvan. "Typology in Puritan New England: The Williams-Cotton Controversy Reassessed." *American Quarterly* 19 (1967): 166–91.

Bolam, C. G.; Goring, Jeremy; Short, H. L.; and Thomas, Roger. *The English Presbyterians: From Elizabethan Puritanism to Modern Unitarianism.* London: George Allen and Unwin, 1968.

Braithwaite, William Charles. *The Beginnings of Quakerism.* London: Macmillan, 1912.

Bridenbaugh, Carl. *Fat Mutton and Liberty of Conscience: Society in Rhode Island, 1636–1690.* New York: Atheneum, 1976.

Brockunier, Samuel Hugh. *The Irrepressible Democrat, Roger Williams.* New York: Ronald Press, 1940.

Brown, Louise Fargo. *The Political Activities of the Baptists and Fifth Monarchy Men in England during the Interregnum.* Washington: American Historical Association, 1912.

Buchan, John. *Oliver Cromwell.* London: Hodder and Stoughton, 1934.

Burrage, Champlin. "The Antecedents of Quakerism." *English Historical Review* 30 (1915): 78–90.

———. *The Early English Dissenters in the Light of Recent Research (1550–1641).* 2 vols. Cambridge: Cambridge University Press, 1912.

Burrell, Sidney A. "The Apocalyptic Vision of the Early Covenanters." *Scottish Historical Review* 43 (April 1964): 1–24.

Calamandrei, Mauro. "Neglected Aspects of Roger Williams' Thought." *Church History* 21 (1952): 239–58.

———. "Theology and Political Thought of Roger Williams." Ph.D. dissertation, University of Chicago, 1953.

Callender, John. *An Historical Discourse, on the Civil and Religious Affairs of the Colony of Rhode-Island.* Edited by Romeo Elton. Collections of the Rhode Island Historical Society 4:47–176 (1838).

Capps, B. S. *The Fifth Monarchy Men: A Study in*

Seventeenth-Century English Millenarianism. London: Faber and Faber, 1972.

Collinson, Patrick. *The Elizabethan Puritan Movement.* Berkeley: University of California Press, 1967.

Covey, Cyclone. *The Gentle Radical: A Biography of Roger Williams.* New York: Macmillan Company, 1966.

Dexter, Henry Martyn. *As to Roger Williams, and His "Banishment" from the Massachusetts Plantation.* Boston: Congregational Publishing Society, 1876.

Ernst, James E. *Roger Williams: New England Firebrand.* New York: Macmillan, 1932.

Frank, Joseph. *The Levellers: A History of the Writings of Three Seventeenth-Century Social Democrats: John Lilburne, Richard Overton, William Walwyn.* Cambridge: Harvard University Press, 1955.

Gardiner, Samuel Rawson. *History of the Commonwealth and Protectorate, 1649–1660.* 4 vols. London: Longmans, Green, 1894–1901.

———. *History of the Great Civil War.* New ed. 4 vols. London: Longmans, Green, 1893.

Garrett, John. *Roger Williams: Witness beyond Christendom, 1603–1683.* New York: Macmillan, 1970.

Haller, William. *The Rise of Puritanism.* New York: Columbia University Press, 1938.

Hill, Christopher. *Antichrist in Seventeenth-Century England.* London: Oxford University Press, 1971.

———. *Society and Puritanism in Pre-Revolutionary England.* New York: Schocken Books, 1964.

———. *The World Turned Upside Down: Radical Ideas during the English Revolution.* New York: Viking Press, 1972.

Jones, Rufus M. *The Quakers in the American Colonies.* London: Macmillan, 1911.

Knappen, Marshall M. *Tudor Puritanism.* Chicago: University of Chicago Press, Phoenix Books, 1966.

Knowles, James D. *Memoir of Roger Williams, the Founder of the State of Rhode Island.* Boston: Lincoln, Edmonds, 1834.

Langdon, George D. *Pilgrim Colony: A History of New Plymouth, 1620–1691.* New Haven: Yale University Press, 1966.

Maclear, James F. "New England and the Fifth Monarchy: The Quest for the Millennium in Early American Puritanism." *William and Mary Quarterly,* 3d ser., 32 (1975): 223–60.

McLoughlin, William G. *New England Dissent, 1630–1833.* 2 vols. Cambridge: Harvard University Press, 1971.

Masson, David. *The Life of John Milton.* New ed. 4 vols. London: Macmillan, 1896.

Miller, Perry. *The New England Mind: The Seventeenth Century*. New York: Macmillan, 1939.

————. *Orthodoxy in Massachusetts, 1630–1650*. Cambridge: Harvard University Press, 1933.

————. *Roger Williams: His Contribution to the American Tradition*. Indianapolis: Bobbs-Merrill, 1953.

Morgan, Edmund S. "Miller's Williams." *New England Quarterly* 38 (1965): 513–23.

————. *Roger Williams: The Church and the State*. New York: Harcourt, Brace and World, 1967.

————. *Visible Saints: The History of a Puritan Idea*. New York: New York University Press, 1963.

Nicholson, J. F. V. "The Office of 'Messenger' amongst British Baptists in the Seventeenth and Eighteenth Centuries." *Baptist Quarterly* 17 (1958): 206–25.

Nuttall, Geoffrey F. *The Holy Spirit in Puritan Faith and Experience*. Oxford: Basil Blackwell, 1946.

————. *Studies in Christian Enthusiasm: Illustrated from Early Quakerism*. Wallingford, Pa.: Pendle Hill, 1948.

————. *The Welsh Saints, 1640–1660*. Cardiff: University of Wales Press, 1957.

Pease, Theodore Calvin. *The Leveller Movement: A Study in the History and Political Theory of the English Great Civil War*. Washington: American Historical Association, 1916.

Rosenmeier, Jesper. "The Teacher and the Witness: John Cotton and Roger Williams." *William and Mary Quarterly*, 3d ser., 25 (1968): 408–31.

Simpson, Alan. "How Democratic Was Roger Williams?" *William and Mary Quarterly*, 3d ser., 13 (1956): 53–67.

————. *Puritanism in Old and New England*. Chicago: University of Chicago Press, 1955.

Solt, Leo F. *Saints in Arms: Puritanism and Democracy in Cromwell's Army*. Stanford: Stanford University Press, 1959.

Stearns, Raymond Phineas. *The Strenuous Puritan: Hugh in Arms: Puritanism and Democracy in Cromwell's Army*. Stanford: Stanford University Press, 1959.

Stearns, Raymond Phineas. *The Strenuous Puritan: Hugh Peter, 1598–1660*. Urbana: University of Illinois Press, 1954.

Tindall, William York. *John Bunyan, Mechanick Preacher*. New York: Columbia University Press, 1934.

Toon, Peter, ed. *Puritans, the Millennium and the Future of Israel: Puritan Eschatology 1600 to 1660*. Cambridge: James Clarke & Co., 1970.

Vann, Richard T. *The Social Development of English Quakerism, 1655–1755*. Cambridge: Harvard University Press, 1969.

Vaughan, Alden T. *New England Frontier: Puritans and Indians, 1620–1675.* Boston: Little, Brown, 1965.

Watkins, Owen C. *The Puritan Experience: Studies in Spiritual Autobiography.* New York: Schocken Books, 1972.

White, B. R. *The English Separatist Tradition.* London: Oxford University Press, 1971.

Williams, George Hunston. *Wilderness and Paradise in Christian Thought.* New York: Harper & Brothers, 1962.

Wilson, John F. *Pulpit in Parliament: Puritanism during the English Civil Wars, 1640–1648.* Princeton: Princeton University Press, 1969.

Winslow, Ola Elizabeth. *Master Roger Williams.* New York: Macmillan, 1957.

Worden, Blair. *The Rump Parliament, 1648–1653.* Cambridge: Cambridge University Press, 1974.

Ziff, Larzer. *The Career of John Cotton: Puritanism and the American Experience.* Princeton: Princeton University Press, 1962.

Index

DATE DUE

14 28 '83	
6 02 '83	
5 31 '84	
MAR 21 '00	
OCT 0 5 1994	
NOV 0 2 1994	
DEC 1 5 1998	
JAN 1 5 2000	
AUG 1 5 2001	

BRODART, INC.

Cat. No. 23-221